SACRED
SPACE

SACRED SPACE

The Prayer Book 2017

from the website www.sacredspace.ie

Prayer from the Irish Jesuits

LOYOLA PRESS.
A JESUIT MINISTRY

Chicago

LOYOLA PRESS.
A JESUIT MINISTRY

3441 N. Ashland Avenue
Chicago, Illinois 60657
(800) 621-1008
www.loyolapress.com

Scripture quotations are from the *New Revised Standard Version Bible: Catholic Edition*, copyright © 1989, 1993 National Council of the Churches of Christ in the United States of America. Used by permission. All rights reserved.

Cover art credit: © iStock/Qweek

ISBN-13: 978-0-8294-4448-3
ISBN-10: 0-8294-4448-3

16 17 18 19 20 21 Versa 10 9 8 7 6 5 4 3 2 1

Contents

Sacred Space Prayer

Bless all who worship you, almighty God,
from the rising of the sun to its setting:
from your goodness enrich us,
by your love inspire us,
by your Spirit guide us,
by your power protect us,
in your mercy receive us,
now and always.

Preface

In 1999 an Irish Jesuit named Alan McGuckian had the simple—but at the time radical—idea of bringing daily prayer to the Internet. No one imagined that his experimental project would grow into a global community with volunteers translating the prayer experience into seventeen different languages.

Millions of people, from numerous Christian traditions, visit www.sacredspace.ie each year, and what they find is an invitation to step away from their busy routine for a few minutes each day to concentrate on what is really important in their lives. Sacred Space offers its visitors the opportunity to grow in prayerful awareness of their friendship with God.

Besides the daily prayer experience, Sacred Space also offers Living Space, with commentaries on the Scripture readings for each day's Catholic Mass. The Chapel of Intentions allows people to add their own prayers, while Pray with the Pope joins the community to the international Apostleship of Prayer. In addition, Sacred Space provides Lenten and Advent retreats, often in partnership with Pray as You Go, an audio prayer service from the British Jesuits.

The contents of this printed edition, first produced in 2004, are taken directly from our Internet site. Despite the increased use of Sacred Space on mobile devices, many people want a book they can hold and carry, and this book has proven especially helpful for prayer groups.

In 2014 the Irish Jesuits entered into an apostolic agreement with the Chicago-Detroit Jesuits, and Sacred Space now operates in partnership with Loyola Press.

I am delighted to bring you the *Sacred Space* book, and I pray that your prayer life will flourish with its help.

Yours in Christ,

Paul Brian Campbell, SJ

Introduction to *Sacred Space*, 2017

Saint Ignatius of Loyola, founder of the Society of Jesus, is famously known for wanting to find God in all things. *Is that even possible?* you might ask. He believed it was, but only as a gift from God and only as the fruit of our paying attention to our experience. Ignatius developed an optimistic spiritual practice that assumed the presence of God at every moment of our existence. While we tend to think of God's presence as a "sometimes thing," Ignatius came to believe that our perception of God's presence as a sometimes occurrence is a major spiritual hindrance. Ignatius believed that God is always creating this universe, always keeping it in existence, always working to bring about God's purpose in creation, and always trying to move us to join God in the great adventure of bringing about what Jesus called the kingdom of God.

In order to experience this ever-present God, we need to develop a regular spiritual practice, a practice Ignatius had learned from his experience as a relatively untutored layman. Ignatius began to teach people and to write down the spiritual practices that helped him move toward uniting himself with God's purposes and thus toward finding God in all things. *Spiritual Exercises* is Ignatius's manual for those who want to follow his example of helping others get in touch with our ever-present God. God wants a close personal relationship with each of us, and he wants each of us to join him in the great work of bringing about a world where peace and justice prevail. Over the almost five centuries since the time of Ignatius, Jesuits and many others have found through these spiritual practices the answer to their own deepest desires.

Over the centuries, the Spiritual Exercises have been adapted in many ways. Jesuits originally followed Ignatius's own practice of giving the Exercises to individuals for thirty days. But they also used the methods of prayer suggested in the Exercises in their preaching, missions, and talks to larger groups. Eventually, houses were set aside for the giving of the Exercises to individuals and large groups. One of the adaptations suggested by Ignatius himself was to make the Exercises in daily life under the direction of someone trained in giving them. In this format, an individual maintained his or her regular daily life and work but promised to devote time every day to the spiritual practices suggested by Ignatius and to see the spiritual director once a week. In the past fifty years, this adaptation has seen a worldwide resurgence and has touched many lives. It has also been used with groups to great advantage. In modern times, the giving of the Spiritual Exercises has become something of a cottage industry in many countries.

Enter the age of the Internet. Could this new tool be used to help large numbers of people move toward finding God in all things? The answer is a resounding *yes*! Many websites, in multiple languages, try to help people become more aware of God's presence in their lives, using practices stemming from the Spiritual Exercises. One example is the book you have in your hands. In 1999 the Irish Jesuits started to offer daily prompts for prayer based on Ignatius's Exercises on the website Sacred Space (www.sacredspace.ie). The English edition was soon translated into other languages, and the site now features twenty-one languages that span the globe.

In my work as a spiritual director and in my travels, I have come across many, many people of various walks of life who use the daily prompts for prayer provided through Sacred Space. People find the site and the daily suggestions to be user-friendly, inviting, and—in keeping with Ignatian spirituality—optimistic. The suggestions help them pay attention to their experience, notice intimations of God's presence in that experience, and engage in an honest conversation with God.

For each week, there is an overarching suggested theme and a method for spending time with God each day. One of the methods is to turn to the Scripture and reflections suggested for each day of the week. Each day's text is taken from the Gospel reading for Mass that day. Thus, someone who follows Sacred Space every day will, in the course of a year, work prayerfully through all four of the Gospels. No wonder that so many have been enthralled by this site.

In spite of the digital age, many of us still like the feel of a book in our hands. The book *Sacred Space*, which you now hold in your hands, was designed for the likes of us. I am very happy to introduce the book and even happier that Loyola Press, a Jesuit institution, is now the publisher. Ignatian spiritual practice has brought me closer to God, for which I am immensely grateful. Through Ignatius's spiritual practices I have experienced God's desire for my friendship, and I figure, if God wants *my* friendship, he wants *everyone's* friendship. If you take this book seriously and engage in the relationship with God that it suggests, you will, I'm sure, find as much joy in God's friendship as I have. Try it—you'll like it.

William A. Barry, SJ

How to Use This Book

During each week of the Liturgical year, begin by reading the "Something to think and pray about each day this week." Then proceed through "The Presence of God," "Freedom," and "Consciousness" steps to prepare yourself to hear the word of God in your heart. In the next step, "The Word," turn to the Scripture reading for each day of the week. Inspiration points are provided if you need them. Then return to the "Conversation" and "Conclusion" steps. Use this process every day of the year.

November 27—December 3, 2016

Something to think and pray about each day this week:

The Dynamic of Hope

A driving dynamic of Advent is hope. If we had nothing to hope for, there would be no point to this season. The original hope was for a child to be born who would bring justice and peace to the world and who would heal the rift between humanity and God. But that larger hope is filled with smaller ones—daily hopes that can shape us as people. Some hopes will shape our relationships. The Christ Child grew to be a man who embodied forgiveness and generosity. A life of hope sees the good in others, is patient with their shortcomings, and tenaciously envisions them at their best. Some hopes will shape our life work. The promised Messiah proclaimed God's realm of justice and mercy. No matter what jobs we do or work positions we hold, as hopeful people we maintain fairness and integrity as short-term and long-term goals. We make our work matter for the common good. Some hopes will shape our character. Jesus exemplified hope that cultivates true interior freedom. A hopeful person cannot continue in anxiety, grasping, need for control, and habitual anger. How is hope visible in your life? Where has it faded?

—Vinita Hampton Wright, Loyola Press blogs

The Presence of God

Be still and know that I am God. Lord, may your spirit guide me to seek your loving presence more and more. For it is there I find rest and refreshment from this busy world.

Freedom

By God's grace I was born to live in freedom. Free to enjoy the pleasures he created for me. Dear Lord, grant that I may live as you intended, with complete confidence in your loving care.

Consciousness

In God's loving presence I unwind the past day,
starting from now and looking back, moment by moment.
I gather in all the goodness and light, in gratitude.
I attend to the shadows and what they say to me,
seeking healing, courage, forgiveness.

The Word

The word of God comes to us through the Scriptures. May the Holy Spirit enlighten my mind and heart to respond to the Gospel teachings. (Please turn to the Scripture on the following pages. Inspiration points are there should you need them. When you are ready, return here to continue.)

Conversation

Jesus, you always welcomed little children when you walked on this earth. Teach me to have a childlike trust in you. To live in the knowledge that you will never abandon me.

Conclusion

Glory be to the Father, and to the Son, and to the Holy Spirit,
As it was in the beginning, is now and ever shall be,
World without end. Amen.

Sunday 27th November
First Sunday of Advent
Matthew 24:37–44

For as the days of Noah were, so will be the coming of the Son of Man. For as in those days before the flood they were eating and drinking, marrying and giving in marriage, until the day Noah entered the ark, and they knew nothing until the flood came and swept them all away, so too will be the coming of the Son of Man. Then two will be in the field; one will be taken and one will be left. Two women will be grinding meal together; one will be taken and one will be left. Keep awake therefore, for you do not know on what day your Lord is coming. But understand this: if the owner of the house had known in what part of the night the thief was coming, he would have stayed awake and would not have let his house be broken into. Therefore you also must be ready, for the Son of Man is coming at an unexpected hour.

- There are tough images here: floods, capture, thieving. These are frightening, life-changing events. We have one life, and it is precious and fragile. We need to be in tune with Jesus constantly, ready for whatever comes our way, not sleepwalking through life.

- Lord, make me present to your daily appearances in my life. As the poet Tagore says, "He comes, comes, ever comes." Lord, do not let me miss you, even in my ordinary routine.

Monday 28th November
Matthew 8:5–11

When Jesus entered Capernaum, a centurion came to him, appealing to him and saying, "Lord, my servant is lying at home paralyzed, in terrible distress." And he said to him, "I will come and cure him." The centurion answered, "Lord, I am not worthy to have you come under my roof; but only speak the word, and my servant will be healed. For I also am a man under authority, with soldiers under me; and I say to one, 'Go,' and he goes, and to another, 'Come,' and he comes, and to my slave, 'Do this,' and the slave does it." When Jesus heard him, he was amazed and said to those who followed him, "Truly I tell you, in no one in Israel have I found such faith. I tell you, many will come from east and west and will eat with Abraham and Isaac and Jacob in the kingdom of heaven."

- The centurion was an officer of the imperial army, a man with power and status. He was begging a favor from a penniless itinerant teacher and declaring himself unworthy even to entertain Jesus in his house. Jesus was amazed, not merely at the trust of the man but at the fact that his love for his servant led him to cut through all the barriers of rank and race. Lord, so much of my life is structured by social conventions and barriers. Give me the grace to listen to my heart and reach out to those that I can help.

- This miracle is unusual for two reasons. Jesus was not actually present when the healing took place: he spoke the word, and the centurion's servant was healed. The servant did not even have to hear Jesus speak the word: it was enough that the word was spoken. Do we realize that when we speak God's word, someone, somewhere, may find healing?

Tuesday 29th November
Luke 10:21–24

Jesus rejoiced in the Holy Spirit and said, "I thank you, Father, Lord of heaven and earth, because you have hidden these things from the wise and the intelligent and have revealed them to infants; yes, Father, for such was your gracious will. All things have been handed over to me by my Father; and no one knows who the Son is except the Father, or who the Father is except the Son and anyone to whom the Son chooses to reveal him." Then turning to the disciples, Jesus said to them privately, "Blessed are the eyes that see what you see! For I tell you that many prophets and kings desired to see what you see, but did not see it, and to hear what you hear, but did not hear it."

- In this scene, Jesus seems to be rejoicing in his disciples, happy that they are with him. He is happy, too, in what God his Father has given to his followers. Jesus rejoices in us just as friends rejoice together and as parents rejoice in the talents and gifts of their children. Perhaps, then, can we rejoice in one another? In prayer we can allow ourselves to be grateful for the goodness, gifts, and faith of others, especially people who are significant in our lives.

- I watch Jesus at his prayer. What is it like to see him rejoicing in the Holy Spirit and thanking his Father? At this moment as I pray, the three divine Persons are present with me, and the Spirit is praying in me. Awareness of this can transform my prayer.

Wednesday 30th November
Matthew 4:18–22

As Jesus walked by the Sea of Galilee, he saw two brothers, Simon, who is called Peter, and Andrew his brother, casting a net into the sea—for they were fishermen. And he said to them, "Follow me, and I will make you fish for people." Immediately they left their nets and followed him. As he went from there, he saw two other brothers, James son of Zebedee and his brother John, in the boat with their father Zebedee, mending their nets, and he called them. Immediately they left the boat and their father, and followed him.

- Jesus called the fishermen, speaking to them in terms they recognized. Jesus calls me as I am, wanting me to use my skills and abilities to draw others to life. Peter, Andrew, James, and John responded to Jesus immediately. I think of how slow my reactions are. I try to see what holds me back, and I talk to Jesus about it.

- In the middle of any ordinary day Jesus walks by, sees me, singles me out from the crowd, speaks to me, and invites my discipleship. What attracts me to Jesus? What helps me respond generously to him? Am I a close follower of his, or do I keep my eye on him only occasionally?

Thursday 1st December
Matthew 7:21, 24–27

Jesus said to the people, "Not everyone who says to me, 'Lord, Lord,' will enter the kingdom of heaven, but only the one who does the will of my Father in heaven. Everyone then who hears these words of mine and acts on them will be like a wise man who built his house on rock. The rain fell, the floods came, and the winds blew and beat on that house, but it did not fall, because it had been founded on rock. And everyone who hears these words of mine and does not act on them will be like a foolish man who built his house on sand. The rain fell, and the floods came, and the winds blew and beat against that house, and it fell—and great was its fall!"

- Saint Ignatius remarks that love is found in deeds rather than in words. Jesus praises good deeds over good intentions that are not carried out. I pray to be like a good servant who does the work God invites me to do.

- Hearing or reading God's word is important, but it is not the end. I take time to let the word of God settle into the shape of my life. I take care not to let it merely stay in my mind but to let it touch my heart and desires as well. I ask God to help me be present to the word. My words are part of my response to God, but I realize that it is not just the saying of words that is important. I ask for sincerity and integrity, that my words will become actions that become my way of life.

Friday 2nd December
Matthew 9:27–31

As Jesus went on his way, two blind men followed him, crying loudly, "Have mercy on us, Son of David!" When he entered the house, the blind men came to him; and Jesus said to them, "Do you believe that I am able to do this?" They said to him, "Yes, Lord." Then he touched their eyes and said, "According to your faith let it be done to you." And their eyes were opened. Then Jesus sternly ordered them, "See that no one knows of this." But they went away and spread the news about him throughout that district.

- How could these men follow Jesus if they could not see? By hearing his voice, perhaps. Or maybe others led them to him. How did they know what to ask for? They knew they needed physical *and* spiritual sight, so they asked for more than sight: they asked for mercy. Their faith in Jesus opened their hearts to appeal to him. Their faith touched power in Jesus, and they were healed. They knew their need for God and for others; they did not hide their need and thus were healed.

- Lord, you do not meet me as one of a multitude, but face to face, on my own, where you can test the truth of my words. You meet me and listen to my desire when it is free from the illusions of mass emotion.

Saturday 3rd December
Matthew 9:35–10:1, 5a, 6–8

Jesus went about all the cities and villages, teaching in their synagogues, and proclaiming the good news of the kingdom, and curing every disease and every sickness. When he saw the crowds, he had compassion for them, because they were harassed and helpless, like sheep without a shepherd. Then he said to his disciples, "The harvest is plentiful, but the laborers are few; therefore ask the Lord of the harvest to send out laborers into his harvest." Then Jesus summoned his twelve disciples and gave them authority over unclean spirits, to cast them out, and to cure every disease and every sickness. These twelve Jesus sent out with the following instructions: "Go to the lost sheep of the house of Israel. As you go, proclaim the good news, 'The kingdom of heaven has come near.' Cure the sick, raise the dead, cleanse the lepers, cast out demons. You received without payment; give without payment."

- This seems to be a really outgoing Gospel reading: we are to look at the big harvest—the sick, the dead, the outcasts. All the needs of people are part of prayer. It is in care and compassion that the kingdom of heaven comes near.

- Lord, the cries of the poor and brokenhearted are evident in the mass migrations daily beamed into my living room. Let me not forget that you summon me today to be your eyes, your ears, and your hands of compassion. May I respond with loving compassion to all who come to me.

The Second Week of Advent
December 4—December 10, 2016

Something to think and pray about each day this week:

God's Big Dreams for Us
Over time, I've come to believe that God and God's people are certainly trying their best to make my life a glorious adventure. Some of the biggest life changes I've experienced were not initiated by me but by my superiors and/or by circumstances. At those moments, I've often found it difficult to see where God is involved, but once I get settled into my new situation and gain a little perspective, I begin to see and appreciate that the move was good and the change was needed for me to stretch and grow. God works through others and through me to lead me to a fuller and better life. I believe that God has big dreams for all of us and is constantly inviting us to choose freedom over fear, generosity over greed, compassion over comparison, and service over selfishness. As such, I'm sure that God is involved in all our decisions, no matter how seemingly trivial. But I'm also sure that God is there plotting to make me happy, so God is not there with a divine remote control but, instead, gently invites us to greater love.
—Paul Brian Campbell, SJ, Loyola Press blogs

The Presence of God
I pause for a moment and think of the love and the grace that God showers on me: I am created in the image and likeness of God; I am God's dwelling place.

Freedom
Lord, you created me to live in freedom. May your Holy Spirit guide me to follow you freely. Instill in my heart a desire to know and love you more each day.

Consciousness
How am I really feeling? Lighthearted? Heavyhearted? I may be very much at peace, happy to be here.
Equally, I may be frustrated, worried, or angry.
I acknowledge how I really am. It is the real me that the Lord loves.

The Word
I read the word of God slowly, a few times over, and I listen to what God is saying to me. (Please turn to the Scripture on the following pages. Inspiration points are there should you need them. When you are ready, return here to continue.)

Conversation
I know with certainty there were times when you carried me, Lord. When it was through your strength I got through the dark times in my life.

Conclusion
I thank God for these moments we have spent together and for any insights I have been given concerning the text.

Sunday 4th December
Second Sunday of Advent
Matthew 3:1–12

In those days John the Baptist appeared in the wilderness of Judea, proclaiming, "Repent, for the kingdom of heaven has come near." This is the one of whom the prophet Isaiah spoke when he said, "The voice of one crying out in the wilderness: 'Prepare the way of the Lord, make his paths straight.'" Now John wore clothing of camel's hair with a leather belt around his waist, and his food was locusts and wild honey. Then the people of Jerusalem and all Judea were going out to him, and all the region along the Jordan, and they were baptized by him in the river Jordan, confessing their sins. But when he saw many Pharisees and Sadducees coming for baptism, he said to them, "You brood of vipers! Who warned you to flee from the wrath to come? Bear fruit worthy of repentance. Do not presume to say to yourselves, 'We have Abraham as our ancestor'; for I tell you, God is able from these stones to raise up children to Abraham. Even now the axe is lying at the root of the trees; every tree therefore that does not bear good fruit is cut down and thrown into the fire. I baptize you with water for repentance, but one who is more powerful than I is coming after me; I am not worthy to carry his sandals. He will baptize you with the Holy Spirit and fire. His winnowing fork is in his hand, and he will clear his threshing floor and will gather his wheat into the granary; but the chaff he will burn with unquenchable fire."

- I may feel uncomfortable when confronted with John's call to repentance, but I let myself listen, acknowledging that I am a sinner in need of God's mercy. If I cannot admit this, then perhaps Advent is not for me.

- God does not want me to receive the Word passively. I work *with* God, preparing the way in my life, expectant and hopefully watching for God's approach.

Monday 5th December
Luke 5:17–26

One day, while Jesus was teaching, Pharisees and teachers of the law were sitting nearby (they had come from every village of Galilee and Judea and from Jerusalem); and the power of the Lord was with him to heal. Just then some men came, carrying a paralyzed man on a bed. They were trying to bring him in and lay him before Jesus; but finding no way to bring him in because of the crowd, they went up on the roof and let him down with his bed through the tiles into the middle of the crowd in front of Jesus. When he saw their faith, he said, "Friend, your sins are forgiven you." Then the scribes and Pharisees began to ask themselves, "Who is this who is speaking blasphemies? Who can forgive sins but God alone?" When Jesus perceived their questionings, he answered them, "Why do you raise such questions in your hearts? Which is easier, to say, 'Your sins are forgiven,' or to say, 'Stand up and walk'? But so that you may know that the Son of Man has authority on earth to forgive sins"—he said to the man who was paralyzed—"I say to you, stand up and take your bed and go to your home." Immediately he stood up before them, picked up what he had been lying on, and went home, glorifying God. Amazement seized all of them, and they glorified God and were filled with awe, saying, "We have seen strange things today."

- What an interesting, colorful, humorous, and yet life-changing scene! The man's friends are not easily put off. They use team effort and creativity to ensure that their paralyzed friend meets Jesus. An encounter happens that heals his body but also frees him from the paralysis of sin. Lord, forgiveness is a pressing need for all. Help me to do all I can to bring people to meet you and know your healing forgiveness in their lives. But help me do it sensitively!

- In this miracle, Jesus performs both a spiritual and a physical healing. Am I a spiritual paralytic? What might be crippling me in following Jesus?

Tuesday 6th December
Matthew 18:12–14

Jesus said, "What do you think? If a shepherd has a hundred sheep, and one of them has gone astray, does he not leave the ninety–nine on the mountains and go in search of the one that went astray? And if he finds it, truly I tell you, he rejoices over it more than over the ninety–nine that never went astray. So it is not the will of your Father in heaven that one of these little ones should be lost."

- Every Gospel passage tells us something about God. Here I learn that God has a particular care for everyone, especially for those who have gone astray. This is a comfort to me because I often lose my way in life. God is watching out for me always.

- I ask the Lord that I, too, may care for the "little ones"—those who are vulnerable and cannot cope with life's demands.

Wednesday 7th December
Matthew 11:28–30

Jesus said, "Come to me, all you that are weary and are carrying heavy burdens, and I will give you rest. Take my yoke upon you, and learn from me; for I am gentle and humble in heart, and you will find rest for your souls. For my yoke is easy, and my burden is light."

- Jesus invites us to come to him just as we are. He recognizes the busyness of our lives, how we labor and are overburdened, and he draws us into his loving and gentle presence. He wants to listen to all our troubles, and he assures us that his yoke is easy and his burden is light. When we spend time with Jesus, we find rest for our souls. He speaks to us in the silence of our hearts and gives us inner peace.

- Sometimes we carry heavy burdens because we want to figure things out on our own, believing there is no one to help us. I pray that people who are weighed down may hear the voice of Jesus. I pray that I may hear it, too, and have the humility I need to ask for and receive help.

Thursday 8th December
The Immaculate Conception of the Blessed Virgin Mary
Luke 1:26–38

In the sixth month the angel Gabriel was sent by God to a town in Galilee called Nazareth, to a virgin engaged to a man whose name was Joseph, of the house of David. The virgin's name was Mary. And he came to her and said, "Greetings, favored one! The Lord is with you." But she was much perplexed by his words and pondered what sort of greeting this might be. The angel said to her, "Do not be afraid, Mary, for you have found favor with God. And now, you will conceive in your womb and bear a son, and you will name him Jesus. He will be great, and will be called the Son of the Most High, and the Lord God will give to him the throne of his ancestor David. He will reign over the house of Jacob forever, and of his kingdom there will be no end." Mary said to the angel, "How can this be, since I am a virgin?" The angel said to her, "The Holy Spirit will come upon you, and the power of the Most High will overshadow you; therefore the child to be born will be holy; he will be called Son of God. And now, your relative Elizabeth in her old age has also conceived a son; and this is the sixth month for her who was said to be barren. For nothing will be impossible with God." Then Mary said, "Here am I, the servant of the Lord; let it be with me according to your word." Then the angel departed from her.

- Like Mary, I came into the world for a purpose. That purpose probably will not be revealed to me as dramatically as it was to her. Perhaps she heard God's message so clearly because she was comfortable with silence. Too often I fear the emptiness, the darkness, the silence within me. Yet it is there that the Spirit lives and works, even when my prayer seems most arid. God, help me go daily into the quiet of my heart, to meet you there, in love and adoration.

- Mary did not receive the angel's message as a total surprise; she was ready to engage in conversation with God's messenger. I turn to God in my prayer and try to see God's finger at work in my life. I draw inspiration from Mary's disposition.

Friday 9th December
Matthew 11:16–19

Jesus spoke to the crowds, "But to what will I compare this generation? It is like children sitting in the marketplaces and calling to one another, 'We played the flute for you, and you did not dance; we wailed, and you did not mourn.' For John came neither eating nor drinking, and they say, 'He has a demon'; the Son of Man came eating and drinking, and they say, 'Look, a glutton and a drunkard, a friend of tax collectors and sinners!' Yet wisdom is vindicated by her deeds."

- Both John and Jesus reveal what God is like, but they are misunderstood and cruelly rejected. I thank Jesus that he does not despair of humankind. He knows what we are like, yet he also sees what we can become. May I never despair over myself or others.

- How much am I willing to put myself out for others, as John and Jesus did? I pray not to be imprisoned in my comfort zones.

Saturday 10th December
Matthew 17:9a, 10–13

The disciples asked Jesus, "Why, then, do the scribes say that Elijah must come first?" He replied, "Elijah is indeed coming and will restore all things; but I tell you that Elijah has already come, and they did not recognize him, but they did to him whatever they pleased. So also the Son of Man is about to suffer at their hands." Then the disciples understood that he was speaking to them about John the Baptist.

- The disciples are bewildered. They believe that Elijah must return before the reign of God comes about. Jesus tries to move them on by telling them that the work of Elijah has already been done by John the Baptist. God moves at a pace that is different from ours. Do I also get stuck and miss the God of Surprises?

- What is preventing me from living as if my savior—my Redeemer—has already come? The philosopher Nietzsche remarked that Jesus' disciples "should look a little more redeemed"!

December 11—December 17, 2016

Something to think and pray about each day this week:

Preparing Our Hearts

"Are you ready for Christmas?" asked a guy I see at the train station every day. I thought of the long list of gifts I still needed to buy and the calendar crammed with holiday events and parties, and I shook my head. "Hardly," I said, and we both laughed knowingly. On my train ride downtown I turned off my iPod and let my mind ponder that question a little deeper. "Am I ready for Christmas?" This time I thought about the meaning of the holiday—the Son of God coming to earth to dwell among us and show us the way to eternal life. Again I shook my head and murmured to myself, "Hardly." It was then that I vowed to take advantage of every opportunity to prepare my heart for the coming of the Christ Child into the world—the world you and I live in. What I discovered was that if we know what we're preparing for, everything we encounter on the way to Christmas can prepare us for the coming of Christ, not only in Bethlehem 2,000 years ago but also in our homes, our families, our workplaces, and our communities. The usual December distractions can instead become holy moments when we find the Christ Child in our midst. Having the right attitude and perspective on the season will help you and your family avoid the excesses that make certain Christmas preparations frantic, yet draining and disappointing. As theologian John Shea says, "The task seems to be the delicate one of learning to make the customs and traditions of Christmas serve the Spirit."

—Tom McGrath, *Loyola Press blogs*

The Presence of God

Jesus, help me to be fully alive to your Holy Presence. Enfold me in your love. Let my heart become one with yours.

Freedom

I will ask God's help,
to be free from my own preoccupations,
to be open to God in this time of prayer,
to come to know, love, and serve God more.

Consciousness

I ask how I am within myself today. Am I particularly tired, stressed, or off form? If any of these characteristics apply, can I try to let go of the concerns that disturb me?

The Word

God speaks to each of us individually. I listen attentively to hear what God is saying to me. Read the text a few times, then listen. (Please turn to the Scripture on the following pages. Inspiration points are there should you need them. When you are ready, return here to continue.)

Conversation

Sometimes I wonder what I might say if I were to meet you in person, Lord.
I think I might say, Thank you, Lord for always being there for me.

Conclusion

Glory be to the Father, and to the Son, and to the Holy Spirit,
As it was in the beginning, is now and ever shall be,
World without end. Amen.

Sunday 11th December
Third Sunday of Advent
Matthew 11:2–11

When John heard in prison what the Messiah was doing, he sent word by his disciples and said to him, "Are you the one who is to come, or are we to wait for another?" Jesus answered them, "Go and tell John what you hear and see: the blind receive their sight, the lame walk, the lepers are cleansed, the deaf hear, the dead are raised, and the poor have good news brought to them. And blessed is anyone who takes no offense at me." As they went away, Jesus began to speak to the crowds about John: "What did you go out into the wilderness to look at? A reed shaken by the wind? What then did you go out to see? Someone dressed in soft robes? Look, those who wear soft robes are in royal palaces. What then did you go out to see? A prophet? Yes, I tell you, and more than a prophet. This is the one about whom it is written, 'See, I am sending my messenger ahead of you, who will prepare your way before you.' Truly I tell you, among those born of women no one has arisen greater than John the Baptist; yet the least in the kingdom of heaven is greater than he."

- There is real comfort in this story. John the Baptist, the powerful, austere man who holds such sway among the Jews, still has his moments of darkness. Imprisoned in Herod's dungeon, he wonders: *Am I a fool? Is this all there is? Was I wrong about Jesus?* He does not just brood on the question; he sends messengers to Jesus. And Jesus does not send back reassurances; rather, he asks the messengers to open their eyes and see the evidence of Jesus' life.

- "Go and tell what you hear and see . . . the blind receive their sight . . ."! What do I see and hear? Do I see the signs of God's kingdom breaking through in the world around me? What does it look like? If I don't see any positive signs, why not? Do I need to look again, or look differently? Am I somehow looking for "soft robes" and "royal palaces" when God is offering me a prophet?

Monday 12th December
Luke 1:26–38

In the sixth month the angel Gabriel was sent by God to a town in Galilee called Nazareth, to a virgin engaged to a man whose name was Joseph, of the house of David. The virgin's name was Mary. And he came to her and said, "Greetings, favored one! The Lord is with you." But she was much perplexed by his words and pondered what sort of greeting this might be. The angel said to her, "Do not be afraid, Mary, for you have found favor with God. And now, you will conceive in your womb and bear a son, and you will name him Jesus. He will be great, and will be called the Son of the Most High, and the Lord God will give to him the throne of his ancestor David. He will reign over the house of Jacob forever, and of his kingdom there will be no end." Mary said to the angel, "How can this be, since I am a virgin?" The angel said to her, "The Holy Spirit will come upon you, and the power of the Most High will overshadow you; therefore the child to be born will be holy; he will be called Son of God. And now, your relative Elizabeth in her old age has also conceived a son; and this is the sixth month for her who was said to be barren. For nothing will be impossible with God." Then Mary said, "Here am I, the servant of the Lord; let it be with me according to your word." Then the angel departed from her.

- Gabriel's message is condensed, intense, and direct. Mary is told that God favors her. She is to become pregnant by the Holy Spirit. She is to be the mother of the long-awaited Messiah. Her aged relative is already expecting a son. Each part of this sequence requires deep reflection, and yet we have the wonder of Mary's immediate consent. What might have prepared her to hear such a message?

- "Let it be with me according to your word." We remember Mary's words whenever we pray the Angelus. Lord, this is not an easy prayer to make. You prayed it yourself in Gethsemane in a sweat of blood: "Not my will but yours be done." Help me make this prayer the pattern of my life. What issues of surrender and trust does it raise for me?

Tuesday 13th December
Matthew 21:28–32

Jesus said, "What do you think? A man had two sons; he went to the first and said, 'Son, go and work in the vineyard today.' He answered, 'I will not'; but later he changed his mind and went. The father went to the second and said the same; and he answered, 'I go, sir'; but he did not go. Which of the two did the will of his father?" They said, "The first." Jesus said to them, "Truly I tell you, the tax collectors and the prostitutes are going into the kingdom of God ahead of you. For John came to you in the way of righteousness and you did not believe him, but the tax collectors and the prostitutes believed him; and even after you saw it, you did not change your minds and believe him."

- Well, which person am I? The smooth but unreliable daddy-pleaser or the guy who, even with a bad attitude, does the job? The kingdom of heaven is not promised to the charmers but to those whose lives would make no sense if God did not exist.

- I review the statements and declarations I may have made. I ask God to help me abide by them and to help me accept forgiveness for wherever I have fallen short. God continually invites me to fullness of life. I do not have to be downhearted because I'm aware that I don't always accept the invitation. Rather, I can be encouraged that God puts trust in me by calling me to serve others.

Wednesday 14th December
Luke 7:18b–23

At that time, John summoned two of his disciples and sent them to the Lord to ask, "Are you the one who is to come, or are we to wait for another?" When the men had come to him, they said, "John the Baptist has sent us to you to ask, 'Are you the one who is to come, or are we to wait for another?'" Jesus had just then cured many people of diseases, plagues, and evil spirits, and had given sight to many who were blind. And he answered them, "Go and tell John what you have seen and heard: the blind receive their sight, the lame walk, the lepers are cleansed, the deaf hear, the dead are raised, the poor have good news brought to them. And blessed is anyone who takes no offense at me."

- The Jews wanted a political Messiah who would dramatically terminate their oppression under Roman rule. But Jesus' good news was not about war or politics. His message was meant especially for the blind, the lame, the lepers, the deaf, the dead, and the poor. I ask Jesus for the wisdom to avoid getting lost in political issues. I pray for the grace to share my love with those who are marginalized and unwanted by the world.

- John has been tossed into prison. As he languishes there, the oil of John's lamp is flickering. He wonders, did I get it right? Was my ministry a waste? Is Jesus the one I believed him to be? Lord, I can identify with John. I find that the wick of my lamp can quiver and splutter when things don't go my way. My desire for a world of peace and justice is met by a world of violence and injustice. This Advent day, refill my inner lamp and let me walk in faith and trust.

Thursday 15th December
Luke 7:24–30

When John's messengers had gone, Jesus began to speak to the crowds about John: "What did you go out into the wilderness to look at? A reed shaken by the wind? What then did you go out to see? Someone dressed in soft robes? Look, those who put on fine clothing and live in luxury are in royal palaces. What then did you go out to see? A prophet? Yes, I tell you, and more than a prophet. This is the one about whom it is written, 'See, I am sending my messenger ahead of you, who will prepare your way before you.' I tell you, among those born of women no one is greater than John; yet the least in the kingdom of God is greater than he." (And all the people who heard this, including the tax collectors, acknowledged the justice of God, because they had been baptized with John's baptism. But by refusing to be baptized by him, the Pharisees and the lawyers rejected God's purpose for themselves.)

- What do I go out to see? What are my true values? What impresses me? Jesus was impressed by John because he expressed God's values and chose simplicity of life. I ask him if he is impressed by me, and I listen in my heart to what he says to me.

- Luke uses a Hebrew poetic form of speaking—with repetition, question, and answer—to emphasize that with Jesus' ministry a new world order is beginning. I thank Jesus that I know the divine project, which John could not have known. I ask that I may help in the unfolding of God's intentions for the world. I can be at least a very minor prophet by living the gospel in my place and time.

Friday 16th December
John 5:33–36

Jesus said, "You sent messengers to John, and he testified to the truth. Not that I accept such human testimony, but I say these things so that you may be saved. He was a burning and shining lamp, and you were willing to rejoice for a while in his light. But I have a testimony greater than John's. The works that the Father has given me to complete, the very works that I am doing, testify on my behalf that the Father has sent me."

- Jesus points out that John's message was indeed a light to the people but that now there is a brighter light, which is Jesus. Sometimes we must transition from one wisdom or enlightenment to another. When do we know it's time to do this? Am I comfortable with the idea that I might need to make such a shift in my spiritual attention?

- What "works" are evidence that God is present? Many people claim to do God's works and deliver God's message, but certainly not all of them speak the truth. Holy Spirit, help me discern when what I am witnessing is a work of God.

Saturday 17th December
Matthew 1:1–17

An account of the genealogy of Jesus the Messiah, the son of David, the son of Abraham. Abraham was the father of Isaac, and Isaac the father of Jacob, and Jacob the father of Judah and his brothers, and Judah the father of Perez and Zerah by Tamar, and Perez the father of Hezron, and Hezron the father of Aram, and Aram the father of Aminadab, and Aminadab the father of Nahshon, and Nahshon the father of Salmon, and Salmon the father of Boaz by Rahab, and Boaz the father of Obed by Ruth, and Obed the father of Jesse, and Jesse the father of King David. And David was the father of Solomon by the wife of Uriah, and Solomon the father of Rehoboam, and Rehoboam the father of Abijah, and Abijah the father of Asaph, and Asaph the father of Jehoshaphat, and Jehoshaphat the father of Joram, and Joram the father of Uzziah, and Uzziah the father of Jotham, and Jotham the father of Ahaz, and Ahaz the father of Hezekiah, and Hezekiah the father of Manasseh, and Manasseh the father of Amos, and Amos the father of Josiah, and Josiah the father of Jechoniah and his brothers, at the time of the deportation to Babylon. And after the deportation to Babylon: Jechoniah was the father of Salathiel, and Salathiel the father of Zerubbabel, and Zerubbabel the father of Abiud, and Abiud the father of Eliakim, and Eliakim the father of Azor, and Azor the father of Zadok, and Zadok the father of Achim, and Achim the father of Eliud, and Eliud the father of Eleazar, and Eleazar the father of Matthan, and Matthan the father of Jacob, and Jacob the father of Joseph the husband of Mary, of whom Jesus was born, who is called the Messiah. So all the generations from Abraham to David are fourteen generations; and from David to the deportation to Babylon, fourteen generations; and from the deportation to Babylon to the Messiah, fourteen generations.

- We all face the challenge to become our best selves. Family tradition and social expectations play their part here, but deepest down we need to know what God is inviting us to be. We are God's beloveds, and a high destiny awaits us. We are to reveal to the world something of God's own self.

- Today's reading looks unsparingly at Jesus' ancestry. Matthew points out that Jesus' forbears included children born of incest (Perez), of mixed races (Boaz), and of adultery (Solomon). God entered our human history with all the episodes that proud people would be ashamed of. Lord, teach me to accept my humanity, my genes, and my relatives, as you did.

The Fourth Week of Advent
December 18—December 24, 2016

Something to think and pray about each day this week:

What Are We Expecting?

How do we prepare our hearts for you, Jesus? Or do we understand our need to prepare? Are we more likely to hurry around once you're here, trying to focus on this guest we weren't expecting? Will we be ready when you appear there in the manger? Or will our hearts and minds be so focused on our immediate struggles that we're unprepared to receive eternal hope and grace? Will we recognize you? Or will we be looking for a savior of our own making? One who is powerful, maybe, who can rule the world by force if necessary? Will we be looking for a savior who looks like we do in race, culture, or religion? Will we stop and gaze upon you, forgetting everything else for just a few moments? Or will we be too distracted by credit card bills, the fallout of family gatherings, the extra pounds we've gained, and all the things we want to buy and do in the coming year? Will we journey through all sorts of weather and landscapes just to get a glimpse of you? Or if it's just too hard to get to the manger, will we flip through the TV channels one more time, get a snack, put on comfortable clothes, and get lost in consoling fantasies? How will we prepare our hearts for the Christ Child?

—Vinita Hampton Wright, Loyola Press blogs

The Presence of God

"I stand at the door and knock," says the Lord. What a wonderful privilege that the Lord of all creation desires to come to me. I welcome his presence.

Freedom

Saint Ignatius thought that a thick and shapeless tree trunk would never believe that it could become a statue, admired as a miracle of sculpture, and would never submit itself to the chisel of the sculptor, who sees by her genius what she can make of it.
I ask for the grace to let myself be shaped by my loving Creator.

Consciousness

Knowing that God loves me unconditionally, I can afford to be honest about how I am. What are my fears and desires? What do I expect from God? What am I willing to give to God—from my emotions and talents, thoughts and energy? And how do I feel now? I share my feelings openly with the Lord.

The Word

I take my time to read the word of God, slowly, a few times, allowing myself to dwell on anything that strikes me. (Please turn to the Scripture on the following pages. Inspiration points are there should you need them. When you are ready, return here to continue.)

Conversation

Do I notice myself reacting as I pray with the word of God? Do I feel challenged, comforted, angry? Imagining Jesus sitting or standing by me, I speak out my feelings, as one trusted friend to another.

Conclusion

I thank God for these moments we have spent together and for any insights I have been given concerning the text.

Sunday 18th December
Fourth Sunday of Advent
Matthew 1:18–24

Now the birth of Jesus the Messiah took place in this way. When his mother Mary had been engaged to Joseph, but before they lived together, she was found to be with child from the Holy Spirit. Her husband Joseph, being a righteous man and unwilling to expose her to public disgrace, planned to dismiss her quietly. But just when he had resolved to do this, an angel of the Lord appeared to him in a dream and said, "Joseph, son of David, do not be afraid to take Mary as your wife, for the child conceived in her is from the Holy Spirit. She will bear a son, and you are to name him Jesus, for he will save his people from their sins." All this took place to fulfill what had been spoken by the Lord through the prophet: "Look, the virgin shall conceive and bear a son, and they shall name him Emmanuel, which means, 'God is with us.'" When Joseph awoke from sleep, he did as the angel of the Lord commanded him; he took her as his wife.

- Joseph is faced with a heartbreaking dilemma. His life is in turmoil because he loves Mary so much. Let me imagine for a few moments how welcome the angel's message must have been to him! How quickly he acts, allowing himself to follow his heart and not allowing his sense of legal obligation to rule.

- How often in Scripture does the quiet prompting of the Spirit come from within, in the form of a dream. How sensitive must the dreamers have been, to recognize the Spirit in their hearts. Do I invite the Spirit to prompt me? How ready am I to hear what the Spirit might suggest?

Monday 19th December
Luke 1:5–25

In the days of King Herod of Judea, there was a priest named Zechariah, who belonged to the priestly order of Abijah. His wife was a descendant of Aaron, and her name was Elizabeth. Both of them were righteous before God, living blamelessly according to all the commandments and regulations of the Lord. But they had no children, because Elizabeth was barren, and both were getting on in years. Once when he was serving as priest before God and his section was on duty, he was chosen by lot, according to the custom of the priesthood, to enter the sanctuary of the

Lord and offer incense. Now at the time of the incense offering, the whole assembly of the people was praying outside. Then there appeared to him an angel of the Lord, standing at the right side of the altar of incense. When Zechariah saw him, he was terrified; and fear overwhelmed him. But the angel said to him, "Do not be afraid, Zechariah, for your prayer has been heard. Your wife Elizabeth will bear you a son, and you will name him John. You will have joy and gladness, and many will rejoice at his birth, for he will be great in the sight of the Lord. He must never drink wine or strong drink; even before his birth he will be filled with the Holy Spirit. He will turn many of the people of Israel to the Lord their God. With the spirit and power of Elijah he will go before him, to turn the hearts of parents to their children, and the disobedient to the wisdom of the righteous, to make ready a people prepared for the Lord." Zechariah said to the angel, "How will I know that this is so? For I am an old man, and my wife is getting on in years." The angel replied, "I am Gabriel. I stand in the presence of God, and I have been sent to speak to you and to bring you this good news. But now, because you did not believe my words, which will be fulfilled in their time, you will become mute, unable to speak, until the day these things occur." Meanwhile the people were waiting for Zechariah, and wondered at his delay in the sanctuary. When he did come out, he could not speak to them, and they realized that he had seen a vision in the sanctuary. He kept motioning to them and remained unable to speak. When his time of service was ended, he went to his home. After those days his wife Elizabeth conceived, and for five months she remained in seclusion. She said, "This is what the Lord has done for me when he looked favorably on me and took away the disgrace I have endured among my people."

- Despite all his prayer, along with reassurance from the angel, Zechariah is unable to put his trust and faith in God's way. The consequence is months of isolation, during which Zechariah is unable to communicate. Despite the man's obstinacy, God's favor is seen in the birth of Zechariah's son. Elizabeth has no difficulty acknowledging the source of new life, saying, "This is what the Lord has done for me." This Advent day, can I reflect back on my life and say likewise?

- Between today and Christmas Day, the liturgy features three biblical women who become pregnant against all the odds: Elizabeth, mother of John the Baptist; the unnamed mother of Samson; and Hannah, mother of Samuel. They remind us that God is in control of the human story and intervenes graciously in favor of the helpless and despised.

Tuesday 20th December
Luke 1:26–38

In the sixth month the angel Gabriel was sent by God to a town in Galilee called Nazareth, to a virgin engaged to a man whose name was Joseph, of the house of David. The virgin's name was Mary. And he came to her and said, "Greetings, favored one! The Lord is with you." But she was much perplexed by his words and pondered what sort of greeting this might be. The angel said to her, "Do not be afraid, Mary, for you have found favor with God. And now, you will conceive in your womb and bear a son, and you will name him Jesus. He will be great, and will be called the Son of the Most High, and the Lord God will give to him the throne of his ancestor David. He will reign over the house of Jacob forever, and of his kingdom there will be no end." Mary said to the angel, "How can this be, since I am a virgin?" The angel said to her, "The Holy Spirit will come upon you, and the power of the Most High will overshadow you; therefore the child to be born will be holy; he will be called Son of God. And now, your relative Elizabeth in her old age has also conceived a son; and this is the sixth month for her who was said to be barren. For nothing will be impossible with God." Then Mary said, "Here am I, the servant of the Lord; let it be with me according to your word." Then the angel departed from her.

- Mary, the young girl of no status, from the village of Nazareth, an utterly insignificant place, is singled out, called, chosen, and overshadowed with God's Spirit. Her response moves from fear to total trust in God's inscrutable designs.

- Lord, may I grow each day in trusting your amazing annunciation to me: I am your "highly favored" one, and I am not to be afraid. You rejoice in me! In the busyness of life, keep these thoughts before me. Like Mary, may I be ready to play my part in bringing you to birth.

Wednesday 21st December
Luke 1:39–45

In those days Mary set out and went with haste to a Judean town in the hill country, where she entered the house of Zechariah and greeted Elizabeth. When Elizabeth heard Mary's greeting, the child leaped in her womb. And Elizabeth was filled with the Holy Spirit and exclaimed with a loud cry, "Blessed are you among women, and blessed is the fruit of your womb. And why has this happened to me, that the mother of my Lord comes to me? For as soon as I heard the sound of your greeting, the child in my womb leaped for joy. And blessed is she who believed that there would be a fulfillment of what was spoken to her by the Lord."

- I marvel at the instinct and insight of mothers. While husband Zechariah is baffled and struck dumb and foster father Joseph has misgivings, it is a woman, Elizabeth, herself pregnant, who recognizes the action of the Lord in her young cousin. She is given the special grace of an intimate appreciation of what is happening and who is really present. In life do I always appreciate what is happening and who is really present?

- John leaped for joy in the presence of his Lord. Centuries earlier, King David "danced before the Lord with all his might." The psalmist tells us to "shout for joy." Saint Paul urges us to "sing and make melody to the Lord with all our heart." It is the child in us who can truly be open to God's constant invitation to be born again and to be part of the creation, which is itself constantly being recreated. The child in us is free to rejoice.

Thursday 22nd December
Luke 1:46–56

And Mary said, "My soul magnifies the Lord, and my spirit rejoices in God my Savior, for he has looked with favor on the lowliness of his servant. Surely, from now on all generations will call me blessed; for the Mighty One has done great things for me, and holy is his name. His mercy is for those who fear him from generation to generation. He has shown strength with his arm; he has scattered the proud in the thoughts of their hearts. He has brought down the powerful from their thrones, and lifted up the lowly; he has filled the hungry with good things, and sent the rich away empty. He has helped his servant Israel, in remembrance of his mercy, according to the promise he made to our ancestors, to Abraham and to his descendants forever." And Mary remained with Elizabeth about three months and then returned to her home.

- I imagine that I am invited to stay with Elizabeth and Mary for the three months they spent together. I observe what they say and do, and how quietly happy they both are, as they each carry the mystery of God in their wombs.

- With Mary, I count my blessings, not as a matter of pride or achievement but to recognize where God is at work in my life. Pride and humility are in the picture as Mary prays her Magnificat. Mary rejoices in being a blessed, lowly servant. I think of how this description relates to how I am now.

Friday 23rd December
Luke 1:57–66

Now the time came for Elizabeth to give birth, and she bore a son. Her neighbors and relatives heard that the Lord had shown his great mercy to her, and they rejoiced with her. On the eighth day they came to circumcise the child, and they were going to name him Zechariah after his father. But his mother said, "No; he is to be called John." They said to her, "None of your relatives has this name." Then they began motioning to his father to find out what name he wanted to give him. He asked for a writing tablet and wrote, "His name is John." And all of them were amazed. Immediately his mouth was opened and his tongue freed, and he began to speak, praising God. Fear came over all their neighbors, and all these things were talked about throughout the entire hill country of Judea. All who heard them pondered them and said, "What then will this child become?" For, indeed, the hand of the Lord was with him.

- How did Elizabeth know that the child was to be called John? Did a small voice tell her this? Do I listen for the small voice that tells me what to do? Elizabeth and Mary were ordinary people, just as I am. God speaks to me as God spoke to them.

- Even in his old age, Zechariah was ready to break from the old patterns. I ask for the help that I need to step away from the usual patterns and to follow God's call. I pray for all children: may the joy and hope that they experience live and grow into a deep appreciation of God's goodness.

Saturday 24th December
Luke 1:67–79

Then his father Zechariah was filled with the Holy Spirit and spoke this prophecy: "Blessed be the Lord God of Israel, for he has looked favorably on his people and redeemed them. He has raised up a mighty savior for us in the house of his servant David, as he spoke through the mouth of his holy prophets from of old, that we would be saved from our enemies and from the hand of all who hate us. Thus he has shown the mercy promised to our ancestors, and has remembered his holy covenant, the oath that he swore to our ancestor Abraham, to grant us that we, being rescued from the hands of our enemies, might serve him without fear, in holiness and righteousness before him all our days. And you, child, will be called the prophet of the Most High; for you will go before the Lord to prepare his ways, to give knowledge of salvation to his people by the forgiveness of their sins. By the tender mercy of our God, the dawn from on high will break upon us, to give light to those who sit in darkness and in the shadow of death, to guide our feet into the way of peace."

- Zechariah is profoundly aware of his heritage and sees God's action in the past as having promise for the future. I draw encouragement from my own story, allowing God to bless me with hope and confidence in continued blessing.

- Allow this psalm of thanks and praise to express what you feel and believe. Zechariah made this prayer for his son. It was a prayer grown and made in love. We are now the ones who go before the Lord; our love and care can become the dawn breaking into others' lives, giving light to all in darkness. We are the ones to walk with the peace that calms those around us and guides them on their journey. Take what is suitable from this great prayer, said each morning throughout the church, and allow it to link you with the living Christ.

The First Week of Christmas
December 25—December 31, 2016

Something to think and pray about each day this week:

Details and Mystery

Some years, during Advent, the concreteness of the nativity story—how normal, how tangible it is—draws me in. The awkward unease of late pregnancy. The human need for shelter and rest. Straw, wood, pieces of cloth. The scent of barn animals. A newborn baby's cry. But this year, it's the swirl of mystery that hovers above and through the narrative that most captures my imagination. In an Advent homily, my priest quoted a theologian who said that thinking about God is like trying to draw a picture of a bird in flight. "You end up with details of its wings caught in a certain position, feathers, eyes, claws frozen in place for careful scrutiny," he explained. "Or you end up with a blur that loses all detail, but captures speed and movement." We're all theologians, he said, and we all envision various concepts of God in detail and others in motion. Do we choose one picture over another, or somehow hold both in tension?

—Jennifer Grant, *Wholehearted Living*

The Presence of God

To be present is to arrive as one is and open up to the other.
At this instant, as I arrive here, God is present waiting for me.
God always arrives before me, desiring to connect with me
even more than my most intimate friend.
I take a moment and greet my loving God.

Freedom

I am free. When I look at these words in writing, they seem to create in me a feeling of awe. Yes, a wonderful feeling of freedom. Thank you, God.

Consciousness

To be conscious about something is to be aware of it.
Dear Lord, help me to remember that you gave me life.
Thank you for the gift of life.
Teach me to slow down, to be still and enjoy the pleasures created for me.
To be aware of the beauty that surrounds me. The marvel of mountains, the calmness of lakes, the fragility of a flower petal. I need to remember that all these things come from you.

The Word

The word of God comes to us through the Scriptures. May the Holy Spirit enlighten my mind and heart to respond to the Gospel teachings. (Please turn to the Scripture on the following pages. Inspiration points are there should you need them. When you are ready, return here to continue.)

Conversation

I begin to talk to Jesus about the piece of Scripture I have just read. What part of it strikes a chord in me? Perhaps the words of a friend—or some story I have heard recently—will slowly rise to the surface in my consciousness. If so, does the story throw light on what the Scripture passage may be trying to say to me?

Conclusion

Glory be to the Father, and to the Son, and to the Holy Spirit,
As it was in the beginning, is now and ever shall be,
World without end. Amen.

Sunday 25th December
The Nativity of the Lord
John 1:1–18

In the beginning was the Word, and the Word was with God, and the Word was God. He was in the beginning with God. All things came into being through him, and without him not one thing came into being. What has come into being in him was life, and the life was the light of all people. The light shines in the darkness, and the darkness did not overcome it. There was a man sent from God, whose name was John. He came as a witness to testify to the light, so that all might believe through him. He himself was not the light, but he came to testify to the light. The true light, which enlightens everyone, was coming into the world. He was in the world, and the world came into being through him; yet the world did not know him. He came to what was his own, and his own people did not accept him. But to all who received him, who believed in his name, he gave power to become children of God, who were born, not of blood or of the will of the flesh or of the will of man, but of God. And the Word became flesh and lived among us, and we have seen his glory, the glory as of a father's only son, full of grace and truth. (John testified to him and cried out, "This was he of whom I said, 'He who comes after me ranks ahead of me because he was before me.'") From his fullness we have all received, grace upon grace. The law indeed was given through Moses; grace and truth came through Jesus Christ. No one has ever seen God. It is God the only Son, who is close to the Father's heart, who has made him known.

- In this hymn, which introduces the fourth Gospel, John proclaims the faith that marks us as Christian. We believe that Jesus is the word of God, God's perfect expression. "No one has ever seen God. It is God the only Son, who is close to the Father's heart, who has made him known." Lord, in the year that starts tonight, let me grow in the knowledge of God. May I receive of your fullness, grace upon grace. You took on this mortal flesh for me and lived among us. May this coming year bring me closer to you.

- In this time of prayer, I let what is at the heart of God reveal itself to me: life and light for all. I acknowledge what comes between me and this life God offers. I identify what darkens my heart and narrows my vision. The goodness and generosity of God are here for me as God longs to become present in the world through me.

Monday 26th December
Matthew 10:17–22

Jesus said, "Beware of them, for they will hand you over to councils and flog you in their synagogues; and you will be dragged before governors and kings because of me, as a testimony to them and the Gentiles. When they hand you over, do not worry about how you are to speak or what you are to say; for what you are to say will be given to you at that time; for it is not you who speak, but the Spirit of your Father speaking through you. Brother will betray brother to death, and a father his child, and children will rise against parents and have them put to death; and you will be hated by all because of my name. But the one who endures to the end will be saved."

- The following advice, attributed to Saint Teresa of Ávila, says that endurance gains us everything:

  Let nothing disturb you.
  Let nothing frighten you.
  All things are passing.
  God never changes.
  Patient endurance attains all things.
  God alone suffices.

- Lord, today we pray for those who are tormented in your name. Martyrs continue to lay down their lives for you, even today. There are also the subtler trials that believers endure: scientific scorn, media distortion, opposition to faith perspectives. Give us the gift of endurance in all of this.

Tuesday 27th December
John 20:1a, 2–8

Mary Magdalene ran and went to Simon Peter and the other disciple, the one whom Jesus loved, and said to them, "They have taken the Lord out of the tomb, and we do not know where they have laid him." Then Peter and the other disciple set out and went towards the tomb. The two were running together, but the other disciple outran Peter and reached the tomb first. He bent down to look in and saw the linen wrappings lying there, but he did not go in. Then Simon Peter came, following him, and went into the tomb. He saw the linen wrappings lying there, and the cloth that had been on Jesus' head, not lying with the linen wrappings but rolled up in a place by itself. Then the other disciple, who reached the tomb first, also went in, and he saw and believed.

- Risen Lord, help me see beyond the obvious and understand your ways. You show me you are alive and active in my moments of joyous discovery, in touches of gladness, in enriching encounters, and in the kindnesses of others. Always you come delicately. As poet Gerard Manley Hopkins wrote: "I greet you the days I meet you, and bless when I understand" (paraphrased).

- John describes how the disciple saw and believed. However, John later points out that it is not enough for us to believe; we must spread the good news, as he himself did: "We are writing these things so that our joy may be complete." I notice that sharing good news brings joy to the sharer as well as to the receiver. Do I experience this?

Wednesday 28th December
Matthew 2:13–18

Now after they had left, an angel of the Lord appeared to Joseph in a dream and said, "Get up, take the child and his mother, and flee to Egypt, and remain there until I tell you; for Herod is about to search for the child, to destroy him." Then Joseph got up, took the child and his mother by night, and went to Egypt, and remained there until the death of Herod. This was to fulfill what had been spoken by the Lord through the prophet, "Out of Egypt I have called my son." When Herod saw that he had been tricked by the wise men, he was infuriated, and he sent and killed all the children in and around Bethlehem who were two years old or under, according to the time that he had learned from the wise men. Then was fulfilled what had been spoken through the prophet Jeremiah: "A voice was heard in Ramah, wailing and loud lamentation, Rachel weeping for her children; she refused to be consoled, because they are no more."

- This is a painful story. What difficult news the angel brings: Joseph and his tiny family have to become refugees and go by night to a foreign land. We ask for his strength of soul today to do what we can to help the world's refugees.

- This morning I pray for the mourning mothers of the Holy Land, weeping to this day for their dead children, because they are no more. Arabs and Jews, all of them one people—Semites—continue to kill one another, in the delusion that bombs and blood will help. I pray for a spirit of peace there.

Thursday 29th December
Luke 2:22–35

When the time came for their purification according to the law of Moses, they brought him up to Jerusalem to present him to the Lord (as it is written in the law of the Lord, "Every firstborn male shall be designated as holy to the Lord"), and they offered a sacrifice according to what is stated in the law of the Lord, "a pair of turtledoves or two young pigeons." Now there was a man in Jerusalem whose name was Simeon; this man was righteous and devout, looking forward to the consolation of Israel, and the Holy Spirit rested on him. It had been revealed to him by the Holy Spirit that he would not see death before he had seen the Lord's Messiah. Guided by the Spirit, Simeon came into the temple; and when the parents brought in the child Jesus, to do for him what was customary under the law, Simeon took him in his arms and praised God, saying, "Master, now you are dismissing your servant in peace, according to your word; for my eyes have seen your salvation, which you have prepared in the presence of all peoples, a light for revelation to the Gentiles and for glory to your people Israel." And the child's father and mother were amazed at what was being said about him. Then Simeon blessed them and said to his mother Mary, "This child is destined for the falling and the rising of many in Israel, and to be a sign that will be opposed so that the inner thoughts of many will be revealed—and a sword will pierce your own soul too."

- Simeon sings his song of farewell after a lifetime of watching for the sign of God's salvation. Attuned to the Holy Spirit, he identifies Jesus from the many children who have come up to Jerusalem. Jesus comes not in power but as a babe in his mother's arms. He comes as a light for all who are in darkness. Lord, may your Holy Spirit rest on me today. Like Simeon, may I recognize that you have come in the form of a vulnerable child.

- Lord, in Simeon I see hope richly rewarded. The years of waiting did not blunt the edge of his faith. His hope and yearning kept him alive to the promptings of God, ready to hear God's voice when it came. Grant that I may learn from him.

Friday 30th December
The Holy Family of Jesus, Mary, and Joseph
Matthew 2:13–15, 19–23

Now after they had left, an angel of the Lord appeared to Joseph in a dream and said, "Get up, take the child and his mother, and flee to Egypt, and remain there until I tell you; for Herod is about to search for the child, to destroy him." Then Joseph got up, took the child and his mother by night, and went to Egypt, and remained there until the death of Herod. This was to fulfill what had been spoken by the Lord through the prophet, "Out of Egypt I have called my son." When Herod died, an angel of the Lord suddenly appeared in a dream to Joseph in Egypt and said, "Get up, take the child and his mother, and go to the land of Israel, for those who were seeking the child's life are dead." Then Joseph got up, took the child and his mother, and went to the land of Israel. But when he heard that Archelaus was ruling over Judea in place of his father Herod, he was afraid to go there. And after being warned in a dream, he went away to the district of Galilee. There he made his home in a town called Nazareth, so that what had been spoken through the prophets might be fulfilled, "He will be called a Nazorean."

- We see that on a number of occasions, angels direct Joseph in his dreams. But we also find that he uses his own common sense! He is cautious that the son of Herod will be as bad as the father and so takes precautions. Joseph is a model of protection and devotion as a husband and a father. Lord, may I be as caring of others as he is.

- Like any newly married couple, Mary and Joseph have their dreams and hopes. He is a skilled carpenter, so their future seems secure. Then, suddenly, everything falls apart: the birth in a stable, the flight into Egypt, and the long wait until they can return to Galilee. But in all the mess, they stay faithful to one another and they bring up the Son of God. Lord, may we support family life no matter how much it is threatened.

Saturday 31st December

John 1:1–18

In the beginning was the Word, and the Word was with God, and the Word was God. He was in the beginning with God. All things came into being through him, and without him not one thing came into being. What has come into being in him was life, and the life was the light of all people. The light shines in the darkness, and the darkness did not overcome it. There was a man sent from God, whose name was John. He came as a witness to testify to the light, so that all might believe through him. He himself was not the light, but he came to testify to the light. The true light, which enlightens everyone, was coming into the world. He was in the world, and the world came into being through him; yet the world did not know him. He came to what was his own, and his own people did not accept him. But to all who received him, who believed in his name, he gave power to become children of God, who were born, not of blood or of the will of the flesh or of the will of man, but of God. And the Word became flesh and lived among us, and we have seen his glory, the glory as of a father's only son, full of grace and truth. (John testified to him and cried out, "This was he of whom I said, 'He who comes after me ranks ahead of me because he was before me.'") From his fullness we have all received, grace upon grace. The law indeed was given through Moses; grace and truth came through Jesus Christ. No one has ever seen God. It is God the only Son, who is close to the Father's heart, who has made him known.

- "The light shines in the darkness, and the darkness did not overcome it." Facing a new calendar year, may we shine with divine light. May this light shine within, so that we believe we are the children of God, loved to the core. May we in turn love others limitlessly and so bring them light and consolation in their everyday lives.

- One theologian wrote, "I searched for God in the heavens but found he had fallen to earth, so I must seek him among my friends." Lord, Emmanuel, I draw near to you today as I celebrate your birth. I thank you for moving house, so to speak, and locating yourself so fully in our human story of loneliness, pain, frailty, and fragility.

The Second Week of Christmas
January 1—January 7, 2017

Something to think and pray about each day this week:

Where Holy Encounter Leads

The story of Christ's coming as a child is filled with miracles: angels coming in person and in dreams; a child born to a virgin; a mysterious star; holy secrets spoken to shepherds and wise men. The glory of this coming has the power to entrance us year after year as we make the journey through Advent and find ourselves, yet again, at the manger. But the child grew up, was baptized by John, and embarked on a life that few if any could fathom or desire. And for each person who encountered this life of God-among-us, the glory and gratitude led also to personal pilgrimage and transformation. Even now, these glorious and enlightening events create holy encounter, which leads us to engagement with God that is personal. Mary and Joseph were forever changed, as were other players in this sacred drama, from the shepherds to John the Baptist and those who would become Jesus' disciples. They invite us by their examples to be courageous enough to stand at the manger but then follow the child to wherever he desires to take us.

—The Editors

The Presence of God

Be still and know that I am God. Lord, may your Spirit guide me to seek your loving presence more and more. For it is there I find rest and refreshment from this busy world.

Freedom

By God's grace I was born to live in freedom. Free to enjoy the pleasures he created for me. Dear Lord, grant that I may live as you intended, with complete confidence in your loving care.

Consciousness

In God's loving presence I unwind the past day,
starting from now and looking back, moment by moment.
I gather in all the goodness and light, in gratitude.
I attend to the shadows and what they say to me,
seeking healing, courage, forgiveness.

The Word

The word of God comes to us through the Scriptures. May the Holy Spirit enlighten my mind and heart to respond to the Gospel teachings. (Please turn to the Scripture on the following pages. Inspiration points are there should you need them. When you are ready, return here to continue.)

Conversation

Jesus, you always welcomed little children when you walked on this earth. Teach me to have a childlike trust in you. To live in the knowledge that you will never abandon me.

Conclusion

Glory be to the Father, and to the Son, and to the Holy Spirit,
As it was in the beginning, is now and ever shall be,
World without end. Amen.

Sunday 1st January
Solemnity of Mary, the Holy Mother of God
Luke 2:16–21

So they went with haste and found Mary and Joseph, and the child lying in the manger. When they saw this, they made known what had been told them about this child; and all who heard it were amazed at what the shepherds told them. But Mary treasured all these words and pondered them in her heart. The shepherds returned, glorifying and praising God for all they had heard and seen, as it had been told them. After eight days had passed, it was time to circumcise the child; and he was called Jesus, the name given by the angel before he was conceived in the womb.

- According to the story, an angel had months ago appeared to Mary, and more angels had now appeared to the shepherds. All the heavenly messengers had conveyed an assurance: "You are going to see that God has sent into the world a prince from heaven's kingdom." The promise filled all with anticipation and the fulfillment filled all—Mary and the shepherds—with thanksgiving. Placing myself alongside Mary before the child, I try to open my heart to thanksgiving for all that God has done in my life.

- We start the year, as we start life, under the protection of a mother. Today we celebrate the most passionate and enduring of all human relationships, that of mother and child. As Mary looked at her baby and gave him her breast, she knew that there was a dimension here beyond her guessing. Christians thought about it for three centuries before the Council of Ephesus, in which they dared to consecrate the title θεοτοκος, mother of God. Like Mary, I treasure the words spoken about Jesus and ponder them in my heart.

Monday 2nd January
John 1:19–28

This is the testimony given by John when the Jews sent priests and Levites from Jerusalem to ask him, "Who are you?" He confessed and did not deny it, but confessed, "I am not the Messiah." And they asked him, "What then? Are you Elijah?" He said, "I am not." "Are you the prophet?" He answered, "No." Then they said to him, "Who are you? Let us have an answer for those who sent us. What do you say about yourself?" He said, "I am the voice of one crying out in the wilderness, 'Make straight the way of the Lord,' as the prophet Isaiah said." Now they had been sent from the Pharisees. They asked him, "Why then are you baptizing if you are neither the Messiah, nor Elijah, nor the prophet?" John answered them, "I baptize with water. Among you stands one whom you do not know, the one who is coming after me; I am not worthy to untie the thong of his sandal." This took place in Bethany across the Jordan where John was baptizing.

- Although he prepared the way for Jesus, John acknowledges that he did not know whom to expect. As I do my best, in my way, to prepare the way for Jesus, I cannot always know just what to be ready for.

- John remained active and vigilant. I pray that I may find the balance to stay occupied in God's service without letting my occupations overwhelm me.

Tuesday 3rd January
John 1:29–34

The next day John saw Jesus coming toward him and declared, "Here is the Lamb of God who takes away the sin of the world! This is he of whom I said, 'After me comes a man who ranks ahead of me because he was before me.' I myself did not know him; but I came baptizing with water for this reason, that he might be revealed to Israel." And John testified, "I saw the Spirit descending from heaven like a dove, and it remained on him. I myself did not know him, but the one who sent me to baptize with water said to me, 'He on whom you see the Spirit descend and remain is the one who baptizes with the Holy Spirit.' And I myself have seen and have testified that this is the Son of God."

- John's mission has reached its completion. His function was to point people in the direction of Jesus, the Lamb of God. With these words John draws back the curtain, and Jesus takes center stage in our human story, inviting us to be with him.

- The witness of John the Baptist depended on what was revealed to him in his prayer and on what he saw with his eyes. Bless me now, Lord, to recognize more clearly where you are moving in my life.

Wednesday 4th January
John 1:35–42

The next day John again was standing with two of his disciples, and as he watched Jesus walk by, he exclaimed, "Look, here is the Lamb of God!" The two disciples heard him say this, and they followed Jesus. When Jesus turned and saw them following, he said to them, "What are you looking for?" They said to him, "Rabbi" (which translated means Teacher), "where are you staying?" He said to them, "Come and see." They came and saw where he was staying, and they remained with him that day. It was about four o'clock in the afternoon. One of the two who heard John speak and followed him was Andrew, Simon Peter's brother. He first found his brother Simon and said to him, "We have found the Messiah" [which translated means Anointed]. He brought Simon to Jesus, who looked at him and said, "You are Simon son of John. You are to be called Cephas" [which translated means Peter].

- John the Baptist, who has an immense following in Jerusalem, does something remarkable here. He points his followers toward Jesus, the Lamb of God. With John's blessing, they walk away from him and follow Jesus. John is not the light but has come to bear witness to the light. He is happy to see his followers leave and to experience his own influence diminishing, because he is witnessing to Jesus. If we bring our ego to people, we bring death. If we bring Jesus, we bring life.

- I hear Jesus ask me, "What are you looking for?" I take time to answer with what is deep in my heart. If I cannot find words, I stay with my mood, being present to Jesus, who knows and loves me. I listen for his invitation to draw closer: "Come and see."

Thursday 5th January
John 1:43–51

The next day Jesus decided to go to Galilee. He found Philip and said to him, "Follow me." Now Philip was from Bethsaida, the city of Andrew and Peter. Philip found Nathanael and said to him, "We have found him about whom Moses in the law and also the prophets wrote, Jesus son of Joseph from Nazareth." Nathanael said to him, "Can anything good come out of Nazareth?" Philip said to him, "Come and see." When Jesus saw Nathanael coming toward him, he said of him, "Here is truly an

Israelite in whom there is no deceit!" Nathanael asked him, "Where did you get to know me?" Jesus answered, "I saw you under the fig tree before Philip called you." Nathanael replied, "Rabbi, you are the Son of God! You are the King of Israel!" Jesus answered, "Do you believe because I told you that I saw you under the fig tree? You will see greater things than these." And he said to him, "Very truly, I tell you, you will see heaven opened and the angels of God ascending and descending upon the Son of Man."

- "Can anything good come out of Nazareth?" How often, Lord, have I tried to pigeonhole people by looking down on their gender, origin, race, or family. Nathanael (identified with Bartholomew from the ninth century on) could have missed the chance to meet you, if not for Philip's gentle invitation: Come and see. Save me, Lord, from the stupidity of those who try to seem smart by despising others. May I heed Philip and fill my vision with you.

- "Where did you get to know me?" Nathanial is surprised not because Jesus saw him under the fig tree but because Jesus read the thoughts of his innermost heart. As I sit with you, Jesus, I ponder, How do you see me? How do you read my innermost heart?

Friday 6th January
Mark 1:7–11

John proclaimed, "The one who is more powerful than I is coming after me; I am not worthy to stoop down and untie the thong of his sandals. I have baptized you with water; but he will baptize you with the Holy Spirit." In those days Jesus came from Nazareth of Galilee and was baptized by John in the Jordan. And just as he was coming up out of the water, he saw the heavens torn apart and the Spirit descending like a dove on him. And a voice came from heaven, "You are my Son, the Beloved; with you I am well pleased."

- Imagine yourself witnessing the scene, perhaps standing in the shallows, the water flowing around your ankles. Picture the scene and allow it to unfold. What is it like? The young man from Nazareth joins the queue waiting for John's baptism, a symbol of purifying but also of birth: coming up out of the waters of the womb into a new life as God's beloved child.

- Jesus' baptism gives us a window into a powerful religious moment. Jesus knows his identity. The imprint of the Spirit has sealed his life. Lord, remind me that I bear your seal of approval. I am marked by your Spirit, called to participate in your mission as your beloved son or daughter.

Saturday 7th January
John 2:1–11

On the third day there was a wedding in Cana of Galilee, and the mother of Jesus was there. Jesus and his disciples had also been invited to the wedding. When the wine gave out, the mother of Jesus said to him, "They have no wine." And Jesus said to her, "Woman, what concern is that to you and to me? My hour has not yet come." His mother said to the servants, "Do whatever he tells you." Now standing there were six stone water jars for the Jewish rites of purification, each holding twenty or thirty gallons. Jesus said to them, "Fill the jars with water." And they filled them up to the brim. He said to them, "Now draw some out, and take it to the chief steward." So they took it. When the steward tasted the water that had become wine, and did not know where it came from (though the servants who had drawn the water knew), the steward called the bridegroom and said to him, "Everyone serves the good wine first, and then the inferior wine after the guests have become drunk. But you have kept the good wine until now." Jesus did this, the first of his signs, in Cana of Galilee, and revealed his glory; and his disciples believed in him.

- It appears that Jesus needed a push from someone who loved and knew him and knew his purpose in the world. Lord, help me listen when others nudge me toward my work and my calling.

- God sent Jesus into this human life, yet Jesus had to embrace his life mission day by day. When was the last time I purposefully embraced a task or goal because I recognized that it was God's will for me and part of my life calling?

Epiphany/The First Week of Ordinary Time
January 8—January 14

Something to think and pray about each day this week:

Empty Boxes

As we move out of the Christmas season and into the New Year, my family is cleaning up the last decorations and storing away extra gift wrap and boxes. It reminds me of a prayer from many Christmases ago, when my spiritual director suggested praying about what gift I'd like to offer to Jesus and what gift I thought he might be offering to me. This suggestion was given at a particularly difficult time in my life when I was experiencing many losses, and the idea that God might still have many graces to offer comforted me. One evening I prayed that Jesus handed me a large wrapped box with purple ribbon. I opened the box and searched around inside with my hand. After a time of searching, I came up only with purple and gold tissue paper. In an instant, I realized that the gift *was* the empty box. The emptiness itself was a beautiful gift: indifference.

—Marina McCoy on *dotMagis*, the blog of IgnatianSpirituality.com

The Presence of God
I pause for a moment and think of the love and the grace that God showers on me: I am created in the image and likeness of God; I am God's dwelling place.

Freedom
Lord, you created me to live in freedom. May your Holy Spirit guide me to follow you freely. Instill in my heart a desire to know and love you more each day.

Consciousness
How am I really feeling? Lighthearted? Heavyhearted? I may be very much at peace, happy to be here.
Equally, I may be frustrated, worried, or angry.
I acknowledge how I really am. It is the real me that the Lord loves.

The Word
I read the word of God slowly, a few times over, and I listen to what God is saying to me. (Please turn to the Scripture on the following pages. Inspiration points are there should you need them. When you are ready, return here to continue.)

Conversation
I know with certainty there were times when you carried me, Lord. When it was through your strength I got through the dark times in my life.

Conclusion
I thank God for these moments we have spent together and for any insights I have been given concerning the text.

Sunday 8th January
The Epiphany of the Lord
Matthew 2:1–12

In the time of King Herod, after Jesus was born in Bethlehem of Judea, wise men from the East came to Jerusalem, asking, "Where is the child who has been born king of the Jews? For we observed his star at its rising, and have come to pay him homage." When King Herod heard this, he was frightened, and all Jerusalem with him; and calling together all the chief priests and scribes of the people, he inquired of them where the Messiah was to be born. They told him, "In Bethlehem of Judea; for so it has been written by the prophet: 'And you, Bethlehem, in the land of Judah, are by no means least among the rulers of Judah; for from you shall come a ruler who is to shepherd my people Israel.'" Then Herod secretly called for the wise men and learned from them the exact time when the star had appeared. Then he sent them to Bethlehem, saying, "Go and search diligently for the child; and when you have found him, bring me word so that I may also go and pay him homage." When they had heard the king, they set out; and there, ahead of them, went the star that they had seen at its rising, until it stopped over the place where the child was. When they saw that the star had stopped, they were overwhelmed with joy. On entering the house, they saw the child with Mary his mother; and they knelt down and paid him homage. Then, opening their treasure chests, they offered him gifts of gold, frankincense, and myrrh. And having been warned in a dream not to return to Herod, they left for their own country by another road.

- The wise men are remembered for their gifts. The gift most worth giving at any age is our love. In prayer, ask God to accept your love for husband or wife, friend, children, neighborhood. Think of those you love, and bring your love for them to the crib where Jesus lies.

- This is the full unveiling (epiphany) of a mystery: The Lord has come among us to take an intimate hand in the future of the human race. We have God's word in Scripture: "I am about to do a new thing." I try to allow this to sink in.

Monday 9th January
The Baptism of the Lord
Matthew 3:13–17

Then Jesus came from Galilee to John at the Jordan, to be baptized by him. John would have prevented him, saying, "I need to be baptized by you, and do you come to me?" But Jesus answered him, "Let it be so now; for it is proper for us in this way to fulfill all righteousness." Then he consented. And when Jesus had been baptized, just as he came up from the water, suddenly the heavens were opened to him and he saw the Spirit of God descending like a dove and alighting on him. And a voice from heaven said, "This is my Son, the Beloved, with whom I am well pleased."

- Jesus came to the river to be baptized, not because he needed to repent but because he wanted to begin our journey of conversion with us, right beside us. He was saying, by this action of being baptized, "This is the way we must go—hearts open to God's forgiveness and healing." When am I most likely to shun acts of repentance, and why?

- The voice from heaven did not say, "This is the Messiah, with whom I am well pleased" or "This is my anointed, with whom I am well pleased." Jesus was the Messiah and God's anointed, but the term God used was "my Son, the Beloved." What does that say to me about the way God sees us and the way God desires to relate to us?

Tuesday 10th January
Mark 1:14–20

Now after John was arrested, Jesus came to Galilee, proclaiming the good news of God, and saying, "The time is fulfilled, and the kingdom of God has come near; repent, and believe in the good news." As Jesus passed along the Sea of Galilee, he saw Simon and his brother Andrew casting a net into the sea—for they were fishermen. And Jesus said to them, "Follow me and I will make you fish for people." And immediately they left their nets and followed him. As he went a little farther, he saw James son of Zebedee and his brother John, who were in their boat mending the nets. Immediately he called them; and they left their father Zebedee in the boat with the hired men, and followed him.

- Had Simon and Andrew, James and John already been in the audience—in the synagogue, or at their mooring by the lakeshore—when Jesus first preached the coming of God's kingdom? Had they already in some way sensed what Jesus was about? Did they already realize that in his work he was going to need followers? Whatever the case, when Jesus called their names, they needed no second invitation. Is there something prompting me about how I could do more for Christ's kingdom?

- If you google "Executive recruitment" on the Web, you are asked to examine résumés; then you are urged to hire expert recruiters to interview on your behalf. By contrast, Jesus moves along the lakeshore, meets dozens of fishermen, and finally picks Simon, Andrew, James, and John. He calls them to a global mission. They have no relevant experience and no training for the job. They are ordinary workers, good men. Their CVs would read: "I grew up here. I fish." Jesus' call is simple: "Follow me." Today his followers form the largest body of believers on the planet. Let me never lose a sense of how extraordinary this moment of calling is—for any of us and all of us.

Wednesday 11th January
Mark 1:29–39

As soon as they left the synagogue, they entered the house of Simon and Andrew, with James and John. Now Simon's mother-in-law was in bed with a fever, and they told him about her at once. He came and took her by the hand and lifted her up. Then the fever left her, and she began to serve them. That evening, at sunset, they brought to him all who were sick or possessed with demons. And the whole city was gathered around the door. And he cured many who were sick with various diseases, and cast out many demons; and he would not permit the demons to speak, because they knew him. In the morning, while it was still very dark, he got up and went out to a deserted place, and there he prayed. And Simon and his companions hunted for him. When they found him, they said to him, "Everyone is searching for you." He answered, "Let us go on to the neighboring towns, so that I may proclaim the message there also; for that is what I came out to do." And he went throughout Galilee, proclaiming the message in their synagogues and casting out demons.

- Jesus does his tour preaching and casting out devils. And we're given to understand that these two are practically the same thing—and that, were it not for the devils (who here want to find their voice!) even disease and sickness would disappear. Jesus is going into battle head to head with the kingdom of evil. When I feel powerless before outside events, and before wayward tendencies in my own heart, I ask Jesus, the strong one, to come to my side.

- There is a moment of truth in the cure of Simon's mother-in-law. This sick woman felt her temperature drop and energy return to her limbs "and she began to serve them." Lord, thank you for my health, not something to luxuriate in but the means by which I can serve others.

Thursday 12th January
Mark 1:40–45

A leper came to him begging Jesus, and kneeling he said to him, "If you choose, you can make me clean." Moved with pity, Jesus stretched out his hand and touched him, and said to him, "I do choose. Be made clean!" Immediately the leprosy left him, and he was made clean. After sternly warning him he sent him away at once, saying to him, "See that you say nothing to anyone; but go, show yourself to the priest, and offer for your cleansing what Moses commanded, as a testimony to them." But he went out and began to proclaim it freely, and to spread the word, so that Jesus could no longer go into a town openly, but stayed out in the country; and people came to him from every quarter.

- "Moved with pity, Jesus stretched out his hand and touched him." Leprosy in the Bible was not precisely what we mean by the term but was a general name for any repulsive, scaly skin disease. That first word in the Greek, σπλαγχυισθείς, connotes a deep, gut-wrenching compassion, which showed itself in the extraordinary (for a man of that time) gesture of touching the leprosy. Touch me, Lord. Touch the ugly parts of me that I do not like to look at. If you will, you can make me clean.

- Jesus affirms the desire of the man with leprosy: "Certainly I want to" is his response to our desire for what is truly for our growth and well-being. The leper knew his need and trusted that Jesus could help him. I pray with the same attitude, not hiding my neediness, not hesitant about bringing it before Jesus, listening for Jesus' encouraging response.

Friday 13th January
Mark 2:1–12

When Jesus returned to Capernaum after some days, it was reported that he was at home. So many gathered around that there was no longer room for them, not even in front of the door; and he was speaking the word to them. Then some people came, bringing to him a paralyzed man, carried by four of them. And when they could not bring him to Jesus because of the crowd, they removed the roof above him; and after having dug through it, they let down the mat on which the paralytic lay. When Jesus saw their faith, he said to the paralytic, "Son, your sins are forgiven." Now some of the scribes were sitting there, questioning in their hearts, "Why does this fellow speak in this way? It is blasphemy! Who can forgive sins but God alone?" At once Jesus perceived in his spirit that they were discussing these questions among themselves; and he said to them, "Why do you raise such questions in your hearts? Which is easier, to say to the paralytic, 'Your sins are forgiven,' or to say, 'Stand up and take your mat and walk'? But so that you may know that the Son of Man has authority on earth to forgive sins"—he said to the paralytic—"I say to you, stand up, take your mat and go to your home." And he stood up, and immediately took the mat and went out before all of them; so that they were all amazed and glorified God, saying, "We have never seen anything like this!"

- I, too, sometimes feel paralyzed by fears or by lack of energy. And I come before Jesus, not disguising my helplessness. I allow the strength of Jesus to take over. Jesus puts my neediness in perspective; he wants me to see that his support is not just for me—it is there for the whole world.

- Lord, sometimes I don't have the courage to act because of some failure or criticism that took the heart out of me. Then I rely on the help of good friends, like the four stretcher-bearers, to bring me to the point where I can hear you say, "Get up and walk." Faith opens a door to a living relationship with God in Jesus. The faith of all helped the sick man. Our faithful time of prayer may help people we know or do not know.

Saturday 14th January

Mark 2:13–17

Jesus went out again beside the sea; the whole crowd gathered around him, and he taught them. As he was walking along, he saw Levi son of Alphaeus sitting at the tax booth, and he said to him, "Follow me." And he got up and followed him. And as he sat at dinner in Levi's house, many tax collectors and sinners were also sitting with Jesus and his disciples—for there were many who followed him. When the scribes of the Pharisees saw that he was eating with sinners and tax collectors, they said to his disciples, "Why does he eat with tax collectors and sinners?" When Jesus heard this, he said to them, "Those who are well have no need of a physician, but those who are sick; I have come to call not the righteous but sinners."

- The job of Levi—collecting the taxes for the Roman government of occupation—never endeared him to his countrymen. Yet it was he who had the more attuned ear for the whole changed relationship with God that Jesus was ushering in. No matter what our circumstances, we can always have an ear open for the higher call.

- Jesus cuts through the carefully constructed assumptions of the Pharisees. What a shock that must have been! Levi, a most unlikely man, despised by the righteous, is the recipient of God's gracious mercy and forgiveness. Jesus sees his hidden potential and invites him into friendship. Hypocrisy, arrogance, and contempt have no place in your table fellowship, Lord. Heal my arrogant, despising, and judging heart so that I can sit at table with you.

The Second Week of Ordinary Time
January 15—January 21

Something to think and pray about each day this week:

Finding Home

The busier seasons can leave us with little time to relax in the armchair, to enjoy the glow of the log fire, to engage in leisurely conversations, and to delight in a shared, unhurried meal. Now is the time for home. But what is home? Not everyone finds "home" where it should be. Not every child is cherished. Not every teenager is listened to. Not every couple makes it through life together. Many long for the touch of a friendly hand and a chance to talk. Inner homelessness has become an epidemic of our time. Just by listening to another's story, reaching out a hand in friendship, just by something as simple as a smile, each of us is able to say to another, "Come on home."

—Margaret Silf, *Daily Inspiration for Women*

The Presence of God
Jesus, help me to be fully alive to your Holy Presence. Enfold me in your love. Let my heart become one with yours.

Freedom
I will ask God's help,
to be free from my own preoccupations,
to be open to God in this time of prayer,
to come to know, love, and serve God more.

Consciousness
I ask how I am within myself today? Am I particularly tired, stressed, or off form? If any of these characteristics apply, can I try to let go of the concerns that disturb me?

The Word
God speaks to each of us individually. I listen attentively to hear what God is saying to me. Read the text a few times, then listen. (Please turn to the Scripture on the following pages. Inspiration points are there should you need them. When you are ready, return here to continue.)

Conversation
Sometimes I wonder what I might say if I were to meet you in person, Lord.
I think I might say, Thank you, Lord, for always being there for me.

Conclusion
Glory be to the Father, and to the Son, and to the Holy Spirit,
As it was in the beginning, is now and ever shall be,
World without end. Amen.

Sunday 15th January
Second Sunday in Ordinary Time
John 1:29–34

The next day John saw Jesus coming towards him and declared, "Here is the Lamb of God who takes away the sin of the world! This is he of whom I said, 'After me comes a man who ranks ahead of me because he was before me.' I myself did not know him; but I came baptizing with water for this reason, that he might be revealed to Israel." And John testified, "I saw the Spirit descending from heaven like a dove, and it remained on him. I myself did not know him, but the one who sent me to baptize with water said to me, 'He on whom you see the Spirit descend and remain is the one who baptizes with the Holy Spirit.' And I myself have seen and have testified that this is the Son of God."

• "Lamb of God" bears biblical overtones of the Passover lamb and of the suffering servant in Isaiah, led like a lamb to the slaughter, bearing our sins. Lord, whenever I hear of some atrocious barbarisms by one of our race, and of the injustice and pain that people suffer through others' wickedness, I remember that this is the world you entered, the burden you took on yourself. You had a strong back to carry the evil that is in the world.

• The witness of John the Baptist depended on what was revealed to him in his prayer and on what he saw with his eyes. Bless me now, Lord, to recognize more clearly where you are moving in my life. Jesus came to take away sin, yet I sometimes hang on to guilt and won't let the past go. Lamb of God, you take away the sins of the world; have mercy on me!

Monday 16th January
Mark 2:18–22

Now John's disciples and the Pharisees were fasting; and people came and said to Jesus, "Why do John's disciples and the disciples of the Pharisees fast, but your disciples do not fast?" Jesus said to them, "The wedding guests cannot fast while the bridegroom is with them, can they? As long as they have the bridegroom with them, they cannot fast. The days will come when the bridegroom is taken away from them, and then they will fast on that day. No one sews a piece of unshrunk cloth on an old cloak; otherwise, the patch pulls away from it, the new from the old, and a worse tear is made. And no one puts new wine into old wineskins; otherwise, the wine will burst the skins, and the wine is lost, and so are the skins; but one puts new wine into fresh wineskins."

- People noticed the contrast between two sorts of religion: the Pharisees' preoccupation with laws and regulations, and Jesus' love of celebrations and feasts. He was seen as somebody who was always ready for a party, somebody who enjoyed life. In his parables, the kingdom of heaven is often a banquet, a wedding, a party. Am I more likely to cling to a set of standards I know well or to join a celebration I don't quite yet understand?

- "New wine, new wineskins." Lord, you caution me against having a closed mind. You challenge me not to cling to old ways and to be receptive to the new. Grant me openness of heart and mind. Let me trust in the depths of your creative Spirit, who is making all things new.

Tuesday 17th January
Mark 2:23–28

One sabbath Jesus was going through the grainfields; and as they made their way his disciples began to pluck heads of grain. The Pharisees said to him, "Look, why are they doing what is not lawful on the sabbath?" And he said to them, "Have you never read what David did when he and his companions were hungry and in need of food? He entered the house of God, when Abiathar was high priest, and ate the bread of the Presence, which it is not lawful for any but the priests to eat, and he gave some to his companions." Then he said to them, "The sabbath was made for humankind, and not humankind for the sabbath; so the Son of Man is lord even of the sabbath."

- The Sabbath was meant to be a day of rest, when people would be free to think of God, to give thanks for God's gifts, and to take care of health and well-being. But some religious authorities gradually encroached on the Sabbath with so many regulations that it risked no longer serving its purpose. Do we sometimes seek security by exercising too much control over other people's lives? Instead, perhaps we can trust ourselves to that freedom we enjoy as God's sons and daughters—sisters and brothers of Jesus.

- When we assemble on the Sabbath, we meet God in many ways. We encounter God in the community itself, in sharing the great story of salvation, and in the meal prepared by God. Our souls are given the chance to catch up, and we go back to our tasks refreshed. Lord, you ask us to show that you are alive by being truly alive ourselves. We are to be the good news in the present tense.

Wednesday 18th January
Mark 3:1–6

Jesus entered the synagogue, and a man was there who had a withered hand. They watched him to see whether he would cure him on the sabbath, so that they might accuse him. And he said to the man who had the withered hand, "Come forward." Then he said to them, "Is it lawful to do good or to do harm on the sabbath, to save life or to kill?" But they were silent. He looked around at them with anger; he was grieved at their hardness of heart and said to the man, "Stretch out your hand." He stretched it out, and his hand was restored. The Pharisees went out and immediately conspired with the Herodians against him, how to destroy him.

- Lord, when you celebrated the Sabbath by healing a person, the Pharisees responded by plotting to kill you. You were stressing that God does not want to make our lives more difficult and does not impose arbitrary rules on us. The great commandment is the law of love. Would people who know me be able to say that I follow the law of love?

- Jesus was being watched to see what he might do, yet it did not stop him from doing good, from bringing life. I ask God for the courage I need to do what I know to be the right thing. The anger of Jesus is passion for life. I let myself imagine how Jesus wants to brush away whatever it is that holds me back from living fully as he calls me to life. For my part I ask for the strength I need to stretch out whatever ails me for healing.

Thursday 19th January
Mark 3:7–12

Jesus departed with his disciples to the sea, and a great multitude from Galilee followed him; hearing all that he was doing, they came to him in great numbers from Judea, Jerusalem, Idumea, beyond the Jordan, and the region around Tyre and Sidon. He told his disciples to have a boat ready for him because of the crowd, so that they would not crush him; for he had cured many, so that all who had diseases pressed upon him to touch him. Whenever the unclean spirits saw him, they fell down before him and shouted, "You are the Son of God!" But he sternly ordered them not to make him known.

- Evil was challenged by Jesus and saw him for the Son of God that he was. The faith of the disciples would grow slowly, and the mystery of his message would take hold gradually. Bring to prayer the ways in which your faith has grown gradually and sometimes with difficulty—and be grateful that even in bad times our faith in the mystery of God's love has grown.

- Jesus needed a boat for his journey. He needs you and me, all of us today, for his journey in our times. The boat in the Gospel is a sign of the self. "Make a boat ready" today means "make yourself ready." We are all part of the divine plan to love and save the universe.

Friday 20th January
Mark 3:13–19

Jesus went up the mountain and called to him those whom he wanted, and they came to him. And he appointed twelve, whom he also named apostles, to be with him, and to be sent out to proclaim the message, and to have authority to cast out demons. So he appointed the twelve: Simon (to whom he gave the name Peter); James son of Zebedee and John the brother of James (to whom he gave the name Boanerges, that is, Sons of Thunder); and Andrew, and Philip, and Bartholomew, and Matthew, and Thomas, and James son of Alphaeus, and Thaddaeus, and Simon the Cananaean, and Judas Iscariot, who betrayed him. Then he went home.

- Imagine the apostles, having been chosen, looking at one another, and James and John turning to Andrew and asking, "Who's this Thaddeus guy?" They could well have been uneasy rubbing shoulders with re-formed tax collector Matthew and fanatical nationalist Simon. The Lord's choice of followers may surprise me, and at times I may have difficulties with them, but they are chosen, with their faults, just as I am.

- I may think I have chosen Jesus, but in fact he has chosen me. Today I pause in gratitude for this.

Saturday 21st January
Mark 3:20–21

Then Jesus went home; and the crowd came together again, so that they could not even eat. When his family heard it, they went out to restrain him, for people were saying, "He has gone out of his mind."

- Jesus' family considers him imbalanced. He has left the security and safety of Nazareth and his carpenter's business. He is on course for a head-on collision with the orthodox leaders, and he has recently gathered a crowd of disciples who would do nothing for his career prospects. He has gone out of his mind!

- Lord, in choosing to live by the Gospel, I, too, run the risk of being misunderstood and ridiculed. You faced opposition with determination and courage. Grant me your grace to follow you resolutely, especially when opposition comes from those near to me.

January 22—January 28

Something to think and pray about each day this week:

The Gift of Breath

Sometimes when I'm anxious or very focused, I hold my breath. I can be watching a thriller, waiting in line at the grocery store, or just sitting in traffic when I realize that my body is very still, my shoulders are locked and tense, and I'm taking in only tiny sips of air. At those moments, I often gulp in a huge mouthful of air and end up in a coughing fit or with a bad case of the hiccups. Other times, I relax my shoulders and take at least three big, whole-body breaths. "Take three cleansing breaths," I used to say to my kids when they seemed perched on the precipice of a temper tantrum. It often worked to calm them down. I knew it would because breathing helps me release tension, too. It recalibrates me. Breathing does so much for us: helps our bodies release toxins, improves posture and mood, reduces our experience of pain, and relaxes us. Don't forget to breathe.

—Jennifer Grant, *Wholehearted Living*

The Presence of God

"I stand at the door and knock," says the Lord. What a wonderful privilege that the Lord of all creation desires to come to me. I welcome his presence.

Freedom

Saint Ignatius thought that a thick and shapeless tree trunk would never believe that it could become a statue, admired as a miracle of sculpture, and would never submit itself to the chisel of the sculptor, who sees by her genius what she can make of it.
I ask for the grace to let myself be shaped by my loving Creator.

Consciousness

Knowing that God loves me unconditionally, I can afford to be honest about how I am. What are my fears and desires? What do I expect from God? What am I willing to give to God—from my emotions and talents, thoughts and energy? And how do I feel now? I share my feelings openly with the Lord.

The Word

I take my time to read the word of God, slowly, a few times, allowing myself to dwell on anything that strikes me. (Please turn to the Scripture on the following pages. Inspiration points are there should you need them. When you are ready, return here to continue.)

Conversation

Do I notice myself reacting as I pray with the word of God? Do I feel challenged, comforted, angry? Imagining Jesus sitting or standing by me, I speak out my feelings, as one trusted friend to another.

Conclusion

I thank God for these moments we have spent together and for any insights I have been given concerning the text.

Sunday 22nd January
Third Sunday in Ordinary Time
Matthew 4:12–17, 23–25

Now when Jesus heard that John had been arrested, he withdrew to Galilee. He left Nazareth and made his home in Capernaum by the lake, in the territory of Zebulun and Naphtali, so that what had been spoken through the prophet Isaiah might be fulfilled:

"Land of Zebulun, land of Naphtali,
on the road by the sea, across the Jordan, Galilee of the Gentiles—
the people who sat in darkness
have seen a great light,
and for those who sat in the region and shadow of death
light has dawned."

From that time Jesus began to proclaim, "Repent, for the kingdom of heaven has come near." . . . Jesus went throughout Galilee, teaching in their synagogues and proclaiming the good news of the kingdom and curing every disease and every sickness among the people. So his fame spread throughout all Syria, and they brought to him all the sick, those who were afflicted with various diseases and pains, demoniacs, epileptics, and paralytics, and he cured them. And great crowds followed him from Galilee, the Decapolis, Jerusalem, Judea, and from beyond the Jordan.

- Jesus ventures into regions where pagan influences are palpable. The demoniacs are in the grip of the prince of darkness; a dark shadow hangs on the lives of the epileptics; and the lives of the sick are blighted also. But Jesus, Lord of light, launches the kingdom of heaven—rolling back the darkness.

- Does some dark influence also tend at times to pull me down in spirit? I open myself to the healing light of Jesus.

Monday 23rd January
Mark 3:22–30

And the scribes who came down from Jerusalem said, "He has Beelzebul, and by the ruler of the demons he casts out demons." And he called them to him, and spoke to them in parables, "How can Satan cast out Satan? If a kingdom is divided against itself, that kingdom cannot stand. And if a house is divided against itself, that house will not be able to stand. And if Satan has risen up against himself and is divided, he cannot stand, but his end has come. But no one can enter a strong man's house and plunder his property without first tying up the strong man; then indeed the house can be plundered. Truly I tell you, people will be forgiven for their sins and whatever blasphemies they utter, but whoever blasphemes against the Holy Spirit can never have forgiveness, but is guilty of an eternal sin"— for they had said, "He has an unclean spirit."

- Jesus cautions the scribes against their clever judgments: Patience and wisdom are needed to allow the Spirit of God to enlighten intelligent observations.

- I pray that my words might never be used to bring division but that, instead, my life may be for the upbuilding of the Body of Christ.

Tuesday 24th January
Mark 3:31–35

The mother and brothers of Jesus arrived and, standing outside, sent in a message asking for him. A crowd was sitting round him at the time the message was passed to him, "Your mother and brothers and sisters are outside asking for you." He replied, "Who are my mother and my brothers?" And looking round at those sitting in a circle about him, he said, "Here are my mother and my brothers. Anyone who does the will of God, that person is my brother and sister and mother."

- Jesus' mother and brothers do not always understand what he is about, but in listening to him, wanting to be close to him, they show us what loving discipleship is. Jesus is ready to count me among his family! Doing the will of God shows how I accept this invitation.

- Is Jesus rejecting his own mother and family? Not at all, but he is reminding his disciples that there is a kinship centered on a radical call to be like him. Relationship with him brings intimacy, like that of a mother, brother, or sister.

Wednesday 25th January
Mark 16:15–18

And he said to them, "Go into all the world and proclaim the good news to the whole creation. The one who believes and is baptized will be saved; but the one who does not believe will be condemned. And these signs will accompany those who believe: by using my name they will cast out demons; they will speak in new tongues; they will pick up snakes in their hands, and if they drink any deadly thing, it will not hurt them; they will lay their hands on the sick, and they will recover."

- Here Jesus sends forth the disciples. They are to be brave, despite their fears. Lord, send me out each day, to witness to you by my actions. I am to minister to you in the sick, the poor, the hungry, the displaced, and the imprisoned of our world.

- Do I ever refer the good news to myself? The good news about me is that I am massively loved and cared for by God. Creation is at my service. Jesus has died for me. I am promised eternal life. God is with me always, so I need not be afraid. Good news indeed!

Thursday 26th January
Mark 4:21–25

He said to them, "Is a lamp brought in to be put under the bushel basket, or under the bed, and not on the lampstand? For there is nothing hidden, except to be disclosed; nor is anything secret, except to come to light. Let anyone with ears to hear listen!" And he said to them, "Pay attention to what you hear; the measure you give will be the measure you get, and still more will be given you. For to those who have, more will be given; and from those who have nothing, even what they have will be taken away."

- When Jesus begins revealing the earth-changing coming of his kingdom, he doesn't want the teaching twisted to their own ends by political agitators or by sensationalists; so he sometimes makes his points in a veiled way—fully explaining them later to a circle of trusted followers. Once these preachers of his message have mastered its true sense, then everything will come out into the light—just as the householder positions the lamp to fill the whole space.

- The light about which Jesus speaks is not a searchlight to expose, shame, or embarrass. When the light of Truth is allowed to shine, all is understood and forgiven. I have no need to hide. O God, I give you this time that you may speak to me. Help me to notice your word among all the signals I receive. Bless me that I may pay attention and receive it in my heart.

Friday 27th January
Mark 4:26–34

Jesus said to the crowd, "The kingdom of God is as if someone would scatter seed on the ground, and would sleep and rise night and day, and the seed would sprout and grow, he does not know how. The earth produces of itself, first the stalk, then the head, then the full grain in the head. But when the grain is ripe, at once he goes in with his sickle, because the harvest has come." He also said, "With what can we compare the kingdom of God, or what parable will we use for it? It is like a mustard seed, which, when sown upon the ground, is the smallest of all the seeds on earth; yet when it is sown it grows up and becomes the greatest of all shrubs, and puts forth large branches, so that the birds of the air can make nests in its shade." With many such parables he spoke the word to them, as they were able to hear it; he did not speak to them except in parables, but he explained everything in private to his disciples.

- Jesus came to inaugurate the kingdom of God, but he never defined what it is. Instead he spoke of it in parables, inviting us to use our imagination to grasp his meaning. These two seed parables draw attention to the hidden and mysterious nature of the kingdom. It grows through a power greater than ours, and its fruitfulness is beyond our expectations.

- Do I see signs of the kingdom in my own life and in today's church? Even in today's world?

Saturday 28th January
Mark 4:35–41

On that day, when evening had come, Jesus said to the disciples, "Let us go across to the other side." And leaving the crowd behind, they took him with them in the boat, just as he was. Other boats were with him. A great windstorm arose, and the waves beat into the boat, so that the boat was already being swamped. But he was in the stern, asleep on the cushion; and they woke him up and said to him, "Teacher, do you not care that we are perishing?" He woke up and rebuked the wind, and said to the sea, "Peace! Be still!" Then the wind ceased, and there was a dead calm. He said to them, "Why are you afraid? Have you still no faith?" And they were filled with great awe and said to one another, "Who then is this, that even the wind and the sea obey him?"

- Imagine that you are in the boat with the disciples. Allow yourself to experience the happy anticipation at the start of the voyage and then the terror as the gale sweeps in. Your life is in danger. You look to Jesus to save you, but he is asleep—as if he doesn't care. Then feel the relief as he speaks with authority and calms the wind and sea. Are you embarrassed when he questions your faith? Is there anything you want to say to him after this adventure?

- Even in the presence of Jesus, with the memory of his words fresh in their minds, the disciples doubted. Like them, I bring my doubts and questions to Jesus and listen for his answer.

The Fourth Week of Ordinary Time
January 29—February 4

Something to think and pray about each day this week:

Possibilities within the Gray
When I think of gray I think of gloom, of low clouds and cold and rain. Perhaps we get what we expect, and I need to adjust my expectations. Perhaps the presence of gray can invite us into solitude to reflect, offering time and space for a good book, a life-giving conversation. Perhaps it can open the gateway to a whole spectrum of subtle colors that we never expected to find hiding in the gray. Everyday life can feel gray for months at a time, especially in the winter season. But what if that drab exterior holds a wealth of unknown possibilities within it? A kind word resonates gently through our day. A time of reflection draws us into deeper reaches of ourselves. A good book opens up vistas invisible in the brighter light.

—Margaret Silf, *Daily Inspiration for Women*

The Presence of God

To be present is to arrive as one is and open up to the other.
At this instant, as I arrive here, God is present waiting for me.
God always arrives before me, desiring to connect with me
even more than my most intimate friend.
I take a moment and greet my loving God.

Freedom

I am free. When I look at these words in writing, they seem to create in me a feeling of awe. Yes, a wonderful feeling of freedom. Thank you, God.

Consciousness

To be conscious about something is to be aware of it.
Dear Lord, help me to remember that you gave me life.
Thank you for the gift of life.
Teach me to slow down, to be still and enjoy the pleasures created for me.
To be aware of the beauty that surrounds me. The marvel of mountains, the calmness of lakes, the fragility of a flower petal. I need to remember that all these things come from you.

The Word

The word of God comes to us through the Scriptures. May the Holy Spirit enlighten my mind and heart to respond to the Gospel teachings. (Please turn to the Scripture on the following pages. Inspiration points are there should you need them. When you are ready, return here to continue.)

Conversation

I begin to talk to Jesus about the piece of Scripture I have just read. What part of it strikes a chord in me? Perhaps the words of a friend—or some story I have heard recently—will slowly rise to the surface in my consciousness. If so, does the story throw light on what the Scripture passage may be trying to say to me?

Conclusion

Glory be to the Father, and to the Son, and to the Holy Spirit,
As it was in the beginning, is now and ever shall be,
World without end. Amen.

Sunday 29th January
Fourth Sunday in Ordinary Time
Matthew 5:1–12

When Jesus saw the crowds, he went up the mountain; and after he sat down, his disciples came to him. Then he began to speak, and taught them, saying:

> "Blessed are the poor in spirit, for theirs is the kingdom of heaven.
> Blessed are those who mourn, for they will be comforted.
> Blessed are the meek, for they will inherit the earth.
> Blessed are those who hunger and thirst for righteousness, for they will be filled.
> Blessed are the merciful, for they will receive mercy.
> Blessed are the pure in heart, for they will see God.
> Blessed are the peacemakers, for they will be called children of God.
> Blessed are those who are persecuted for righteousness' sake, for theirs is the kingdom of heaven.
> Blessed are you when people revile you and persecute you and utter all kinds of evil against you falsely on my account. Rejoice and be glad, for your reward is great in heaven, for in the same way they persecuted the prophets who were before you."

- Often compared with the Ten Commandments, the Beatitudes are quite different: They are blessings or gifts offered by God. They are not to be observed as commandments but, rather, desired and nurtured in prayer. So ponder them slowly and see if they resonate with your own life experiences.

- Think of the affirmation that Jesus gives to what is fragile, weak, and overlooked in the eyes of the world. I might choose two of these Beatitudes to be a backdrop to my prayer and reflection today: one that affirms me and one that calls me further.

Monday 30th January
Mark 5:1–20

They came to the other side of the lake, to the country of the Gerasenes. And when he had stepped out of the boat, immediately a man out of the tombs with an unclean spirit met him. . . . When he saw Jesus from a distance, he ran and bowed down before him; and he shouted at the top of his voice, "What have you to do with me, Jesus, Son of the Most High God? I adjure you by God, do not torment me." For he had said to him, "Come out of the man, you unclean spirit!" Then Jesus asked him, "What is your name?" He replied, "My name is Legion; for we are many." He begged him earnestly not to send them out of the country. Now there on the hillside a great herd of swine was feeding; and the unclean spirits begged him, "Send us into the swine; let us enter them." So he gave them permission. And the unclean spirits came out and entered the swine; and the herd, numbering about two thousand, rushed down the steep bank into the lake, and were drowned in the lake. The swineherds ran off and told it in the city and in the country. Then people came to see what it was that had happened. They came to Jesus and saw the demoniac sitting there, clothed and in his right mind, the very man who had had the legion; and they were afraid. Those who had seen what had happened to the demoniac and to the swine reported it. Then they began to beg Jesus to leave their neighborhood. As he was getting into the boat, the man who had been possessed by demons begged him that he might be with him. But Jesus refused, and said to him, "Go home to your friends, and tell them how much the Lord has done for you, and what mercy he has shown you." And he went away and began to proclaim in the Decapolis how much Jesus had done for him; and everyone was amazed.

- Jesus speaks with the demons who have taken over this tormented person. They recognize the identity of the one who has power over them. If I am in the crowd of bystanders, what do I see, and how do I react? And in my real life, here and now, do I consider the spiritual battles going on around me?

- Why do the people want Jesus to leave? Are they frightened by his show of power? Angry that he has destroyed their cash crop of pigs? Why do we resist Jesus' presence, in dramatic situations or ones more ordinary?

Tuesday 31st January
Mark 5:21–43

When Jesus had crossed again in the boat to the other side, a great crowd gathered around him; and he was by the sea. Then one of the leaders of the synagogue named Jairus came and, when he saw him, fell at his feet and begged him repeatedly, "My little daughter is at the point of death. Come and lay your hands on her, so that she may be made well, and live." So he went with him. And a large crowd followed him and pressed in on him. Now there was a woman who had been suffering from hemorrhages for twelve years. She had endured much under many physicians, and had spent all that she had; and she was no better, but rather grew worse. She had heard about Jesus, and came up behind him in the crowd and touched his cloak, for she said, "If I but touch his clothes, I will be made well." Immediately her hemorrhage stopped; and she felt in her body that she was healed of her disease. Immediately aware that power had gone forth from him, Jesus turned about in the crowd and said, "Who touched my clothes?" And his disciples said to him, "You see the crowd pressing in on you; how can you say, Who touched me?" He looked all around to see who had done it. But the woman, knowing what had happened to her, came in fear and trembling, fell down before him, and told him the whole truth. He said to her, "Daughter, your faith has made you well; go in peace, and be healed of your disease." While he was still speaking, some people came from the leader's house to say, "Your daughter is dead. Why trouble the teacher any further?" But overhearing what they said, Jesus said to the leader of the synagogue, "Do not fear, only believe." He allowed no one to follow him except Peter, James, and John, the brother of James. When they came to the house of the leader of the synagogue, he saw a commotion, people weeping and wailing loudly. When he had entered, he said to them, "Why do you make a commotion and weep? The child is not dead but sleeping." And they laughed at him. Then he put them all outside, and took the child's father and mother and those who were with him, and went in where the child was. He took her by the hand and said to her, "Talitha cum," which means, "Little girl, get up!" And immediately the girl got up and began to walk about (she was twelve years of age). At this they were overcome with amazement. He strictly ordered them that no one should know this, and told them to give her something to eat.

- You might allow yourself to identify with Jairus or his wife (or even with their daughter) or with the distressed woman—inserting yourself into the world's suffering but also experiencing the world's hope.

Throughout, keep your focus on Jesus, becoming aware of his deep compassion as well as of his healing power.

- Jesus is tender to the two women, calling one "Daughter!" and the other "Little girl (literally, "Little lamb"). In my need I, too, can turn to him and find healing. Then I can in turn become a tender and healing presence to those around me.

Wednesday 1st February
Mark 6:1–6

Jesus left that place and came to his hometown, and his disciples followed him. On the sabbath he began to teach in the synagogue, and many who heard him were astounded. They said, "Where did this man get all this? What is this wisdom that has been given to him? What deeds of power are being done by his hands! Is not this the carpenter, the son of Mary and brother of James and Joses and Judas and Simon, and are not his sisters here with us?" And they took offense at him. Then Jesus said to them, "Prophets are not without honor, except in their hometown, and among their own kin, and in their own house." And he could do no deed of power there, except that he laid his hands on a few sick people and cured them. And he was amazed at their unbelief. Then he went about among the villages teaching.

- The French author Francois Mauriac wrote in his life of Jesus: "It is baffling to record that, for a period of thirty years, the Son of Man did not appear to be anything other than a man." Those who lived with him thought they knew him. He fixed their tables and chairs. When he stepped outside the role they had fixed for him, they put him down as just a workman. Lord, there are depths in each of us, even those we think we know well, that only you can glimpse. Help me see others with your gaze.

- Jesus moved on—he did not dig in and insist on convincing those whose minds were closed. I pray for the same freedom: that I may offer truth, hope, and life and leave the rest to God.

Thursday 2nd February
The Presentation of the Lord
Luke 2:22–40

When the time came for their purification according to the law of Moses, they brought him up to Jerusalem to present him to the Lord (as it is written in the law of the Lord, "Every firstborn male shall be designated as holy to the Lord"), and they offered a sacrifice according to what is stated in the law of the Lord, "a pair of turtledoves or two young pigeons." Now there was a man in Jerusalem whose name was Simeon; this man was righteous and devout, looking forward to the consolation of Israel, and the Holy Spirit rested on him. It had been revealed to him by the Holy Spirit that he would not see death before he had seen the Lord's Messiah. Guided by the Spirit, Simeon came into the temple; and when the parents brought in the child Jesus, to do for him what was customary under the law, Simeon took him in his arms and praised God, saying, "Master, now you are dismissing your servant in peace, / according to your word; / for my eyes have seen your salvation, / which you have prepared in the presence of all peoples, / a light for revelation to the Gentiles / and for glory to your people Israel." And the child's father and mother were amazed at what was being said about him. Then Simeon blessed them and said to his mother Mary, "This child is destined for the falling and the rising of many in Israel, and to be a sign that will be opposed so that the inner thoughts of many will be revealed—and a sword will pierce your own soul too." There was also a prophet, Anna the daughter of Phanuel, of the tribe of Asher. She was of a great age, having lived with her husband for seven years after her marriage, then as a widow to the age of eighty-four. She never left the temple but worshipped there with fasting and prayer night and day. At that moment she came, and began to praise God and to speak about the child to all who were looking for the redemption of Jerusalem. When they had finished everything required by the law of the Lord, they returned to Galilee, to their own town of Nazareth. The child grew and became strong, filled with wisdom; and the favor of God was upon him.

- The Holy Spirit helps the old man Simeon recognize and praise God and bless the parents of Jesus. What about me? The Holy Spirit dwells in me, too: I am his temple! But is he perhaps only a quiet lodger whom

I hardly notice? Have I locked him up? Can he become my mentor whom I look to for advice and support? Can the Spirit and I create life together?

- The feast of the Presentation can happen every day if I wish it so. This is because when I pray, I am presenting myself before God. God and I meet directly.

Friday 3rd February
Mark 6:14–29

King Herod heard of it, for Jesus' name had become known. Some were saying, "John the baptizer has been raised from the dead; and for this reason these powers are at work in him." But others said, "It is Elijah." And others said, "It is a prophet, like one of the prophets of old." But when Herod heard of it, he said, "John, whom I beheaded, has been raised." For Herod himself had sent men who arrested John, bound him, and put him in prison on account of Herodias, his brother Philip's wife, because Herod had married her. For John had been telling Herod, "It is not lawful for you to have your brother's wife." And Herodias had a grudge against him, and wanted to kill him. But she could not, for Herod feared John, knowing that he was a righteous and holy man, and he protected him. When he heard him, he was greatly perplexed; and yet he liked to listen to him. But an opportunity came when Herod on his birthday gave a banquet for his courtiers and officers and for the leaders of Galilee. When the daughter of this same Herodias came in and danced, she pleased Herod and his guests; and the king said to the girl, "Ask me for whatever you wish, and I will give it." And he solemnly swore to her, "Whatever you ask me, I will give you, even half of my kingdom." She went out and said to her mother, "What should I ask for?" She replied, "The head of John the baptizer." Immediately she rushed back to the king and requested, "I want you to give me at once the head of John the Baptist on a platter." The king was deeply grieved; yet out of regard for his oaths and for the guests, he did not want to refuse her. Immediately the king sent a soldier of the guard with orders to bring John's head. He went and beheaded him in the prison, brought his head on a platter, and gave it to the girl. Then the girl gave it to her mother. When his disciples heard about it, they came and took his body, and laid it in a tomb.

- The Gospel tells the sordid story of the final hours of John the Baptist, beheaded for a frivolous promise of Herod's. Lord Jesus, you spent your last night before your crucifixion in prison. Bring comfort to the thousands of good people who are languishing behind bars. They are my sisters and brothers.

- John the Baptist was a channel of grace for King Herod, and the king "liked to listen to him." But the people around Herod, and his own unruly appetites, got in the way. Do I get trapped, too, and then act out of my lack of freedom?

Saturday 4th February
Mark 6:30–34

The apostles gathered around Jesus, and told him all that they had done and taught. He said to them, "Come away to a deserted place all by yourselves and rest a while." For many were coming and going, and they had no leisure even to eat. And they went away in the boat to a deserted place by themselves. Now many saw them going and recognized them, and they hurried there on foot from all the towns and arrived ahead of them. As he went ashore, he saw a great crowd; and he had compassion for them, because they were like sheep without a shepherd; and he began to teach them many things.

- The apostles return from their missions like children from a party. They are so full of what happened on their journeys and are anxious to tell Jesus all about it. Do I take a little time each evening to chat with him about how the day has gone?

- When I give time to prayer, I am responding to the invitation of Jesus to "come away" to a quiet place. I meet God, who answers my need for rest and nourishment. I notice that I never regret the time I give to prayer, even though sometimes, little seems to happen. It seems my heart is made for prayer, just as my body is made for healthy air.

The Fifth Week of Ordinary Time
February 5—February 11

Something to think and pray about each day this week:

Spiritual Repetition

Repetition is the return to a previous period of prayer for the purpose of allowing the movements of God to deepen within the heart. Through repetitions, we fine-tune our sensitivities to God and to how he speaks in our prayer and in our life circumstances. The prayer of repetition teaches us to understand who we are in light of how God sees us and who God is revealing himself to be for us. Repetition is a way of honoring God's word to us in the earlier prayer period. It is recalling and pondering an earlier conversation with one we love. It is as if we say to God, "Tell me that again; what did I hear you saying?" In this follow-up conversation or repetition, we open ourselves to a healing presence that often transforms whatever sadness and confusion we may have experienced the first time we prayed. In repetitions, not only does the consolation (joy, warmth, peace) deepen, but the desolation (pain, sadness, confusion) frequently moves to a new level of understanding and acceptance within God's plan for us.

—Jacqueline Syrup Bergan and Sister Marie Schwan, CSJ,
Love: A Guide for Prayer

The Presence of God
I pause for a moment and think of the love and the grace that God showers on me: I am created in the image and likeness of God; I am God's dwelling place.

Freedom
Lord, you created me to live in freedom. May your Holy Spirit guide me to follow you freely. Instill in my heart a desire to know and love you more each day.

Consciousness
How am I really feeling? Lighthearted? Heavyhearted? I may be very much at peace, happy to be here.
Equally, I may be frustrated, worried, or angry.
I acknowledge how I really am. It is the real me that the Lord loves.

The Word
I read the word of God slowly, a few times over, and I listen to what God is saying to me. (Please turn to the Scripture on the following pages. Inspiration points are there should you need them. When you are ready, return here to continue.)

Conversation
I know with certainty there were times when you carried me, Lord. When it was through your strength I got through the dark times in my life.

Conclusion
I thank God for these moments we have spent together and for any insights I have been given concerning the text.

Sunday 5th February
Fifth Sunday in Ordinary Time
Matthew 5:13–16

Jesus said to the crowds, "You are the salt of the earth; but if salt has lost its taste, how can its saltiness be restored? It is no longer good for anything, but is thrown out and trampled under foot. You are the light of the world. A city built on a hill cannot be hid. No one after lighting a lamp puts it under the bushel basket, but on the lampstand, and it gives light to all in the house. In the same way, let your light shine before others, so that they may see your good works and give glory to your Father in heaven."

- The two metaphors of salt and light can apply to the individual believer and to the church as a whole. The saltiness points to the need for passion and dynamism at the heart of faith. The brightness of light points to the witness quality of the believer's life. Others are meant to sense the faith that motivates our good works and so be led to praise God. Faith is personal but not private. Is this true for me?

- People do not usually praise a meal for its saltiness, but many will miss salt if it is absent. How do I contribute something vital to the world—something that does not draw attention to me but that is needed?

Monday 6th February
Mark 6:53–56

When Jesus and the disciples had crossed over, they came to land at Gennesaret and moored the boat. When they got out of the boat, people at once recognized him, and rushed about that whole region and began to bring the sick on mats to wherever they heard he was. And wherever he went, into villages or cities or farms, they laid the sick in the marketplaces, and begged him that they might touch even the fringe of his cloak; and all who touched it were healed.

- How the people of Gennesaret must have rejoiced over Jesus' visit. It was such a wondrous time of healing. They welcomed him as a healer. How do I welcome Jesus? How do I see him—as healer, friend, advocate?

- I imagine Jesus playing his part in rowing the boat and then mooring it. I watch as the word spreads that he has arrived. People rush about;

they grab this chance to have their friends healed. Where am I in the scene? Am I helping others to reach him, or am I perhaps waiting for someone to bring me to Jesus? Can I let Jesus touch me?

Tuesday 7th February
Mark 7:1–13

Now when the Pharisees and some of the scribes who had come from Jerusalem gathered around him, they noticed that some of his disciples were eating with defiled hands, that is, without washing them. (For the Pharisees, and all the Jews, do not eat unless they thoroughly wash their hands, thus observing the tradition of the elders; and they do not eat anything from the market unless they wash it; and there are also many other traditions that they observe, the washing of cups, pots, and bronze kettles.) So the Pharisees and the scribes asked him, "Why do your disciples not live according to the tradition of the elders, but eat with defiled hands?" He said to them, "Isaiah prophesied rightly about you hypocrites, as it is written,

'This people honors me with their lips,
but their hearts are far from me;
in vain do they worship me,
teaching human precepts as doctrines.'

You abandon the commandment of God and hold to human tradition." Then he said to them, "You have a fine way of rejecting the commandment of God in order to keep your tradition! For Moses said, 'Honor your father and your mother'; and, 'Whoever speaks evil of father or mother must surely die.' But you say that if anyone tells father or mother, 'Whatever support you might have had from me is Corban' (that is, an offering to God)—then you no longer permit doing anything for a father or mother, thus making void the word of God through your tradition that you have handed on. And you do many things like this."

- How often do we choose to be distracted by little things in order to avoid or admit to the real problem? Lord, help me to focus on your love for me and mine and for my neighbor!

- Is my heart far from God? Do I give more time to keeping a clean house than a clean heart? I pray for church leaders. In these difficult times, they need a deep understanding of how God wants them to serve. May they not get lost in distractions and obsessions.

Wednesday 8th February
Mark 7:14–23

Then he called the crowd again and said to them, "Listen to me, all of you, and understand: there is nothing outside a person that by going in can defile, but the things that come out are what defile." When he had left the crowd and entered the house, his disciples asked him about the parable. He said to them, "Then do you also fail to understand? Do you not see that whatever goes into a person from outside cannot defile, since it enters, not the heart but the stomach, and goes out into the sewer?" (Thus he declared all foods clean.) And he said, "It is what comes out of a person that defiles. For it is from within, from the human heart, that evil intentions come: fornication, theft, murder, adultery, avarice, wickedness, deceit, licentiousness, envy, slander, pride, folly. All these evil things come from within, and they defile a person."

- For Jesus, the battlefield between good and evil is the human heart, and my heart is included! How clean is my heart?
- We can be grasping, we can spoil things for others, and leave our smudge on them. We can make things difficult for others, humiliate them, reduce them to tears. Lord, you list twelve "evil intentions" that defile a person. Reveal to me the one I need to address right now!

Thursday 9th February
Mark 7:24–30

From there Jesus set out and went away to the region of Tyre. He entered a house and did not want anyone to know he was there. Yet he could not escape notice, but a woman whose little daughter had an unclean spirit immediately heard about him, and she came and bowed down at his feet. Now the woman was a Gentile, of Syrophoenician origin. She begged him to cast the demon out of her daughter. He said to her, "Let the children be fed first, for it is not fair to take the children's food and throw it to the dogs." But she answered him, "Sir, even the dogs under the table eat the children's crumbs." Then he said to her, "For saying that, you may go—the demon has left your daughter." So she went home, found the child lying on the bed, and the demon gone.

- The prayer of the woman was not answered immediately. Her persistence shows Jesus how serious she was. Jesus, forgive me for my trivial requests. Help me listen to my prayers that I might learn what is really closest to my heart.

- This is a brave and determined woman! She risks her self-respect and dignity to save her sick daughter. She is the only woman in this Gospel to win an argument with Jesus. She gets him to change his mind about the scope of his ministry. Lord, may I have courage to do what I can so that the gifts women bring to the church may be more fully appreciated.

Friday 10th February
Mark 7:31–37

Then Jesus returned from the region of Tyre, and went by way of Sidon towards the Sea of Galilee, in the region of the Decapolis. They brought to him a deaf man who had an impediment in his speech; and they begged him to lay his hand on him. He took him aside in private, away from the crowd, and put his fingers into his ears, and he spat and touched his tongue. Then looking up to heaven, he sighed and said to him, "Ephphatha, that is, 'Be opened.'" And immediately his ears were opened, his tongue was released, and he spoke plainly. Then Jesus ordered them to tell no one; but the more he ordered them, the more zealously they proclaimed it. They were astounded beyond measure, saying, "He has done everything well; he even makes the deaf to hear and the mute to speak."

- Nobody is excluded from the healing touch of God. This man is doubly afflicted—being a foreigner he suffers isolation, and he is also excluded by his physical impairment. Jesus' action initiates a new age. He doesn't heal from a distance. He comes close enough to touch us, one by one.

- I can hear the word of God but not put it into practice; I can receive the Eucharist but not be nourished by it. So I take this time with Jesus and ask him to touch the ears of my heart and loosen my tongue so that I may hear his life-giving words and speak clearly about how God is working in my life.

Saturday 11th February
Mark 8:1–10

In those days when there was again a great crowd without anything to eat, Jesus called his disciples and said to them, "I have compassion for the crowd, because they have been with me now for three days and have nothing to eat. If I send them away hungry to their homes, they will faint on the way—and some of them have come from a great distance." His disciples replied, "How can one feed these people with bread here in the desert?" He asked them, "How many loaves do you have?" They said, "Seven." Then he ordered the crowd to sit down on the ground; and he took the seven loaves, and after giving thanks he broke them and gave them to his disciples to distribute; and they distributed them to the crowd. They had also a few small fish; and after blessing them, he ordered that these too should be distributed. They ate and were filled; and they took up the broken pieces left over, seven baskets full. Now there were about four thousand people.

- I think of how Jesus has compassion on me and wants to feed me. He sees the distance I have come and wants to give me strength. Even for very little, Jesus gave thanks. The needs are great, my resources small. I give thanks for what I have.

- Lord, today let me see some of the miracles that surround me. I have food and drink. Someone treats me kindly. I have the freedom and ability to read this book in my hand. And I meet you, my God, in this time of prayer. Others support me with their prayer, and I support them, too. Thank you, Lord—for everything!

The Sixth Week of Ordinary Time
February 12—February 18

Something to think and pray about each day this week:

Love Visible

God's love is an effective love. It changes us—our way of seeing and our way of responding. Although we cannot see God, we can see the effect of his love in the circumstances of our lives. His love becomes visible in an awareness of his caring for us through all the people who have loved us. It becomes visible in the realization of the many times we have been spared the consequences of our sin and foolishness. Most of all, God's love becomes visible when we feel our fears dissipating and our hearts expanding with love and concern for others. Even if our personal experiences of being loved have sometimes been disappointing, there is within the core of us, always alive, always yearning, the Spirit of love, the Spirit of God, which continues to create us and to hold us in being. God is love; he has first loved us.

—Jacqueline Syrup Bergan and Sister Marie Schwan, CSJ,
Love: A Guide for Prayer

The Presence of God
Jesus, help me to be fully alive to your Holy Presence. Enfold me in your love. Let my heart become one with yours.

Freedom
I will ask God's help,
to be free from my own preoccupations,
to be open to God in this time of prayer,
to come to know, love, and serve God more.

Consciousness
I ask how I am within myself today? Am I particularly tired, stressed, or off form? If any of these characteristics apply, can I try to let go of the concerns that disturb me?

The Word
God speaks to each of us individually. I listen attentively to hear what God is saying to me. Read the text a few times, then listen. (Please turn to the Scripture on the following pages. Inspiration points are there should you need them. When you are ready, return here to continue.)

Conversation
Sometimes I wonder what I might say if I were to meet you in person, Lord.
I think I might say, Thank you, Lord, for always being there for me.

Conclusion
Glory be to the Father, and to the Son, and to the Holy Spirit,
As it was in the beginning, is now and ever shall be,
World without end. Amen.

Sunday 12th February
Sixth Sunday in Ordinary Time
Matthew 5:17–37

Jesus said, "Do not think that I have come to abolish the law or the prophets; I have come not to abolish but to fulfill. For truly I tell you, until heaven and earth pass away, not one letter, not one stroke of a letter, will pass from the law until all is accomplished. Therefore, whoever breaks one of the least of these commandments, and teaches others to do the same, will be called least in the kingdom of heaven; but whoever does them and teaches them will be called great in the kingdom of heaven. For I tell you, unless your righteousness exceeds that of the scribes and Pharisees, you will never enter the kingdom of heaven."

- Jesus is not careless about the requirements of the law. He wants us, too, to be attentive and careful and asks us to bring all aspects of our lives before God. I pray that I might respect the voice of my conscience as I try to hear how God is speaking to me.

- I am often told who are the winners and losers; I hear about the great, I am taught to ignore the small. Jesus shows me a different way of thinking about who is great. I ask Jesus to show me who really deserves my attention.

Monday 13th February
Mark 8:11–13

The Pharisees came and began to argue with Jesus, asking him for a sign from heaven, to test him. And he sighed deeply in his spirit and said, "Why does this generation ask for a sign? Truly I tell you, no sign will be given to this generation." And he left them, and getting into the boat again, he went across to the other side.

- All the wonders that Jesus is doing are the "sign from heaven" that the Pharisees are demanding. But their hearts are closed. If a new sign came, they would look for yet another. Jesus realizes he can't satisfy the demanding, grasping search for evidence.

- Lord, what about me? Am I always looking for something more from you? You reveal yourself as being totally on my side, through your

Passion and Resurrection. Let me accept these great signs. Let me trust that you are on my side even when smaller things do not go well.

Tuesday 14th February
Mark 8:14–21

Now the disciples had forgotten to bring any bread; and they had only one loaf with them in the boat. And he cautioned them, saying, "Watch out—beware of the yeast of the Pharisees and the yeast of Herod." They said to one another, "It is because we have no bread." And becoming aware of it, Jesus said to them, "Why are you talking about having no bread? Do you still not perceive or understand? Are your hearts hardened? Do you have eyes, and fail to see? Do you have ears, and fail to hear? And do you not remember? When I broke the five loaves for the five thousand, how many baskets full of broken pieces did you collect?" They said to him, "Twelve." "And the seven for the four thousand, how many baskets full of broken pieces did you collect?" And they said to him, "Seven." Then he said to them, "Do you not yet understand?"

- I take these moments of prayer and ask Jesus to be honest with me. What questions does he ask me as his lackluster disciple? "Is your faith bland?" "Do you know what it is like to live by the Gospel?" "If you want to be alive, why not follow me closely?" "You are limitlessly loved—do you know that?"

- I think of Jesus looking at me lovingly, speaking to me gently, inviting me to understand and to receive his good news into my heart.

Wednesday 15th February
Mark 8:22–26

Jesus and the disciples came to Bethsaida. Some people brought a blind man to Jesus and begged him to touch him. He took the blind man by the hand and led him out of the village; and when he had put saliva on his eyes and laid his hands on him, he asked him, "Can you see anything?" And the man looked up and said, "I can see people, but they look like trees, walking." Then Jesus laid his hands on his eyes again; and he looked intently and his sight was restored, and he saw everything clearly. Then he sent him away to his home, saying, "Do not even go into the village."

- Jesus took the blind man out of the village and, having healed him, told him not to return there. This time of prayer for me is a time of stepping apart, of being alone with Jesus. Are there some concerns I have from which I can step away for a while? Are there some things about which I worry that I might leave in the hands of the Lord?

- This miracle is unusual in that it is gradual. Mark uses it to highlight the blindness embedded in our minds and heart, which can hinder God's working in us. I reflect on my own slow struggle to believe fully in Jesus, and I ask his help. Lord, may I see people as you see them— each a sister or brother for whom you died.

Thursday 16th February
Mark 8:27–33

Jesus went on with his disciples to the villages of Caesarea Philippi; and on the way he asked his disciples, "Who do people say that I am?" And they answered him, "John the Baptist; and others, Elijah; and still others, one of the prophets." He asked them, "But who do you say that I am?" Peter answered him, "You are the Messiah." And he sternly ordered them not to tell anyone about him. Then he began to teach them that the Son of Man must undergo great suffering, and be rejected by the elders, the chief priests, and the scribes, and be killed, and after three days rise again. He said all this quite openly. And Peter took him aside and began to rebuke him. But turning and looking at his disciples, he rebuked Peter and said, "Get behind me, Satan! For you are setting your mind not on divine things but on human things."

- We can sympathize with Peter because who among us can bear the thought of our best friend being tortured and killed? But Jesus tells Peter that God's plans are so much bigger than he imagines. Someone has said that God's dreams come to us several sizes too large! It takes us time to grow into them.

- What about my inner growth: have I stopped growing at some point, so that God cannot do more creative work with me? Lord, let me be open to your unrestricted dreams for me, even though they involve change and pain and, ultimately, death. This is the way to eternal joy.

Friday 17th February
Mark 8:34—9:1

Jesus called the crowd with his disciples, and said to them, "If any want to become my followers, let them deny themselves and take up their cross and follow me. For those who want to save their life will lose it, and those who lose their life for my sake, and for the sake of the Gospel, will save it. For what will it profit them to gain the whole world and forfeit their life? Indeed, what can they give in return for their life? Those who are ashamed of me and of my words in this adulterous and sinful generation, of them the Son of Man will also be ashamed when he comes in the glory of his Father with the holy angels." And he said to them, "Truly I tell you, there are some standing here who will not taste death until they see that the kingdom of God has come with power."

- Much of life seems to be about collecting, gathering, saving, and preparing. Jesus speaks of another way: letting go. If there is something to which I am too attached—possessions, opinions, relationships—I ask for God's help.

- If I choose living for others, and keep that decision alive by constant renewal, then my relationships take on a new quality. It is then that I am fully alive.

Saturday 18th February
Mark 9:2–13

Six days later, Jesus took with him Peter and James and John, and led them up a high mountain apart, by themselves. And he was transfigured before them, and his clothes became dazzling white, such as no one on earth could bleach them. And there appeared to them Elijah with Moses, who were talking with Jesus. Then Peter said to Jesus, "Rabbi, it is good for us to be here; let us make three dwellings, one for you, one for Moses, and one for Elijah." He did not know what to say, for they were terrified. Then a cloud overshadowed them, and from the cloud there came a voice, "This is my Son, the Beloved; listen to him!" Suddenly when they looked around, they saw no one with them any more, but only Jesus. As they were coming down the mountain, he ordered them to tell no one about what they had seen, until after the Son of Man had risen from the dead.

So they kept the matter to themselves, questioning what this rising from the dead could mean.

- In our journey to God we have peak moments, when the ground is holy. Like Peter, we want them to last forever. But Jesus, only Jesus, brings us down the mountain and prepares us for the hard times ahead, living on the memory of brief transfigurations. Can I recall any of my peak moments?

- The divine is hidden within each of us. Sometimes my goodness shines out, and sometimes it is hidden. But everyone I meet, at home, on the streets, at work, in the hospital and the supermarket, is a daughter or son of God.

The Seventh Week of Ordinary Time
February 19—February 25

Something to think and pray about each day this week:

Beyond Our Comfort
Whether Jesus was teaching about true generosity, a more profound meaning of justice, or the truth of his own identity and mission, he nearly always made someone uncomfortable. He asked questions that caused discomfort, such as "What were you arguing about?" or "But who do you say that I am?" He asks those questions still—and we should imagine his gaze going straight to our own hearts. We can be thankful for this grace of discomfort because it means that Jesus considers us true followers, and he asks a lot of us. He asks that we search our motives, that we learn from wisdom and example, and that we change our default attitudes from standard human reactions to kingdom-of-God responses.

—The Editors

The Presence of God

"I stand at the door and knock," says the Lord. What a wonderful privilege that the Lord of all creation desires to come to me. I welcome his presence.

Freedom

Saint Ignatius thought that a thick and shapeless tree trunk would never believe that it could become a statue, admired as a miracle of sculpture, and would never submit itself to the chisel of the sculptor,
who sees by her genius what she can make of it.
I ask for the grace to let myself be shaped by my loving Creator.

Consciousness

Knowing that God loves me unconditionally, I can afford to be honest about how I am. What are my fears and desires? What do I expect from God? What am I willing to give to God—from my emotions and talents, thoughts and energy? And how do I feel now? I share my feelings openly with the Lord.

The Word

I take my time to read the word of God, slowly, a few times, allowing myself to dwell on anything that strikes me. (Please turn to the Scripture on the following pages. Inspiration points are there should you need them. When you are ready, return here to continue.)

Conversation

Do I notice myself reacting as I pray with the word of God? Do I feel challenged, comforted, angry? Imagining Jesus sitting or standing by me, I speak out my feelings, as one trusted friend to another.

Conclusion

I thank God for these moments we have spent together and for any insights I have been given concerning the text.

Sunday 19th February
Seventh Sunday in Ordinary Time
Matthew 5:38–48

Jesus said to the crowds, "You have heard that it was said, 'An eye for an eye and a tooth for a tooth.' But I say to you, Do not resist an evildoer. But if anyone strikes you on the right cheek, turn the other also; and if anyone wants to sue you and take your coat, give your cloak as well; and if anyone forces you to go one mile, go also the second mile. Give to everyone who begs from you, and do not refuse anyone who wants to borrow from you." . . .

- The principle of an eye for an eye and a tooth for a tooth served to prevent excessive retaliation for an offense. But Jesus wants no retaliation at all. Instead he looks for a generosity of spirit that forgives the offender and returns good for evil. Take each of his examples into your prayer in turn and see how it might apply to you.

- Think about the world as you experience it: Where do you notice attitudes that are defensive, reactive, and self-protecting; where do you meet surprising generosity, graciousness, and hope? To which of these ways of seeing do you give the most attention?

Monday 20th February
Mark 9:14–29

When the crowd saw Jesus, they were immediately overcome with awe, and they ran forward to greet him. He asked them, "What are you arguing about with them?" Someone from the crowd answered him, "Teacher, I brought you my son; he has a spirit that makes him unable to speak; and whenever it seizes him, it dashes him down; and he foams and grinds his teeth and becomes rigid; and I asked your disciples to cast it out, but they could not do so." He answered them, "You faithless generation, how much longer must I be among you? How much longer must I put up with you? Bring him to me." And they brought the boy to him. When the spirit saw him, immediately it threw the boy into convulsions, and he fell on the ground and rolled about, foaming at the mouth. Jesus asked the father, "How long has this been happening to him?" And he said, "From childhood. It has often cast him into the fire and into the water, to destroy him; but if you are able to do anything, have pity on us and help us." Jesus said to him, "If you are able!—All things can be done for the one who believes." Immediately the father of the child cried out, "I believe; help my unbelief!" When Jesus saw that a crowd came running together, he rebuked the unclean spirit, saying to it, "You spirit that keeps this boy from speaking and hearing, I command you, come out of him, and never enter him again!" After crying out and convulsing him terribly, it came out, and the boy was like a corpse, so that most of them said, "He is dead." But Jesus took him by the hand and lifted him up, and he was able to stand. When he had entered the house, his disciples asked him privately, "Why could we not cast it out?" He said to them, "This kind can come out only through prayer."

- Notice Jesus' impatience in this situation. In it we can find resonance with our own human impatience and also find the strength to persevere. Doubt can be an important part of belief and can add to our growth.

- Jesus' disciples prove to be a disappointment. Lord, I sometimes feel let down and disappointed by the church or its ministers. When I am discouraged, help me to look beyond the institution and its ministers. Let me turn in faith to you, O healer and giver of life.

Tuesday 21st February
Mark 9:30–37

Then Jesus and the disciples came to Capernaum; and when he was in the house he asked them, "What were you arguing about on the way?" But they were silent, for on the way they had argued with one another who was the greatest. He sat down, called the twelve, and said to them, "Whoever wants to be first must be last of all and servant of all." Then he took a little child and put it among them; and taking it in his arms, he said to them, "Whoever welcomes one such child in my name welcomes me, and whoever welcomes me welcomes not me but the one who sent me."

- The apostles were just as people still are: competitive, making comparisons, wanting to be right. If I notice these patterns in myself, I ask for the healing I need. I pray that I may realize that all that matters is how I welcome God's reign.

- I ask God to bless my memory and to show me how I, as a child, was innocent and trusting. I consider this not sentimentally but so that I might appreciate what Jesus is saying. I ask that I now receive God's word in trust and faith.

Wednesday 22nd February
Matthew 16:13–19

Now when Jesus came into the district of Caesarea Philippi, he asked his disciples, "Who do people say that the Son of Man is?" And they said, "Some say John the Baptist, but others Elijah, and still others Jeremiah or one of the prophets." He said to them, "But who do you say that I am?" Simon Peter answered, "You are the Messiah, the Son of the living God." And Jesus answered him, "Blessed are you, Simon son of Jonah! For flesh and blood has not revealed this to you, but my Father in heaven. And I tell you, you are Peter, and on this rock I will build my church, and the gates of Hades will not prevail against it. I will give you the keys of the kingdom of heaven, and whatever you bind on earth will be bound in heaven, and whatever you loose on earth will be loosed in heaven."

- We are not, as is sometimes phrased, "followers of the church." We *are* the church, served by bishops and others, but with our own wisdom. Lord, you did not leave us orphans. We are the people of God, with a leader, and the support of the Holy Spirit. I am not alone.

- "But who do you say that I am?" It is not enough to quote the Catechism of the Catholic Church or the views of one or another theologian. Try to answer not only from the head but from the heart. You might helpfully rephrase the question as: Who is Jesus for me?

Thursday 23rd February
Mark 9:41–50

Jesus said to his disciples, "If anyone gives you a cup of water to drink just because you belong to Christ, then I tell you solemnly, he will most certainly not lose his reward. But anyone who is an obstacle to bring down one of these little ones who have faith, would be better thrown into the sea with a great millstone round his neck. And if your hand should cause you to sin, cut it off; it is better for you to enter into life crippled, than to have two hands and go to hell, into the fire that cannot be put out. And if your foot should cause you to sin, cut it off; it is better for you to enter into life lame, than to have two feet and be thrown into hell. And if your eye should cause you to sin, tear it out; it is better for you to enter into the kingdom of God with one eye, than to have two eyes and be thrown into hell where their worm does not die nor their fire go out. For everyone will be salted with fire. Salt is a good thing, but if salt has become insipid, how can you season it again? Have salt in yourselves and be at peace with one another."

- "Have salt in yourselves and be at peace with one another." What does Jesus mean by this? Salt was a preservative and a seasoning. A certain spiritual "saltiness" leads to good works and to peace. How do I develop this quality of life?

- Jesus is describing a lack of spiritual freedom: "If your foot [or eye or hand] should cause you to sin, cut it off." He uses harsh language to emphasize that we should allow nothing to get in our way of entering life with God. Am I free to love God and others? Is there any aspect of my life that prevents this?

Friday 24th February
Mark 10:1–12

. . . Some Pharisees came, and to test him they asked, "Is it lawful for a man to divorce his wife?" He answered them, "What did Moses command you?" They said, "Moses allowed a man to write a certificate of dismissal and to divorce her." But Jesus said to them, "Because of your hardness of heart he wrote this commandment for you. But from the beginning of creation, God made them male and female. For this reason a man shall leave his father and mother and be joined to his wife, and the two shall become one flesh. So they are no longer two, but one flesh. Therefore what God has joined together, let no one separate." Then in the house the disciples asked him again about this matter. He said to them, "Whoever divorces his wife and marries another commits adultery against her; and if she divorces her husband and marries another, she commits adultery."

- The unity and love of a happy marriage are gifts from God. Unfortunately, many married people, for various reasons, have been unable to live this gift fully. I can pray today for all married couples. May the compassion of Christ touch all those who are experiencing or have experienced difficulty in married life.

- Jesus denounces any hardness of heart that can bring about divorce. Spouses must not treat each other as worthless property to be discarded. They are called instead to a life of mutual respect and interdependence.

Saturday 25th February
Mark 10:13–16

People were bringing little children to Jesus in order that he might touch them; and the disciples spoke sternly to them. But when Jesus saw this, he was indignant and said to them, "Let the little children come to me; do not stop them; for it is to such as these that the kingdom of God belongs. Truly I tell you, whoever does not receive the kingdom of God as a little child will never enter it." And he took them up in his arms, laid his hands on them, and blessed them.

- Welcoming children requires patience, openness, and respect for vulnerable lives. Lord Jesus, help me notice children more and honor who they are, even if they try my patience or disrupt my schedule. Help me learn from them how to love life with an open heart.

- This scene shows that Jesus understood how to love children. A crowd of them interrupted his preaching, and the apostles were shooing them away. But he gave the children time and affection, two high priorities indeed.

The Eighth Week of Ordinary Time
February 26—March 4

Something to think and pray about each day this week:

Desired into Existence

I maintain that God—out of the abundance of divine relational life, not any need for us—desires humans into existence for the sake of friendship. This thesis may sound strange, because it runs counter to much teaching about God. To be honest, I questioned it myself when I first began to think it through. But over the years, as my own relationship with God has deepened and I have listened to people talk about how God relates to them, I have become convinced that the best analogy for the relationship God wants with us is friendship.

—William A. Barry, SJ, *Lenten Meditations*

The Presence of God

To be present is to arrive as one is and open up to the other.
At this instant, as I arrive here, God is present waiting for me.
God always arrives before me, desiring to connect with me
even more than my most intimate friend.
I take a moment and greet my loving God.

Freedom

I am free. When I look at these words in writing, they seem to create in
me a feeling of awe. Yes, a wonderful feeling of freedom. Thank you,
God.

Consciousness

To be conscious about something is to be aware of it.
Dear Lord, help me to remember that you gave me life.
Thank you for the gift of life.
Teach me to slow down, to be still and enjoy the pleasures created for me.
To be aware of the beauty that surrounds me. The marvel of mountains,
the calmness of lakes, the fragility of a flower petal. I need to remember
that all these things come from you.

The Word

The word of God comes to us through the Scriptures. May the Holy Spirit
enlighten my mind and heart to respond to the Gospel teachings. (Please
turn to the Scripture on the following pages. Inspiration points are there
should you need them. When you are ready, return here to continue.)

Conversation

I begin to talk to Jesus about the piece of Scripture I have just read. What
part of it strikes a chord in me? Perhaps the words of a friend—or some
story I have heard recently—will slowly rise to the surface in my consciousness. If so, does the story throw light on what the Scripture passage
may be trying to say to me?

Conclusion

Glory be to the Father, and to the Son, and to the Holy Spirit,
As it was in the beginning, is now and ever shall be,
World without end. Amen.

Sunday 26th February
Eighth Sunday in Ordinary Time
Matthew 6:24–34

. . . Jesus said, "Therefore I tell you, do not worry about your life, what you will eat or what you will drink, or about your body, what you will wear. Is not life more than food, and the body more than clothing? Look at the birds of the air; they neither sow nor reap nor gather into barns, and yet your heavenly Father feeds them. Are you not of more value than they? And can any of you by worrying add a single hour to your span of life? And why do you worry about clothing? Consider the lilies of the field, how they grow; they neither toil nor spin, yet I tell you, even Solomon in all his glory was not clothed like one of these. But if God so clothes the grass of the field, which is alive today and tomorrow is thrown into the oven, will he not much more clothe you—you of little faith? Therefore do not worry, saying, 'What will we eat?' or 'What will we drink?' or 'What will we wear?' For it is the Gentiles who strive for all these things; and indeed your heavenly Father knows that you need all these things. But strive first for the kingdom of God and his righteousness, and all these things will be given to you as well. So do not worry about tomorrow, for tomorrow will bring worries of its own. Today's trouble is enough for today."

- There are so many messages all around me telling me what I should wear, what I should eat. Jesus reminds me that I am more than a consumer. My identity lies in my relationship with God, who loves me and causes me to trust.

- This passage is one of great beauty. Let me savor it for a few moments and find peace and joy in it. Jesus promises us that God is generous. God can be trusted to provide what we need as we "strive first for the kingdom of God."

Monday 27th February
Mark 10:17–27

As Jesus was setting out on a journey, a man ran up and knelt before him, and asked him, "Good Teacher, what must I do to inherit eternal life?" Jesus said to him, "Why do you call me good? No one is good but God alone. You know the commandments: You shall not murder; You shall not commit adultery; You shall not steal; You shall not bear false witness; You shall not defraud; Honor your father and mother." He said to him, "Teacher, I have kept all these since my youth." Jesus, looking at him, loved him and said, "You lack one thing; go, sell what you own, and give the money to the poor, and you will have treasure in heaven; then come, follow me." When he heard this, he was shocked and went away grieving, for he had many possessions. Then Jesus looked around and said to his disciples, "How hard it will be for those who have wealth to enter the kingdom of God!" And the disciples were perplexed at these words. But Jesus said to them again, "Children, how hard it is to enter the kingdom of God! It is easier for a camel to go through the eye of a needle than for someone who is rich to enter the kingdom of God." They were greatly astounded and said to one another, "Then who can be saved?" Jesus looked at them and said, "For mortals it is impossible, but not for God; for God all things are possible."

- "Jesus, looking at him, loved him"; something in Jesus' gaze was unforgettable. I consider this scene and wonder what it was that Jesus loved about the man. I allow myself time to think about what he loves about me—and I don't move on until I do!

- Mark does not spare us the shock and grief of the man as he hears, and rejects, Jesus' invitation, or Jesus' calm acceptance of that refusal. He will not do violence to our freedom. Jesus may show me the one thing that is holding me back from freedom. I can walk away or I can ask for help to deal with it.

Tuesday 28th February
Mark 10:28–31

Peter began to say to Jesus, "Look, we have left everything and followed you." Jesus said, "Truly I tell you, there is no one who has left house or brothers or sisters or mother or father or children or fields, for my sake and for the sake of the good news, who will not receive a hundredfold now in this age—houses, brothers and sisters, mothers and children, and fields, with persecutions—and in the age to come eternal life. But many who are first will be last, and the last will be first."

- I reflect on this exchange as Saint Peter might have done at the end of his life. What has it meant to me to follow Jesus? What have I given up? What was my hundredfold, in the way of joy, contentment, peace of soul?

- Jesus does not ask that we turn our back on our responsibilities. Rather, he invites us to cultivate a freedom and generosity of spirit centered on the greater good. When our concern is for others' well-being, we are already in the kingdom. Can I ask Jesus to help me face with courage and generosity any responsibilities I might be running away from?

Wednesday 1st March
Ash Wednesday
Matthew 6:1–6,16–18

Jesus said, "Beware of practicing your piety before others in order to be seen by them; for then you have no reward from your Father in heaven. So whenever you give alms, do not sound a trumpet before you, as the hypocrites do in the synagogues and in the streets, so that they may be praised by others. Truly I tell you, they have received their reward. But when you give alms, do not let your left hand know what your right hand is doing, so that your alms may be done in secret; and your Father who sees in secret will reward you. And whenever you pray, do not be like the hypocrites; for they love to stand and pray in the synagogues and at the street corners, so that they may be seen by others. Truly I tell you, they have received their reward. But whenever you pray, go into your room and shut the door and pray to your Father who is in secret; and your Father who sees in secret will reward you. . . . And whenever you fast, do not look dismal, like the hypocrites, for they disfigure their faces so as to show others that they are fasting. Truly I tell you, they have received their reward. But when you fast, put oil on your head and wash your face, so that your fasting may be seen not by others but by your Father who is in secret; and your Father who sees in secret will reward you."

- At this time of year, the church invites us to test our inner freedom— concerning food and drink, pornography, complaining, gossiping, and so on. What habits make you hard to live with? Lent is about regaining control of our own lives, especially in those areas that damage other people.

- Do I have a secret room in which I meet God? Am I happy to have God see all that I do? The kingdom of God becomes visible through my public religious practices and also through my private works of charity and acts of faith.

Thursday 2nd March
Luke 9:22–25

Jesus said to his disciples, "The Son of Man must undergo great suffering, and be rejected by the elders, chief priests, and scribes, and be killed, and on the third day be raised." Then he said to them all, "If any want to become my followers, let them deny themselves and take up their cross daily and follow me. For those who want to save their life will lose it, and those who lose their life for my sake will save it. What does it profit them if they gain the whole world, but lose or forfeit themselves?"

- *Deny yourself and take up your cross daily.* Lord, I used to think this meant looking for mortifications. You have taught me that my cross is myself, my ego, the pains in my body, my awkwardness, my mistakes. To follow you is to move beyond ego trips. It means coping with the business of life without trampling on others or making them suffer.

- The Gospel is unambiguous: suffering and self-displacement are the hallmarks of a disciple. Jesus goes the way of the cross. He does not hoard his life, even though living must have had a special quality for him. I am called not to hoard my life but to live generously.

Friday 3rd March
Matthew 9:14–15

Then the disciples of John came to him, saying, "Why do we and the Pharisees fast often, but your disciples do not fast?" And Jesus said to them, "The wedding guests cannot mourn as long as the bridegroom is with them, can they? The days will come when the bridegroom is taken away from them, and then they will fast."

- Spend some time each day allowing the joy of God to fill your heart. Spend some time mourning with him, as joy is lost for so many. Any fasting is to remind us that the Lord of all joy suffers in his people, perhaps in people who are near to us. Prayer brings us near to others and near to God.

- Here Jesus uses the notion of fasting to reveal that the God whom the Jews hunger for has arrived. Rejoicing, not mourning, is the appropriate response to the presence of divine mercy revealed in Jesus. Lord, this Lent may my prayer and my fasting reveal my inner hunger for you.

Saturday 4th March
Luke 5:27–32

After this Jesus went out and saw a tax collector named Levi, sitting at the tax booth; and he said to him, "Follow me." And he got up, left everything, and followed him. Then Levi gave a great banquet for him in his house; and there was a large crowd of tax collectors and others sitting at the table with them. The Pharisees and their scribes were complaining to his disciples, saying, "Why do you eat and drink with tax collectors and sinners?" Jesus answered, "Those who are well have no need of a physician, but those who are sick; I have come to call not the righteous but sinners to repentance."

- Whom Jesus eats and drinks with is a distraction from what his mission is—to call us into a change of life. When we are focused on Jesus, we can eat and drink with anyone. We can invite anyone into our prayer and allow prayer to be a time of healing and forgiveness.

- Where are the Levis in my world? The drug pushers, greedy CEOs, abusers, rapists, those who cheat on taxes or social welfare. Lord, these are the sick who need you as physician. How can I help you to reach out to them?

The First Week of Lent
March 5—March 11

Something to think and pray about each day this week:

Truth and Discernment
It's difficult to make a good decision when you don't have all the information. It's also difficult to move forward while trying to deny part of your reality. Jesus came from a tradition that was brutally honest; just read a bit from any of Israel's prophets to see how forcefully they spoke the truth. Jesus continued in this vein as he talked about what it really took to be people of God, to participate in the kingdom of God. Jesus knew what John the Baptist knew before him and what the prophets knew before both of them: without truth, people cannot heal. If we ignore the root cause of our wounds, we will continue to be wounded, even if we heal some of the damage. We might fix what has been harmed. But if we continue doing what caused the harm in the first place, we will simply acquire (or inflict) new wounds because the core activity has not changed. Lent is a good time to stop our activity long enough to look at it carefully, prayerfully, and to determine the specific truths of the situation.

—Vinita Hampton Wright, *Praying Freedom*

The Presence of God

Be still and know that I am God. Lord, may your spirit guide me to seek your loving presence more and more. For it is there I find rest and refreshment from this busy world.

Freedom

By God's grace I was born to live in freedom. Free to enjoy the pleasures he created for me. Dear Lord, grant that I may live as you intended, with complete confidence in your loving care.

Consciousness

In God's loving presence I unwind the past day,
starting from now and looking back, moment by moment.
I gather in all the goodness and light, in gratitude.
I attend to the shadows and what they say to me,
seeking healing, courage, forgiveness.

The Word

The word of God comes to us through the Scriptures. May the Holy Spirit enlighten my mind and heart to respond to the Gospel teachings. (Please turn to the Scripture on the following pages. Inspiration points are there should you need them. When you are ready, return here to continue.)

Conversation

Jesus, you always welcomed little children when you walked on this earth. Teach me to have a childlike trust in you. To live in the knowledge that you will never abandon me.

Conclusion

Glory be to the Father, and to the Son, and to the Holy Spirit,
As it was in the beginning, is now and ever shall be,
World without end. Amen.

Sunday 5th March
First Sunday of Lent
Matthew 4:1–11

Then Jesus was led up by the Spirit into the wilderness to be tempted by the devil. He fasted for forty days and forty nights, and afterwards he was famished. The tempter came and said to him, "If you are the Son of God, command these stones to become loaves of bread." But he answered, "It is written, 'One does not live by bread alone, but by every word that comes from the mouth of God.'"

- Our real hungers are fed by the meaning and the love of the word of God. One form of prayer is to allow ourselves to be addressed in the heart by the word of God. Let a phrase or word from this passage of Scripture echo in your mind today.

- That Jesus was tempted meant that he truly desired what the devil offered him. Of course he was hungry. His body desired what it needed. In what ways might the devil use my legitimate, real desires to lead me astray? Open my eyes, Lord, so that I can recognize temptation when it comes.

Monday 6th March
Matthew 25:31–46

Jesus said to his disciples, "When the Son of Man comes in his glory, and all the angels with him, then he will sit on the throne of his glory. All the nations will be gathered before him, and he will separate people one from another as a shepherd separates the sheep from the goats, and he will put the sheep at his right hand and the goats at the left. Then the king will say to those at his right hand, 'Come, you that are blessed by my Father, inherit the kingdom prepared for you from the foundation of the world; for I was hungry and you gave me food, I was thirsty and you gave me something to drink, I was a stranger and you welcomed me, I was naked and you gave me clothing, I was sick and you took care of me, I was in prison and you visited me.' Then the righteous will answer him, 'Lord, when was it that we saw you hungry and gave you food, or thirsty and gave you something to drink? And when was it that we saw you a stranger and welcomed you, or naked and gave you clothing? And when was it that we saw you sick or in prison and visited you?' And the king will answer them, 'Truly I tell you, just as you did it to one of the least of these who are members of my family, you did it to me.' Then he will say to those at his left hand, 'You that are accursed, depart from me into the eternal fire prepared for the devil and his angels; for I was hungry and you gave me no food, I was thirsty and you gave me nothing to drink, I was a stranger and you did not welcome me, naked and you did not give me clothing, sick and in prison and you did not visit me.' Then they also will answer, 'Lord, when was it that we saw you hungry or thirsty or a stranger or naked or sick or in prison, and did not take care of you?' Then he will answer them, 'Truly I tell you, just as you did not do it to one of the least of these, you did not do it to me. And these will go away into eternal punishment, but the righteous into eternal life.'"

- This message is simple, Lord. You will judge me on my love for and service to others. You are there in the poor, the sick, the prisoners, the strangers. May I recognize your face.

- The story does not use fancy words about justice and solidarity but speaks of food, clothing, something to drink, protection from elements. What matters is not a theoretical love but compassion that helps the person in need.

Tuesday 7th March
Matthew 6:7–15

Jesus said, "When you are praying, do not heap up empty phrases as the Gentiles do; for they think that they will be heard because of their many words. Do not be like them, for your Father knows what you need before you ask him. Pray then in this way: Our Father in heaven, hallowed be your name. Your kingdom come. Your will be done, on earth as it is in heaven. Give us this day our daily bread. And forgive us our debts, as we also have forgiven our debtors. And do not bring us to the time of trial, but rescue us from the evil one. For if you forgive others their trespasses, your heavenly Father will also forgive you; but if you do not forgive others, neither will your Father forgive your trespasses."

- This simple prayer that Jesus taught is as new and fresh today as when it was first spoken. It reveals how things are to be between God and ourselves, and also with one another. Let me slowly say the Our Father, as if I were praying it for the first time.

- Jesus calls his disciples to pray and teaches them how. Prayer, he says, is not a magic formula but a trusting relationship between God and myself. The Our Father invites me to simplicity and sincerity of heart. It expresses an attitude of complete dependency on God. Jesus, the petitions in this prayer put God at the center of everything. That is how you lived. Help me do the same.

Wednesday 8th March
Luke 11:29–32

When the crowds were increasing, Jesus began to say, "This generation is an evil generation; it asks for a sign, but no sign will be given to it except the sign of Jonah. For just as Jonah became a sign to the people of Nineveh, so the Son of Man will be to this generation. The queen of the South will rise at the judgment with the people of this generation and condemn them, because she came from the ends of the earth to listen to the wisdom of Solomon, and see, something greater than Solomon is here! The people of Nineveh will rise up at the judgment with this generation and condemn it, because they repented at the proclamation of Jonah, and see, something greater than Jonah is here!"

- Jonah converted the great city of Nineveh by his godliness and his preaching, not by miracles. Holiness is a greater marvel than special effects but less easily recognized. Lord, your hand is more evident in saintliness than in extraordinary signs. Open my eyes to your work in my sisters and brothers.

- Jesus, you stand before me as a sign. Like Jonah, you are swallowed up by death, but you rise from the dead and challenge me to walk in newness of life. Stay with me in my times of blindness and usher me back into your saving presence.

Thursday 9th March
Matthew 7:7–12

Jesus said, "Ask, and it will be given to you; search, and you will find; knock, and the door will be opened for you. For everyone who asks receives, and everyone who searches finds, and for everyone who knocks, the door will be opened. Is there anyone among you who, if your child asks for bread, will give a stone? Or if the child asks for a fish, will give a snake? If you then, who are evil, know how to give good gifts to your children, how much more will your Father in heaven give good things to those who ask him! In everything do to others as you would have them do to you; for this is the law and the prophets."

- In the very act of praying we receive something from God. As we open our hearts to God in prayer, God's hands are open to give us good gifts. We leave a time of prayer with an increase of faith, hope, and love, which is the consolation of God.

- Parent/child is only a metaphor for what happens in prayer. I know, Lord, that you always hear my cry, but I do not always understand your answer. I will still go on praying to you, happy to fall back on the "Our Father."

Friday 10th March
Matthew 5:20–26

Jesus said, "For I tell you, unless your righteousness exceeds that of the scribes and Pharisees, you will never enter the kingdom of heaven. You have heard that it was said to those of ancient times, 'You shall not murder; and whoever murders shall be liable to judgment.' But I say to you that if you are angry with a brother or sister, you will be liable to judgment; and if you insult a brother or sister, you will be liable to the council; and if you say, 'You fool,' you will be liable to the hell of fire. So when you are offering your gift at the altar, if you remember that your brother or sister has something against you, leave your gift there before the altar and go; first be reconciled to your brother or sister, and then come and offer your gift. Come to terms quickly with your accuser while you are on the way to court with him, or your accuser may hand you over to the judge, and the judge to the guard, and you will be thrown into prison. Truly I tell you, you will never get out until you have paid the last penny."

- Lord, you are pushing my conscience inward. I will be judged not just by what I have done on the exterior but also by the voluntary movements of my heart. God sees the heart and sees how far I go along with hatred, lust, or pride. I should be responding more to God's gaze than to anyone else's.

- Jesus is unhappy with taking the prohibition of murder too literally or restrictively. He wants it to include any kind of psychological or verbal abuse of another human being. Life is meant to be about relationships that are peaceful and harmonious. Hence the need for reconciliation when relationships break down. Am I in need of reconciliation with anyone today?

Saturday 11th March
Matthew 5:43–48

Jesus said to the disciples, "You have heard that it was said, 'You shall love your neighbor and hate your enemy.' But I say to you, Love your enemies and pray for those who persecute you, so that you may be children of your Father in heaven; for he makes his sun rise on the evil and on the good, and sends rain on the righteous and on the unrighteous. For if you love those who love you, what reward do you have? Do not even the tax collectors do the same? And if you greet only your brothers and sisters, what more are you doing than others? Do not even the Gentiles do the same? Be perfect, therefore, as your heavenly Father is perfect."

- Jesus emphasizes that the easy option is not the correct one. How simple to love and be happy with those who love you! But the kingdom of God is much bigger than that: You must love all. Lord, you call us out of our comfort zones. Our growth is measured by the breadth of our love. Help us to grow in love!

- Loving our enemies is among the most challenging precepts taught by Jesus. Notice how he finds motivation and a standard in the love shown by our Father in heaven—a love that is all-embracing, non-discriminating, inclusive. Ponder how Jesus himself modelled this love. Do I want to live and love like him?

The Second Week of Lent
March 12—March 18

Something to think and pray about each day this week:

The Communal Journey

Lent is indeed how God draws us home as individuals, but it is also a very communal journey. We never journey alone, no matter how lonely we may feel. We are always journeying together. If we can experience our journey in communion with others, it makes it so much clearer that we are on a journey together. When we can share our experiences with a close friend or our worship community, we can enjoy support that allows grace to flourish. Let us pray for one another on this journey, especially for those who need and desire a change of heart on this pilgrimage to Easter joy. Choosing and acting Lent are so important because we are body-persons. We experience things with our senses, relish them with our imaginations, and we share in God's own creative and loving activity when our hearts and hands work together for and with others.

—Andy Alexander, SJ and Maureen McCann Waldron, *Praying Lent*

The Presence of God

I pause for a moment and think of the love and the grace that God showers on me: I am created in the image and likeness of God; I am God's dwelling place.

Freedom

Lord, you created me to live in freedom. May your Holy Spirit guide me to follow you freely. Instill in my heart a desire to know and love you more each day.

Consciousness

How am I really feeling? Lighthearted? Heavyhearted? I may be very much at peace, happy to be here.
Equally, I may be frustrated, worried, or angry.
I acknowledge how I really am. It is the real me that the Lord loves.

The Word

I read the word of God slowly, a few times over, and I listen to what God is saying to me. (Please turn to the Scripture on the following pages. Inspiration points are there should you need them. When you are ready, return here to continue.)

Conversation

I know with certainty there were times when you carried me, Lord. When it was through your strength I got through the dark times in my life.

Conclusion

I thank God for these moments we have spent together and for any insights I have been given concerning the text.

Sunday 12th March
The Second Sunday of Lent
Matthew 17:1–9

Six days later, Jesus took with him Peter and James and his brother John and led them up a high mountain, by themselves. And he was transfigured before them, and his face shone like the sun, and his clothes became dazzling white. Suddenly there appeared to them Moses and Elijah, talking with him. Then Peter said to Jesus, "Lord, it is good for us to be here; if you wish, I will make three dwellings here, one for you, one for Moses, and one for Elijah." While he was still speaking, suddenly a bright cloud overshadowed them, and from the cloud a voice said, "This is my Son, the Beloved; with him I am well pleased; listen to him!" When the disciples heard this, they fell to the ground and were overcome by fear. But Jesus came and touched them, saying, "Get up and do not be afraid." And when they looked up, they saw no one except Jesus himself alone. As they were coming down the mountain, Jesus ordered them, "Tell no one about the vision until after the Son of Man has been raised from the dead."

- The disciples were privileged to see Jesus in glory, to recognize that their friend could be fully present to them and to God. Jesus saw that the experience was too much for them and told them to keep it in their hearts as they headed back toward the everyday. I thank God for the inspiration and encouragement I discover in my prayer and ask that I may know how best to carry it into everyday life.

- A listening heart is a heart warmed by the love of God and taught by his words. Prayer is better described as listening than speaking. Spend some time echoing his words, or just listening to the mood of love and peace in prayer.

Monday 13th March
Luke 6:36–38

Jesus said to the disciples, "Be merciful, just as your Father is merciful. Do not judge, and you will not be judged; do not condemn, and you will not be condemned. Forgive, and you will be forgiven; give, and it will be given to you. A good measure, pressed down, shaken together, running over, will be put into your lap; for the measure you give will be the measure you get back."

- What a beautiful, challenging Lenten program! Let us strive each day for the remainder of Lent not to judge or condemn; to forgive and tell others that they are forgiven; and to do one daily act of generosity. What transformed people we will be by Easter!

- Jesus stresses once again the primary importance of good relationships with others. The world would be a different place if we were merciful and non-condemning. Lord, my poor heart is very small, and it can also be very hard. Your heart is large and also very tender and compassionate. When I try to forgive others, my heart becomes a bit more like yours, and you swamp me with your overflowing generosity.

Tuesday 14th March
Matthew 23:1–12

Then Jesus said to the crowds and to his disciples, "The scribes and the Pharisees sit on Moses' seat; therefore, do whatever they teach you and follow it; but do not do as they do, for they do not practice what they teach. They tie up heavy burdens, hard to bear, and lay them on the shoulders of others; but they themselves are unwilling to lift a finger to move them. They do all their deeds to be seen by others; for they make their phylacteries broad and their fringes long. They love to have the place of honor at banquets and the best seats in the synagogues, and to be greeted with respect in the marketplaces, and to have people call them rabbi. But you are not to be called rabbi, for you have one teacher, and you are all students. And call no one your father on earth, for you have one Father—the one in heaven. Nor are you to be called instructors, for you have one instructor, the Messiah. The greatest among you will be your servant. All who exalt themselves will be humbled, and all who humble themselves will be exalted."

- In the mysterious way that Scripture works, I am growing daily in knowledge of God's ways. You, Lord, are my teacher. I remember in prayer a moment when I felt humbled as I served somebody or did something really relevant for them. I offer this memory to God in thanks.

- Jesus does not take issue with how the Pharisees live, but he sees how they have become distracted from God by using human measures and assessments. Could it be that I am sometimes misled by wanting my way, by trying too hard to measure my own worth?

Wednesday 15th March
Matthew 20:17–28

While Jesus was going up to Jerusalem, he took the twelve disciples aside by themselves, and said to them on the way, "See, we are going up to Jerusalem, and the Son of Man will be handed over to the chief priests and scribes, and they will condemn him to death; then they will hand him over to the Gentiles to be mocked and flogged and crucified; and on the third day he will be raised." Then the mother of the sons of Zebedee came to him with her sons, and kneeling before him, she asked a favor of him. And he said to her, "What do you want?" She said to him, "Declare that these two sons of mine will sit, one at your right hand and one at your left, in your kingdom." But Jesus answered, "You do not know what you are asking. Are you able to drink the cup that I am about to drink?" They said to him, "We are able." He said to them, "You will indeed drink my cup, but to sit at my right hand and at my left, this is not mine to grant, but it is for those for whom it has been prepared by my Father." When the ten heard it, they were angry with the two brothers. But Jesus called them to him and said, "You know that the rulers of the Gentiles lord it over them, and their great ones are tyrants over them. It will not be so among you; but whoever wishes to be great among you must be your servant, and whoever wishes to be first among you must be your slave; just as the Son of Man came not to be served but to serve, and to give his life a ransom for many."

- Jesus describes vividly the degrading ways in which he will be treated in his Passion. He does this to strengthen his disciples. When we decide to act lovingly in all we do, we become vulnerable. People will take advantage of us. But love will have the final word. We will be raised up as Jesus was. I thank God for this.

- Jesus, you abhor all forms of domination. The kingdom of God is to be a domination-free community. I can see how Christian churches fall into the trap of domination. But do I dominate anyone? Even in an argument? Do I even think I am better than anyone else?

Thursday 16th March

Luke 16:19–31

Jesus said to the Pharisees, "There was a rich man who was dressed in purple and fine linen and who feasted sumptuously every day. And at his gate lay a poor man named Lazarus, covered with sores, who longed to satisfy his hunger with what fell from the rich man's table; even the dogs would come and lick his sores. The poor man died and was carried away by the angels to be with Abraham. The rich man also died and was buried. In Hades, where he was being tormented, he looked up and saw Abraham far away with Lazarus by his side. He called out, 'Father Abraham, have mercy on me, and send Lazarus to dip the tip of his finger in water and cool my tongue; for I am in agony in these flames.' But Abraham said, 'Child, remember that during your lifetime you received your good things, and Lazarus in like manner evil things; but now he is comforted here, and you are in agony. Besides all this, between you and us a great chasm has been fixed, so that those who might want to pass from here to you cannot do so, and no one can cross from there to us.' He said, 'Then, father, I beg you to send him to my father's house—for I have five brothers—that he may warn them, so that they will not also come into this place of torment.' Abraham replied, 'They have Moses and the prophets; they should listen to them.' He said, 'No, father Abraham; but if someone goes to them from the dead, they will repent.' He said to him, 'If they do not listen to Moses and the prophets, neither will they be convinced even if someone rises from the dead.'"

- The poor are brought straight into the kingdom of God, while the rich have to endure the pain of conversion. I ponder the mysterious workings of God's providence. I pray for the rich that they be converted, and I ask to be shown how to share my own possessions with the needy.

- During Lent I try to hear the call to come back home to God. I join the great pilgrimage of people who, through the ages, have been called by Moses and the prophets to listen to the word of the Lord.

Friday 17th March
Matthew 21:33–43, 45–46

Jesus said, "Listen to another parable. There was a landowner who planted a vineyard, put a fence around it, dug a wine press in it, and built a watchtower. Then he leased it to tenants and went to another country. When the harvest time had come, he sent his slaves to the tenants to collect his produce. But the tenants seized his slaves and beat one, killed another, and stoned another. Again he sent other slaves, more than the first; and they treated them in the same way. Finally he sent his son to them, saying, 'They will respect my son.' But when the tenants saw the son, they said to themselves, 'This is the heir; come, let us kill him and get his inheritance. So they seized him, threw him out of the vineyard, and killed him. Now when the owner of the vineyard comes, what will he do to those tenants?" They said to him, "He will put those wretches to a miserable death, and lease the vineyard to other tenants who will give him the produce at the harvest time." Jesus said to them, "Have you never read in the Scriptures: 'The stone that the builders rejected has become the cornerstone; this was the Lord's doing, and it is amazing in our eyes'? Therefore I tell you, the kingdom of God will be taken away from you and given to a people that produces the fruits of the kingdom." . . . When the chief priests and the Pharisees heard his parables, they realized that he was speaking about them. They wanted to arrest him, but they feared the crowds, because they regarded him as a prophet.

- We are the tenants in the parable. God provides everything we need to make our vineyard prosper. God gives us the freedom to run the vineyard as we choose—but it is God's. This is what prayer is about—coming to know the mind of God about our lives. What fruits will I produce for the Lord?

- One of the saddest statements in the Gospels is this innocent comment by the father: "They will respect my son." I am frightened to think what would happen if Jesus came into our world today. His message about the kingdom of God would put him in direct opposition to so many other kingdoms. He would become an enemy to be got rid of. Jesus, you were thrown out and killed. But you took no revenge. Instead, by your love you reconciled everyone with God. May I always wish others well and pray for them, even if they hurt me.

Saturday 18th March

Luke 15:1–3, 11–32

Now all the tax collectors and sinners were coming near to listen to him. And the Pharisees and the scribes were grumbling and saying, "This fellow welcomes sinners and eats with them." So he told them this parable: . . . "There was a man who had two sons. The younger of them said to his father, 'Father, give me the share of the property that will belong to me.' So he divided his property between them. A few days later the younger son gathered all he had and traveled to a distant country, and there he squandered his property in dissolute living. When he had spent everything, a severe famine took place throughout that country, and he began to be in need. So he went and hired himself out to one of the citizens of that country, who sent him to his fields to feed the pigs. He would gladly have filled himself with the pods that the pigs were eating; and no one gave him anything. But when he came to himself he said, 'How many of my father's hired hands have bread enough and to spare, but here I am dying of hunger! I will get up and go to my father, and I will say to him, "Father, I have sinned against heaven and before you; I am no longer worthy to be called your son; treat me like one of your hired hands." So he set off and went to his father. But while he was still far off, his father saw him and was filled with compassion; he ran and put his arms around him and kissed him. Then the son said to him, 'Father, I have sinned against heaven and before you; I am no longer worthy to be called your son.' But the father said to his slaves, 'Quickly, bring out a robe—the best one—and put it on him; put a ring on his finger and sandals on his feet. And get the fatted calf and kill it, and let us eat and celebrate; for this son of mine was dead and is alive again; he was lost and is found!' And they began to celebrate. Now his elder son was in the field; and when he came and approached the house, he heard music and dancing. He called one of the slaves and asked what was going on. He replied, 'Your brother has come, and your father has killed the fatted calf, because he has got him back safe and sound.' Then he became angry and refused to go in. His father came out and began to plead with him. But he answered his father, 'Listen! For all these years I have been working like a slave for you, and I have never disobeyed your command; yet you have never given me even a young goat so that I might celebrate with my friends. But when this son of yours came back, who has devoured your property with prostitutes, you killed the fatted calf for him!' Then the father said to him, 'Son, you are always with me, and all that is mine is yours. But we had to celebrate and rejoice, because this brother of yours was dead and has come to life; he was lost and has been found.'"

- Jesus told a rather elaborate story. If you could not use a story but had to create a rational argument, how would you explain what Jesus was trying to say?

- Jesus, remind me that I am part of the eternal sacred story. And teach me how to communicate to others that their individual stories are also sacred.

The Third Week of Lent
March 19—March 25

Something to think and pray about each day this week:

Friendship Characteristics
It might help your reflection on friendship with God to think about your friendships with others. Who are your friends? What makes you say that they are your friends? You tell them things about yourself that you would not tell a stranger. You know that they will not tell others the secrets you share with them, that they will not hold against you what you tell them or hold it over your head as a threat. At the deepest level, you trust that they will remain your friends even when they know some of the less savory aspects of your past life and your character. You also trust that they will stick with you through thick and thin, through good times and tough times. And at least some of these characteristics will also be true of the relationship God wants with you. *What is the most important characteristic I look for in a friend? Can I also find this characteristic in my friendship with God?*

—William A. Barry, SJ, *Lenten Meditations*

The Presence of God
Jesus, help me to be fully alive to your Holy Presence. Enfold me in your love. Let my heart become one with yours.

Freedom
I will ask God's help,
to be free from my own preoccupations,
to be open to God in this time of prayer,
to come to know, love, and serve God more.

Consciousness
I ask how I am within myself today? Am I particularly tired, stressed, or off form? If any of these characteristics apply, can I try to let go of the concerns that disturb me?

The Word
God speaks to each of us individually. I listen attentively to hear what God is saying to me. Read the text a few times, then listen. (Please turn to the Scripture on the following pages. Inspiration points are there should you need them. When you are ready, return here to continue.)

Conversation
Sometimes I wonder what I might say if I were to meet you in person, Lord.
I think I might say, Thank you, Lord, for always being there for me.

Conclusion
Glory be to the Father, and to the Son, and to the Holy Spirit,
As it was in the beginning, is now and ever shall be,
World without end. Amen.

Sunday 19th March
Third Sunday of Lent
John 4:5–15, 19b–26, 39a, 40–42

So Jesus came to a Samaritan city called Sychar, near the plot of ground that Jacob had given to his son Joseph. Jacob's well was there, and Jesus, tired out by his journey, was sitting by the well. It was about noon. A Samaritan woman came to draw water, and Jesus said to her, "Give me a drink." (His disciples had gone to the city to buy food.) The Samaritan woman said to him, "How is it that you, a Jew, ask a drink of me, a woman of Samaria?" (Jews do not share things in common with Samaritans.) Jesus answered her, "If you knew the gift of God, and who it is that is saying to you, 'Give me a drink,' you would have asked him, and he would have given you living water." The woman said to him, "Sir, you have no bucket, and the well is deep. Where do you get that living water? Are you greater than our ancestor Jacob, who gave us the well, and with his sons and his flocks drank from it?" Jesus said to her, "Everyone who drinks of this water will be thirsty again, but those who drink of the water that I will give them will never be thirsty. The water that I will give will become in them a spring of water gushing up to eternal life." The woman said to him, "Sir, give me this water, so that I may never be thirsty or have to keep coming here to draw water." . . .

- Jesus begins with his own physical thirst and ends up talking about the woman's soul thirst. What can I learn from this conversation about sharing the good news?

- In speaking with a woman to whom he was not related, and to a Samaritan, who was considered apostate by the Jewish community, Jesus crossed two cultural boundaries. What boundaries do I face in a normal day?

Monday 20th March
Saint Joseph, Spouse of the Blessed Virgin Mary
Matthew 1:16, 18–21, 24a

Jacob [was] the father of Joseph the husband of Mary, of whom Jesus was born, who is called the Messiah. . . . Now the birth of Jesus the Messiah took place in this way. When his mother Mary had been engaged to Joseph, but before they lived together, she was found to be with child from the Holy Spirit. Her husband Joseph, being a righteous man and unwilling to expose her to public disgrace, planned to dismiss her quietly. But just when he had resolved to do this, an angel of the Lord appeared to him in a dream and said, "Joseph, son of David, do not be afraid to take Mary as your wife, for the child conceived in her is from the Holy Spirit. She will bear a son, and you are to name him Jesus, for he will save his people from their sins." . . . When Joseph awoke from sleep, he did as the angel of the Lord commanded him; he took her as his wife . . .

- A great quality of Joseph was his openness to God. Something happened in a dream that led him to trust in the call of God even in the strange circumstances of the pregnancy of his wife-to-be. Lord, help me open my thoughts, dreams, and desires to your influence.

- Saint Matthew tells the story of Jesus from Joseph's viewpoint. He is shown as an ordinary, good Jew, obedient to the Law. God intervenes and shatters his expectations. He is called to a new level of obedience. Lord, am I open to letting you break in on my life?

Tuesday 21st March
Matthew 18:21–35

Then Peter came and said to him, "Lord, if another member of the church sins against me, how often should I forgive? As many as seven times?" Jesus said to him, "Not seven times, but, I tell you, seventy-seven times. For this reason the kingdom of heaven may be compared to a king who wished to settle accounts with his slaves. When he began the reckoning, one who owed him ten thousand talents was brought to him; and, as he could not pay, his lord ordered him to be sold, together with his wife and children and all his possessions, and payment to be made. So the slave fell on his knees before him, saying, 'Have patience with me, and I will pay you everything.' And out of pity for him, the lord of that slave released him and forgave him the debt. But that same slave, as he went out, came upon one of his fellow slaves who owed him a hundred denarii; and seizing him by the throat, he said, 'Pay what you owe.' Then his fellow slave fell down and pleaded with him, 'Have patience with me, and I will pay you.' But he refused; then he went and threw him into prison until he would pay the debt. When his fellow slaves saw what had happened, they were greatly distressed, and they went and reported to their lord all that had taken place. Then his lord summoned him and said to him, 'You wicked slave! I forgave you all that debt because you pleaded with me. Should you not have had mercy on your fellow slave, as I had mercy on you?' And in anger his lord handed him over to be tortured until he would pay his entire debt. So my heavenly Father will also do to every one of you, if you do not forgive your brother or sister from your heart."

- Only those who forgive belong in God's kingdom. Lord, to forgive from the heart is a grace I must pray for. I can't do it on my own, and I know this. I can be so hard-hearted with those who offend me. Have mercy on me and change my heart!

- When God is at work, there is no purely private benefit; the effects spread widely. As I acknowledge that what is good in my life comes from God, I pray for the generosity I need to be a blessing to others.

Wednesday 22nd March
Matthew 5:17–19

Jesus said to the crowds, "Do not think that I have come to abolish the law or the prophets; I have come not to abolish but to fulfill. For truly I tell you, until heaven and earth pass away, not one letter, not one stroke of a letter, will pass from the law until all is accomplished. Therefore, whoever breaks one of the least of these commandments, and teaches others to do the same, will be called least in the kingdom of heaven; but whoever does them and teaches them will be called great in the kingdom of heaven."

- Lord, you were not turning your back on the past but deepening our sense of where we stand before God: not as scrupulous rule keepers but as loving children.

- Christians continue to reverence the Old Testament as a source of revelation—for instance, by praying the psalms. Do I appreciate how such prayer brings me into harmony with my Jewish brothers and sisters today?

Thursday 23rd March
Luke 11:14–23

Now Jesus was casting out a demon that was mute; when the demon had gone out, the one who had been mute spoke, and the crowds were amazed. But some of them said, "He casts out demons by Beelzebul, the ruler of the demons." Others, to test him, kept demanding from him a sign from heaven. But he knew what they were thinking and said to them, "Every kingdom divided against itself becomes a desert, and house falls on house. If Satan also is divided against himself, how will his kingdom stand?—for you say that I cast out the demons by Beelzebul. Now if I cast out the demons by Beelzebul, by whom do your exorcists cast them out? Therefore they will be your judges. But if it is by the finger of God that I cast out the demons, then the kingdom of God has come to you. When a strong man, fully armed, guards his castle, his property is safe. But when one stronger than he attacks him and overpowers him, he takes away his armour in which he trusted and divides his plunder. Whoever is not with me is against me, and whoever does not gather with me scatters."

- With whom do I identify in the crowd that witnesses Jesus' miracle? With those who watch in amazed belief? With those who reject him? Or with those who hedge their bets, looking for further signs? Jesus forces us off the middle ground. Today, Jesus, do I believe in your power in my life?

- Jesus' mission is to overcome evil in all its forms. I thank God for this. *Satan* means "adversary" and refers to all that stands against the goodness of God. I may live under a corrupt government, where bad legislation oppresses the innocent and unfair taxes enrich the powerful. I may be called by God to protest against wrongdoing. I can also pray!

Friday 24th March
Mark 12:28–34

One of the scribes came near and heard them disputing with one another, and seeing that Jesus answered them well, he asked him, "Which commandment is the first of all?" Jesus answered, "The first is, 'Hear, O Israel: the Lord our God, the Lord is one; you shall love the Lord your God with all your heart, and with all your soul, and with all your mind, and with all your strength.' The second is this, 'You shall love your neighbor as yourself.' There is no other commandment greater than these." Then the scribe said to him, "You are right, Teacher; you have truly said that 'he is one, and besides him there is no other'; and 'to love him with all the heart, and with all the understanding, and with all the strength,' and 'to love one's neighbor as oneself,'—this is much more important than all whole burnt offerings and sacrifices." When Jesus saw that he answered wisely, he said to him, "You are not far from the kingdom of God." After that no one dared to ask him any question.

- Are you comfortable with the designation of love as a *commandment*? That word can sound cold and legalistic, whereas the word *love* evokes warmth and freedom. Could you suggest an alternative to commandment? Or would you want to?

- Lord, with what affection and regard you answered this scribe. Unlike others, he was seeking wisdom, not an argument. He relished Jesus' answer and placed it in the context of the Scriptures. Is my search as serious as that scribe's?

Saturday 25th March
The Annunciation of the Lord
Luke 1:26–38

In the sixth month the angel Gabriel was sent by God to a town in Galilee called Nazareth, to a virgin engaged to a man whose name was Joseph, of the house of David. The virgin's name was Mary. And he came to her and said, "Greetings, favored one! The Lord is with you." But she was much perplexed by his words and pondered what sort of greeting this might be. The angel said to her, "Do not be afraid, Mary, for you have found favor with God. And now, you will conceive in your womb and bear a son, and you will name him Jesus. He will be great, and will be called the Son of the Most High, and the Lord God will give to him the throne of his ancestor David. He will reign over the house of Jacob forever, and of his kingdom there will be no end." Mary said to the angel, "How can this be, since I am a virgin?" The angel said to her, "The Holy Spirit will come upon you, and the power of the Most High will overshadow you; therefore the child to be born will be holy; he will be called Son of God. And now, your relative Elizabeth in her old age has also conceived a son; and this is the sixth month for her who was said to be barren. For nothing will be impossible with God." Then Mary said, "Here am I, the servant of the Lord; let it be with me according to your word." Then the angel departed from her.

- Mary is not flattered but perplexed, and she voices her perplexity. She hears God's messenger but wonders, *Can this be true?* She knows that she is free to say yes or no. She ponders the invitation in her heart, then gives her response. Seat of Wisdom, teach me how to use my head and heart in a crisis.

- "Let it be with me according to your word." Lord, this is not an easy prayer to make. You prayed it yourself in Gethsemane in a sweat of blood: Not my will but yours be done. Help me make it the pattern of my life.

The Fourth Week of Lent
March 26—April 1

Something to think and pray about each day this week:

Jesus' Humanity

In contemplating the Gospels during Lent, take this advice to heart: Be sure to take Jesus' humanity seriously even as you reflect on his divine attributes. God took humanity seriously enough to become one of us, and we do God a disservice if we downplay what God has done in becoming human. When we use our imagination in contemplating Jesus, we trust that God's Spirit will use it to reveal something about Jesus that is important for us so that we will love him and want to follow him. The only way we can get to know another person is through revelation; the other must reveal him- or herself to us. In contemplating the Gospels, we are asking Jesus to reveal himself to us.

—William A. Barry, SJ, *Lenten Meditations*

The Presence of God

"I stand at the door and knock," says the Lord. What a wonderful privilege that the Lord of all creation desires to come to me. I welcome his presence.

Freedom

Saint Ignatius thought that a thick and shapeless tree trunk would never believe that it could become a statue, admired as a miracle of sculpture, and would never submit itself to the chisel of the sculptor, who sees by her genius what she can make of it.
I ask for the grace to let myself be shaped by my loving Creator.

Consciousness

Knowing that God loves me unconditionally, I can afford to be honest about how I am. What are my fears and desires? What do I expect from God? What am I willing to give to God—from my emotions and talents, thoughts and energy? And how do I feel now? I share my feelings openly with the Lord.

The Word

I take my time to read the word of God, slowly, a few times, allowing myself to dwell on anything that strikes me. (Please turn to the Scripture on the following pages. Inspiration points are there should you need them. When you are ready, return here to continue.)

Conversation

Do I notice myself reacting as I pray with the word of God? Do I feel challenged, comforted, angry? Imagining Jesus sitting or standing by me, I speak out my feelings, as one trusted friend to another.

Conclusion

I thank God for these moments·we have spent together and for any insights I have been given concerning the text.

Sunday 26th March
Fourth Sunday of Lent

John 9:1, 6–9, 13–17, 34–38

As he walked along, he saw a man blind from birth. . . . When he had said this, he spat on the ground and made mud with the saliva and spread the mud on the man's eyes, saying to him, "Go, wash in the pool of Siloam" (which means Sent). Then he went and washed and came back able to see. The neighbors and those who had seen him before as a beggar began to ask, "Is this not the man who used to sit and beg?" Some were saying, "It is he." Others were saying, "No, but it is someone like him." He kept saying, "I am the man." . . . They brought to the Pharisees the man who had formerly been blind. Now it was a sabbath day when Jesus made the mud and opened his eyes. Then the Pharisees also began to ask him how he had received his sight. He said to them, "He put mud on my eyes. Then I washed, and now I see." Some of the Pharisees said, "This man is not from God, for he does not observe the sabbath." But others said, "How can a man who is a sinner perform such signs?" And they were divided. So they said again to the blind man, "What do you say about him? It was your eyes he opened." He said, "He is a prophet." . . . They answered him, "You were born entirely in sins, and are you trying to teach us?" And they drove him out. Jesus heard that they had driven him out, and when he found him, he said, "Do you believe in the Son of Man?" He answered, "And who is he, sir? Tell me, so that I may believe in him." Jesus said to him, "You have seen him, and the one speaking with you is he." He said, "Lord, I believe." And he worshipped him.

- The opening question of the disciples was, "Who is to blame?" This is a common question in the media today; perhaps it is part of my own vocabulary. Jesus reminds us that sometimes no one is to blame but that difficult situations present an opportunity for us to be drawn into God's presence.

- Lord there were times I was lost and found, was blind and then could see. Thank you. The man's blindness is cured, but the blindness of those who won't believe in Jesus remains. I think of how I grope, stumble, and am unsure of my direction unless I can rely on Jesus, the light of the world.

Monday 27th March

John 4:43–54

When the two days were over, he went from that place to Galilee (for Jesus himself had testified that a prophet has no honor in the prophet's own country). When he came to Galilee, the Galileans welcomed him, since they had seen all that he had done in Jerusalem at the festival; for they too had gone to the festival. Then he came again to Cana in Galilee where he had changed the water into wine. Now there was a royal official whose son lay ill in Capernaum. When he heard that Jesus had come from Judea to Galilee, he went and begged him to come down and heal his son, for he was at the point of death. Then Jesus said to him, "Unless you see signs and wonders you will not believe." The official said to him, "Sir, come down before my little boy dies." Jesus said to him, "Go; your son will live." The man believed the word that Jesus spoke to him and started on his way. As he was going down, his slaves met him and told him that his child was alive. So he asked them the hour when he began to recover, and they said to him, "Yesterday at one in the afternoon the fever left him." The father realized that this was the hour when Jesus had said to him, "Your son will live." So he himself believed, along with his whole household. Now this was the second sign that Jesus did after coming from Judea to Galilee.

- This prayer was made humbly and wholeheartedly, and by a Gentile. Jesus saw true faith in this man's prayer; the boy was healed through the faith of his father. May I readily bring people of all sorts of people to Jesus for healing.

- This is the first recorded healing miracle of Jesus. Do I believe in miracles? More important, do I believe that Jesus is the greatest miracle of the universe? He is all the love of God contained in a human heart and a human face (Pope Benedict XVI).

Tuesday 28th March

John 5:1–16

There was a festival of the Jews, and Jesus went up to Jerusalem. Now in Jerusalem by the Sheep Gate there is a pool, called in Hebrew Beth-zatha, which has five porticoes. In these lay many invalids—blind, lame, and paralyzed. One man was there who had been ill for thirty-eight years.

When Jesus saw him lying there and knew that he had been there a long time, he said to him, "Do you want to be made well?" The sick man answered him, "Sir, I have no one to put me into the pool when the water is stirred up; and while I am making my way, someone else steps down ahead of me." Jesus said to him, "Stand up, take your mat and walk." At once the man was made well, and he took up his mat and began to walk. Now that day was a sabbath. So the Jews said to the man who had been cured, "It is the sabbath; it is not lawful for you to carry your mat." But he answered them, "The man who made me well said to me, Take up your mat and walk." They asked him, "Who is the man who said to you, Take it up and walk?" Now the man who had been healed did not know who it was, for Jesus had disappeared in the crowd that was there. Later Jesus found him in the temple and said to him, "See, you have been made well! Do not sin any more, so that nothing worse happens to you." The man went away and told the Jews that it was Jesus who had made him well. Therefore the Jews started persecuting Jesus, because he was doing such things on the sabbath.

- The man on the mat is obviously ill, and yet Jesus asks if he wants to be made well. In truth, sometimes we prefer to remain as we are rather than change for the better. We fear what the change will bring, or we have grown comfortable with our "illness." I imagine Jesus asking me, right now, "Do you want to be made well?" What is my response?

- By healing people on the Sabbath, Jesus was breaking not the law of Moses but subsequent laws created to help people know how to fulfill the law of Moses. It can seem simpler to stick with rigid and complicated systems than to rely on our own discernment of what God asks of us. What discernment is required of me today?

Wednesday 29th March
John 5:17–30

Jesus answered them, "My Father is still working, and I also am working." For this reason the Jews were seeking all the more to kill him, because he was not only breaking the sabbath, but was also calling God his own Father, thereby making himself equal to God. Jesus said to them, "Very truly, I tell you, the Son can do nothing on his own, but only what he sees the Father doing; for whatever the Father does, the Son does likewise.

The Father loves the Son and shows him all that he himself is doing; and he will show him greater works than these, so that you will be astonished. Indeed, just as the Father raises the dead and gives them life, so also the Son gives life to whomsoever he wishes. The Father judges no one but has given all judgment to the Son, so that all may honor the Son just as they honor the Father. Anyone who does not honor the Son does not honor the Father who sent him. Very truly, I tell you, anyone who hears my word and believes him who sent me has eternal life, and does not come under judgment, but has passed from death to life. Very truly, I tell you, the hour is coming, and is now here, when the dead will hear the voice of the Son of God, and those who hear will live. For just as the Father has life in himself, so he has granted the Son also to have life in himself; and he has given him authority to execute judgment, because he is the Son of Man. Do not be astonished at this; for the hour is coming when all who are in their graves will hear his voice and will come out—those who have done good, to the resurrection of life, and those who have done evil, to the resurrection of condemnation. I can do nothing on my own. As I hear, I judge; and my judgment is just, because I seek to do not my own will but the will of him who sent me."

- Note the striking statement: "My Father is still working, and I also am working." God is present among us, but this is not a passive presence. It is an active presence through which God is involved in the drama of our lives.

- It is hard to understand the relationships between divinity and humanity, but we can enter prayer with the willingness and hope to fulfill the will of God. Our time in prayer, silent or verbal, is our wish that God's will be done and that the love of his reign be made visible on earth.

Thursday 30th March
John 5:31–47

Jesus said, "If I testify about myself, my testimony is not true. There is another who testifies on my behalf, and I know that his testimony to me is true. You sent messengers to John, and he testified to the truth. Not that I accept such human testimony, but I say these things so that you may be saved. He was a burning and shining lamp, and you were willing to rejoice for a while in his light. But I have a testimony greater than John's. . . ."

- Jesus appeals to the minds of those who seek to disregard him. He reminds them of what they have seen, of the witnesses they have heard, and of the words of the prophets. I pray that I be blessed with deeper faith as I review the evidence to which Jesus draws my attention. As I believe in Jesus who was sent by God, the word of God is alive in me.

- John the Baptist prepared the way for people to hear Jesus. He brought people near to God, and some of them recognized Jesus when he arrived. Some people we meet make it easier to recognize Jesus. It is good to have met people who are like Jesus—just as John the Baptist prepared the way of Jesus by the way he lived. Give thanks for such people in prayer!

Friday 31st March
John 7:1–2, 10, 25–30

Jesus went about in Galilee. He did not wish to go about in Judea because the Jews were looking for an opportunity to kill him. Now the Jewish festival of Booths was near. . . . But after his brothers had gone to the festival, then he also went, not publicly but as it were in secret. . . . Now some of the people of Jerusalem were saying, "Is not this the man whom they are trying to kill? And here he is, speaking openly, but they say nothing to him! Can it be that the authorities really know that this is the Messiah? Yet we know where this man is from; but when the Messiah comes, no one will know where he is from." Then Jesus cried out as he was teaching in the temple, "You know me, and you know where I am from. I have not come on my own. But the one who sent me is true, and you do not know him. I know him, because I am from him, and he sent me." Then they tried to arrest him, but no one laid hands on him, because his hour had not yet come.

- Jesus knew throughout his passion where he came from—the heart of God the Father. He knew he would return there. He always knew he was not on his own. Can we walk with him in his passion of today? Where people suffer, Jesus suffers.

- The arguments go to and fro about Jesus: Some say that they know nothing about him, others that they know everything. It seems that nowadays, too, there are experts on every side. I realize that Lent calls me, not to be convinced in my mind but to accept Jesus in my heart. Show me how to learn of you in that way, Jesus.

Saturday 1st April
John 7:40–53

When they heard Jesus' words, some in the crowd said, "This is really the prophet." Others said, "This is the Messiah." But some asked, "Surely the Messiah does not come from Galilee, does he? Has not the Scripture said that the Messiah is descended from David and comes from Bethlehem, the village where David lived?" So there was a division in the crowd because of him. Some of them wanted to arrest him, but no one laid hands on him. Then the temple police went back to the chief priests and Pharisees, who asked them, "Why did you not arrest him?" The police answered, "Never has anyone spoken like this!" Then the Pharisees replied, "Surely you have not been deceived too, have you? Has any one of the authorities or of the Pharisees believed in him? But this crowd, which does not know the law—they are accursed." Nicodemus, who had gone to Jesus before, and who was one of them, asked, "Our law does not judge people without first giving them a hearing to find out what they are doing, does it?" They replied, "Surely you are not also from Galilee, are you? Search and you will see that no prophet is to arise from Galilee." Then each of them went home.

- Prayer can allow us to be surprised by Jesus Christ—or to be questioned by him. We can end our prayer with the question, "Who is this man, and what have I learned about him today?" He gives no easy answers but walks with us while we ask the questions.

- The police were sent to Jesus to arrest him, but they came back empty-handed, exclaiming, "Never has anyone spoken like this!" Familiarity can blunt us to the revolutionary power of Christ's words. Lord, grant that I may hear and understand and be turned inside out.

The Fifth Week of Lent
April 2—April 8

Something to think and pray about each day this week:

The Eternal Broken Heart

In Jesus, God saves us by becoming so vulnerable that we are able to kill him in a vile and humiliating way. The crucifixion and resurrection of Jesus assure us that God's offer of friendship will never be withdrawn, no matter what we do. If the cross did not result in a withdrawal of the offer, then nothing we do will lead to a change of God's heart. We can, however, refuse the offer. Friendship is a mutual relationship, and a person has to accept the offer; he or she cannot be coerced or tricked into it. And any human being's final refusal of God's friendship breaks God's heart. Still, God does not turn away from such a person in anger and rage. God lives eternally with a broken heart. That's how vulnerable God wants to be.

—William A. Barry, SJ, *Lenten Meditations*

The Presence of God

To be present is to arrive as one is and open up to the other.
At this instant, as I arrive here, God is present waiting for me.
God always arrives before me, desiring to connect with me
even more than my most intimate friend.
I take a moment and greet my loving God.

Freedom

I am free. When I look at these words in writing, they seem to create in me a feeling of awe. Yes, a wonderful feeling of freedom. Thank you, God.

Consciousness

To be conscious about something is to be aware of it.
Dear Lord, help me to remember that you gave me life.
Thank you for the gift of life.
Teach me to slow down, to be still and enjoy the pleasures created for me.
To be aware of the beauty that surrounds me. The marvel of mountains, the calmness of lakes, the fragility of a flower petal. I need to remember that all these things come from you.

The Word

The word of God comes to us through the Scriptures. May the Holy Spirit enlighten my mind and heart to respond to the Gospel teachings. (Please turn to the Scripture on the following pages. Inspiration points are there should you need them. When you are ready, return here to continue.)

Conversation

I begin to talk to Jesus about the Scripture I have just read. What part of it strikes a chord in me? Perhaps the words of a friend—or some story I have heard recently—will slowly rise to the surface in my consciousness. If so, does the story throw light on what the Scripture passage may be trying to say to me?

Conclusion

Glory be to the Father, and to the Son, and to the Holy Spirit,
As it was in the beginning, is now and ever shall be,
World without end. Amen.

Sunday 2nd April
Fifth Sunday of Lent
John 11:3–7, 17, 20–27, 33b–45

So the sisters sent a message to Jesus, "Lord, he whom you love is ill." But when Jesus heard it, he said, "This illness does not lead to death; rather it is for God's glory, so that the Son of God may be glorified through it." Accordingly, though Jesus loved Martha and her sister and Lazarus, after having heard that Lazarus was ill, he stayed two days longer in the place where he was. Then after this he said to the disciples, "Let us go to Judea again." . . . When Jesus arrived, he found that Lazarus had already been in the tomb for four days. . . . When Martha heard that Jesus was coming, she went and met him, while Mary stayed at home. Martha said to Jesus, "Lord, if you had been here, my brother would not have died. But even now I know that God will give you whatever you ask of him." Jesus said to her, "Your brother will rise again." Martha said to him, "I know that he will rise again in the resurrection on the last day." Jesus said to her, "I am the resurrection and the life. Those who believe in me, even though they die, will live, and everyone who lives and believes in me will never die. Do you believe this?" She said to him, "Yes, Lord, I believe that you are the Messiah, the Son of God, the one coming into the world." . . . When Jesus saw her weeping, and the Jews who came with her also weeping, he was greatly disturbed in spirit and deeply moved. He said, "Where have you laid him?" They said to him, "Lord, come and see." Jesus began to weep. So the Jews said, "See how he loved him!" But some of them said, "Could not he who opened the eyes of the blind man have kept this man from dying?" Then Jesus, again greatly disturbed, came to the tomb. It was a cave, and a stone was lying against it. Jesus said, "Take away the stone." Martha, the sister of the dead man, said to him, "Lord, already there is a stench because he has been dead for four days." Jesus said to her, "Did I not tell you that if you believed, you would see the glory of God?" So they took away the stone. And Jesus looked upwards and said, "Father, I thank you for having heard me. I knew that you always hear me, but I have said this for the sake of the crowd standing here, so that they may believe that you sent me." When he had said this, he cried with a loud voice, "Lazarus, come out!" The dead man came out, his hands and feet bound with strips of cloth, and his face wrapped in a cloth. Jesus said to them, "Unbind him, and let him go." Many of the Jews therefore, who had come with Mary and had seen what Jesus did, believed in him.

- I hear you asking me the same question, Lord: "Do you believe that I am the resurrection and the life?" In the long run, nothing is more important than my answer to this. I cannot grasp your words in my imagination, Lord, but I believe. Help my unbelief.

- "Unbind him, and let him go." Even a man resurrected from the dead needed the help of community. Show me, Lord, how I can participate in others' unbinding and freedom.

Monday 3rd April
John 8:1–11

Early in the morning Jesus came again to the temple. All the people came to him and he sat down and began to teach them. The scribes and the Pharisees brought a woman who had been caught in adultery; and making her stand before all of them, they said to him, "Teacher, this woman was caught in the very act of committing adultery. Now in the law Moses commanded us to stone such women. Now what do you say?" They said this to test him, so that they might have some charge to bring against him. Jesus bent down and wrote with his finger on the ground. When they kept on questioning him, he straightened up and said to them, "Let anyone among you who is without sin be the first to throw a stone at her." And once again he bent down and wrote on the ground. When they heard it, they went away, one by one, beginning with the elders; and Jesus was left alone with the woman standing before him. Jesus straightened up and said to her, "Woman, where are they? Has no one condemned you?" She said, "No one, sir." And Jesus said, "Neither do I condemn you. Go your way, and from now on do not sin again."

- With whom do you most identify in this story? The adulterous woman who, though guilty, did not deserve death by stoning? (Besides, where was her partner in adultery? Was he not equally guilty?) Or do you see yourself in those who condemned her, shamed her publicly, and were willing to stone her?

- As I reflect on my life and consider my need for forgiveness, I realize that I need to draw closer to Jesus, who loves me. I hear Jesus speaking to me—not condemning me, but giving me a new mission and a new vision of myself.

Tuesday 4th April
John 8:21–30

Jesus said to them, "I am going away, and you will search for me, but you will die in your sin. Where I am going, you cannot come." Then the Jews said, "Is he going to kill himself? Is that what he means by saying, Where I am going, you cannot come?" He said to them, "You are from below, I am from above; you are of this world, I am not of this world. I told you that you would die in your sins, for you will die in your sins unless you believe that I am he." They said to him, "Who are you?" Jesus said to them, "Why do I speak to you at all? I have much to say about you and much to condemn; but the one who sent me is true, and I declare to the world what I have heard from him." They did not understand that he was speaking to them about the Father. So Jesus said, "When you have lifted up the Son of Man, then you will realize that I am he, and that I do nothing on my own, but I speak these things as the Father instructed me. And the one who sent me is with me; he has not left me alone, for I always do what is pleasing to him." As he was saying these things, many believed in him.

- The readings of these days may need to be simplified when brought to prayer. You might take a single verse, or even a single phrase. For example, "The one who sent me is with me; he has not left me alone." Or sit quietly with the overall mystery of who Jesus is.

- When I knock on God's door, Jesus opens it and invites me in to meet his Father! "I always do what is pleasing to the Father." This reveals the heart of Jesus' spirituality. I pray that it may become the truth of my life, too, because God is so good to me.

Wednesday 5th April
John 8:31–42

Then Jesus said to the Jews who had believed in him, "If you continue in my word, you are truly my disciples; and you will know the truth, and the truth will make you free." They answered him, "We are descendants of Abraham and have never been slaves to anyone. What do you mean by saying, 'You will be made free'?" Jesus answered them, "Very truly, I tell you, everyone who commits sin is a slave to sin. The slave does not have a permanent place in the household; the son has a place there forever. So if the Son makes you free, you will be free indeed. I know that you are descendants of Abraham; yet you look for an opportunity to kill me, because there is no place in you for my word. I declare what I have seen in the Father's presence; as for you, you should do what you have heard from the Father." They answered him, "Abraham is our father." Jesus said to them, "If you were Abraham's children, you would be doing what Abraham did, but now you are trying to kill me, a man who has told you the truth that I heard from God. This is not what Abraham did. You are indeed doing what your father does." They said to him, "We are not illegitimate children; we have one father, God himself." Jesus said to them, "If God were your Father, you would love me, for I came from God and now I am here. I did not come on my own, but he sent me."

- "Abiding" ("continue in") means that we draw life from the word of God. This life is Christ himself; he is the love of the Father. Being a disciple, a listener, is living and abiding in truth, knowing that the Jesus of our prayer comes from God and is with God.

- Our love indicates our spiritual pedigree. Jesus, help me follow you and thus accept truth and demonstrate it through love.

Thursday 6th April
John 8:51–59

Jesus said, "Very truly, I tell you, whoever keeps my word will never see death." The Jews said to him, "Now we know that you have a demon. Abraham died, and so did the prophets; yet you say, Whoever keeps my word will never taste death. Are you greater than our father Abraham, who died? The prophets also died. Who do you claim to be?" Jesus answered, "If I glorify myself, my glory is nothing. It is my Father who glorifies me, he of whom you say, He is our God, though you do not know him. But I know him; if I were to say that I do not know him, I would be a liar like you. But I do know him and I keep his word. Your ancestor Abraham rejoiced that he would see my day; he saw it and was glad." Then the Jews said to him, "You are not yet fifty years old, and have you seen Abraham?" Jesus said to them, "Very truly, I tell you, before

Abraham was, I am." So they picked up stones to throw at him, but Jesus hid himself and went out of the temple.

- Note yet another "I am" statement: *Before Abraham was, I am.* Jesus claims both pre-existence and oneness with God. How does such information influence the way I think about life and death and what it means to be a spiritual being?

- Jesus is saying, "If you want to see God, here I am!" What should be a wonderful moment of revelation becomes horribly negative. Execution by stoning was the punishment for asserting that one is equal to God. Lord, I find you in some safe place and try to comfort you. What more can you do to show people who you are?

Friday 7th April
John 10:31–42

The Jews took up stones again to stone him. Jesus replied, "I have shown you many good works from the Father. For which of these are you going to stone me?" The Jews answered, "It is not for a good work that we are going to stone you, but for blasphemy, because you, though only a human being, are making yourself God." Jesus answered, "Is it not written in your law, 'I said, you are gods'? If those to whom the word of God came were called 'gods'—and the Scripture cannot be annulled—can you say that the one whom the Father has sanctified and sent into the world is blaspheming because I said, 'I am God's Son'? If I am not doing the works of my Father, then do not believe me. But if I do them, even though you do not believe me, believe the works, so that you may know and understand that the Father is in me and I am in the Father." Then they tried to arrest him again, but he escaped from their hands. He went away again across the Jordan to the place where John had been baptizing earlier, and he remained there. Many came to him, and they were saying, John performed no sign, but everything that John said about this man was true. And many believed in him there.

- Jesus often impresses upon us the need to act. One can argue with words, but deeds speak for themselves. The word is planted deep in me, and I pray according to the words of the apostle James, "Let me be a doer of the word and not a forgetful hearer."

- The world watches the deeds of Christians and is often not impressed. The people in today's reading condemn Jesus because of their particular image of God. What is my image of God? Have I ever condemned someone because I nursed a warped image of God?

Saturday 8th April

John 11:45–56

Many of the Jews therefore, who had come with Mary and had seen what Jesus did, believed in him. But some of them went to the Pharisees and told them what he had done. So the chief priests and the Pharisees called a meeting of the council, and said, "What are we to do? This man is performing many signs. If we let him go on like this, everyone will believe in him, and the Romans will come and destroy both our holy place and our nation." But one of them, Caiaphas, who was high priest that year, said to them, "You know nothing at all! You do not understand that it is better for you to have one man die for the people than to have the whole nation destroyed." He did not say this on his own, but being high priest that year he prophesied that Jesus was about to die for the nation, and not for the nation only, but to gather into one the dispersed children of God. So from that day on they planned to put him to death. Jesus therefore no longer walked about openly among the Jews, but went from there to a town called Ephraim in the region near the wilderness; and he remained there with the disciples. Now the Passover of the Jews was near, and many went up from the country to Jerusalem before the Passover to purify themselves. They were looking for Jesus and were asking one another as they stood in the temple, "What do you think? Surely he will not come to the festival, will he?"

- Caiaphas is ruthless, political, and determined to buttress the status quo and the privileges of his wealthy class. He uses the argument of the powerful in every age: We must eliminate the awkward troublemaker in the name of the common good. But he says more than he knows. One man, Jesus, will die for the people—and for all of us.

- Caiaphas is afraid that the popularity of Jesus will draw down the wrath of Rome and destroy both the temple—the holy place—and the nation. In his blindness he cannot see that the Jewish people are themselves the temple. Do I appreciate that I, too, am a temple of the living God? Lord, take away my blindness so that I can see myself as you see me.

April 9—April 15

Something to think and pray about each day this week:

Facing Evil

Jesus lived a human life as God's true Son, overcoming the temptations all of us inherit by being born into this world. On Good Friday, Jesus went to his death trusting that his dear Father would bring victory out of what seemed the total defeat of his mission. In the garden on the night before his death, he seems to have faced for the last time the temptation to fear, but he was able to hand over his life in trust to his Father. He went to his death believing that his way of being Messiah was the way to bring about God's Kingdom, and he absorbed human evil without passing it on. His faith made this possible. *Jesus, help me face the evil of the world with the faith you demonstrated on Good Friday.*

—William A. Barry, SJ, Lenten Meditations

The Presence of God

Be still and know that I am God. Lord, may your Spirit guide me to seek your loving presence more and more. For it is there I find rest and refreshment from this busy world.

Freedom

By God's grace I was born to live in freedom. Free to enjoy the pleasures he created for me. Dear Lord, grant that I may live as you intended, with complete confidence in your loving care.

Consciousness

In God's loving presence I unwind the past day,
starting from now and looking back, moment by moment.
I gather in all the goodness and light, in gratitude.
I attend to the shadows and what they say to me,
seeking healing, courage, forgiveness.

The Word

The word of God comes to us through the Scriptures. May the Holy Spirit enlighten my mind and heart to respond to the Gospel teachings. (Please turn to the Scripture on the following pages. Inspiration points are there should you need them. When you are ready, return here to continue.)

Conversation

Jesus, you always welcomed little children when you walked on this earth. Teach me to have a childlike trust in you. To live in the knowledge that you will never abandon me.

Conclusion

Glory be to the Father, and to the Son, and to the Holy Spirit,
As it was in the beginning, is now and ever shall be,
World without end. Amen.

Sunday 9th April
Palm Sunday of the Passion of the Lord
Matthew 26:14—27:66

Then one of the twelve, who was called Judas Iscariot, went to the chief priests and said, "What will you give me if I betray him to you?" They paid him thirty pieces of silver. And from that moment he began to look for an opportunity to betray him. On the first day of Unleavened Bread the disciples came to Jesus, saying, "Where do you want us to make the preparations for you to eat the Passover?" He said, "Go into the city to a certain man, and say to him, 'The Teacher says, My time is near; I will keep the Passover at your house with my disciples.'" So the disciples did as Jesus had directed them, and they prepared the Passover meal. When it was evening, he took his place with the twelve; and while they were eating, he said, "Truly I tell you, one of you will betray me." And they became greatly distressed and began to say to him one after another, "Surely not I, Lord?" He answered, "The one who has dipped his hand into the bowl with me will betray me. The Son of Man goes as it is written of him, but woe to that one by whom the Son of Man is betrayed! It would have been better for that one not to have been born." Judas, who betrayed him, said, "Surely not I, Rabbi?" He replied, "You have said so.". . .

- Look at Judas and watch him—fearfully betraying Jesus. Look at Jesus as his heart goes out to the weakness of his disciples. In all sorts of weakness in our lives, the love of God is triumphant. Let him be the strength in your weakness and sinfulness.

- Is Judas motivated by anger and disappointment? Had he a different vision of the messianic kingdom than Jesus? Did he resent that Jesus saw through him when he protested at the waste of Mary's costly ointment at the feast? One thing is clear: He refused to accept Jesus as he was. Like us, he didn't see that it is we, not God, who must change.

Monday 10th April
John 12:1–11

Six days before the Passover Jesus came to Bethany, the home of Lazarus, whom he had raised from the dead. There they gave a dinner for him. Martha served, and Lazarus was one of those at the table with him. Mary took a pound of costly perfume made of pure nard, anointed Jesus' feet, and wiped them with her hair. The house was filled with the fragrance of the perfume. But Judas Iscariot, one of his disciples (the one who was about to betray him), said, "Why was this perfume not sold for three hundred denarii and the money given to the poor?" (He said this not because he cared about the poor, but because he was a thief; he kept the common purse and used to steal what was put into it.) Jesus said, "Leave her alone. She bought it so that she might keep it for the day of my burial. You always have the poor with you, but you do not always have me." When the great crowd of the Jews learned that he was there, they came not only because of Jesus but also to see Lazarus, whom he had raised from the dead. So the chief priests planned to put Lazarus to death as well, since it was on account of him that many of the Jews were deserting and were believing in Jesus.

- We join the dinner party and are struck by the surpassing generosity of Mary's gesture, and then by the bitter begrudging with which Judas interprets the gift. We might allow moments of prayer this week to reach the zones within us that need tolerance, healing, and forgiveness.

- The generosity of Mary appeared wasteful and misplaced. Mary knew that Jesus was worthy of her honor and service, even when it cost. She was not held back by the judgments of others. Jesus, may I give to you freely and not care about others' opinions and reactions.

Tuesday 11th April
John 13:21–33, 36–38

Jesus was troubled in spirit, and declared, "Very truly, I tell you, one of you will betray me." The disciples looked at one another, uncertain of whom he was speaking. One of his disciples—the one whom Jesus loved—was reclining next to him; Simon Peter therefore motioned to him to ask Jesus of whom he was speaking. So while reclining next to Jesus, he asked him, "Lord, who is it?" Jesus answered, "It is the one to whom I give this piece of bread when I have dipped it in the dish." So when he had dipped the piece of bread, he gave it to Judas son of Simon Iscariot. After he received the piece of bread, Satan entered into him. Jesus said to him, "Do quickly what you are going to do." Now no one at the table knew why he said this to him. Some thought that, because Judas had the common purse, Jesus was telling him, "Buy what we need for the festival"; or, that he should give something to the poor. So, after receiving the piece of bread, he immediately went out. And it was night. When he had gone out, Jesus said, "Now the Son of Man has been glorified, and God has been glorified in him. If God has been glorified in him, God will also glorify him in himself and will glorify him at once. . . . Simon Peter said to him, "Lord, where are you going?" Jesus answered, "Where I am going, you cannot follow me now; but you will follow afterwards." Peter said to him, "Lord, why can I not follow you now? I will lay down my life for you." Jesus answered, "Will you lay down your life for me? Very truly, I tell you, before the cock crows, you will have denied me three times."

- Imagine yourself at the table during the Last Supper. Are you picking up the tensions among the other participants? Do you notice how Jesus is troubled in spirit? Let the drama of the scene draw you into it. What are your predominant feelings? Speak freely to Jesus about the whole situation and your reactions to it.

- Two treacheries: Judas went out to grab his money, betray Jesus, and kill himself in despair. Peter denied his Lord, faced his own appalling guilt, and wept bitterly—but failure was not the end of his mission but the beginning. Success is what I do with my failures. Teach me to trust in your love, Lord, and to learn from my mistakes and treacheries.

Wednesday 12th April
Matthew 26:14–25

Then one of the twelve, who was called Judas Iscariot, went to the chief priests and said, "What will you give me if I betray him to you?" They paid him thirty pieces of silver. And from that moment he began to look for an opportunity to betray him. On the first day of Unleavened Bread the disciples came to Jesus, saying, "Where do you want us to make the preparations for you to eat the Passover?" He said, "Go into the city to a certain man, and say to him, 'The Teacher says, My time is near; I will keep the Passover at your house with my disciples.'" So the disciples did as Jesus had directed them, and they prepared the Passover meal. When it was evening, he took his place with the twelve; and while they were eating, he said, "Truly I tell you, one of you will betray me." And they became greatly distressed and began to say to him one after another, "Surely not I, Lord?" He answered, "The one who has dipped his hand into the bowl with me will betray me. The Son of Man goes as it is written of him, but woe to that one by whom the Son of Man is betrayed! It would have been better for that one not to have been born." Judas, who betrayed him, said, "Surely not I, Rabbi?" He replied, "You have said so."

- In some places this day is known as Spy Wednesday. Judas is the spy or sly, sneaky person who secretly approaches the chief priests with the intention of betraying Jesus to them. Jesus uses only words to persuade Judas not to carry out his pact with the chief priests. He takes no other measures to prevent his arrest. What is your reaction to this?

- Like us, Judas didn't see that it is we, not God, who must change. The real sin of Judas was not his betrayal but his rejection of the light. Judas refused to believe in the possibility of forgiveness. Let us not imitate him. No matter what wrong we have done, we can turn to Jesus for forgiveness and healing.

Thursday 13th April
Thursday of Holy Week (Holy Thursday)
John 13:1–15

Now before the festival of the Passover, Jesus knew that his hour had come to depart from this world and go to the Father. Having loved his own who were in the world, he loved them to the end. The devil had already put it into the heart of Judas son of Simon Iscariot to betray him. And during supper Jesus, knowing that the Father had given all things into his hands, and that he had come from God and was going to God, got up from the table, took off his outer robe, and tied a towel around himself. Then he poured water into a basin and began to wash the disciples' feet and to wipe them with the towel that was tied around him. He came to Simon Peter, who said to him, "Lord, are you going to wash my feet?" Jesus answered, "You do not know now what I am doing, but later you will understand." Peter said to him, "You will never wash my feet." Jesus answered, "Unless I wash you, you have no share with me." Simon Peter said to him, "Lord, not my feet only but also my hands and my head!" Jesus said to him, "One who has bathed does not need to wash, except for the feet, but is entirely clean. And you are clean, though not all of you." For he knew who was to betray him; for this reason he said, "Not all of you are clean." After he had washed their feet, had put on his robe, and had returned to the table, he said to them, "Do you know what I have done to you? You call me Teacher and Lord—and you are right, for that is what I am. So if I, your Lord and Teacher, have washed your feet, you also ought to wash one another's feet. For I have set you an example, that you also should do as I have done to you."

- There's much in the Gospel story or words of Jesus that we can't immediately understand. He says little about the meaning of the washing of the feet, except that it's about service, and then just that we should do it too. By doing something in the example or name of Jesus, we often find its meaning.

- I ask to learn what I need to learn from this scene. I note how I feel as I see Jesus rise from table and approach me, kneel before me, and prepare to wash my feet. Help me, Lord, graciously to allow myself to be served and to recognize you in those who care for me.

Friday 14th April
Friday of the Passion of the Lord (Good Friday)
John 18:1—19:42

. . . So the soldiers, their officer, and the Jewish police arrested Jesus and bound him. . . . Then Pilate entered the headquarters again, summoned Jesus, and asked him, "Are you the King of the Jews?" Jesus answered, "Do you ask this on your own, or did others tell you about me?" Pilate replied, "I am not a Jew, am I? Your own nation and the chief priests have handed you over to me. What have you done?" Jesus answered, "My kingdom is not from this world. If my kingdom were from this world, my followers would be fighting to keep me from being handed over to the Jews. But as it is, my kingdom is not from here." Pilate asked him, "So you are a king?" Jesus answered, "You say that I am a king. For this I was born, and for this I came into the world, to testify to the truth. Everyone who belongs to the truth listens to my voice." Pilate asked him, "What is truth?" After he had said this, he went out to the Jews again and told them, "I find no case against him." . . . Then Pilate took Jesus and had him flogged. . . . And the soldiers wove a crown of thorns and put it on his head, and they dressed him in a purple robe. . . . and carrying the cross by himself, he went out to what is called The Place of the Skull, which in Hebrew is called Golgotha. There they crucified him, and with him two others, one on either side, with Jesus between them. Pilate also had an inscription written and put on the cross. It read, "Jesus of Nazareth, the King of the Jews." . . . After this, when Jesus knew that all was now finished, he said (in order to fulfill the Scripture), "I am thirsty." A jar full of sour wine was standing there. So they put a sponge full of the wine on a branch of hyssop and held it to his mouth. When Jesus had received the wine, he said, "It is finished." Then he bowed his head and gave up his spirit. . . . They took the body of Jesus and wrapped it with the spices in linen cloths, according to the burial custom of the Jews.

- All of us will one day give up our spirit. In prayer we can offer our death to God; we can do so with Mary: "Holy Mary, mother of God, pray for us, sinners; now and at the hour of our death."

- I watch Jesus as he moves through these acts of the Passion: arrest, interrogation, trial, and crucifixion. I observe how he seems calm, and I note the impact he has on others. His sense of vocation, of following the Father's will, never wavers.

Saturday 15th April
Holy Saturday
Matthew 28:1–10

After the sabbath, as the first day of the week was dawning, Mary Magdalene and the other Mary went to see the tomb. And suddenly there was a great earthquake; for an angel of the Lord, descending from heaven, came and rolled back the stone and sat on it. His appearance was like lightning, and his clothing white as snow. For fear of him the guards shook and became like dead men. But the angel said to the women, "Do not be afraid; I know that you are looking for Jesus who was crucified. He is not here; for he has been raised, as he said. Come, see the place where he lay. Then go quickly and tell his disciples, 'He has been raised from the dead, and indeed he is going ahead of you to Galilee; there you will see him.' This is my message for you." So they left the tomb quickly with fear and great joy, and ran to tell his disciples. Suddenly Jesus met them and said, "Greetings!" And they came to him, took hold of his feet, and worshipped him. Then Jesus said to them, "Do not be afraid; go and tell my brothers to go to Galilee; there they will see me."

- The angel and Jesus say to the women, "Do not be afraid." Change, revelation, and enlightenment tempt us to be anxious because we have encountered something so beyond our understanding. Jesus, help me remember "Do not be afraid" when I sense a transformation beginning in my life.

- Another point in common between the angel and Jesus is that they instructed the women to go tell the other disciples. Our life with Jesus is personal but not private; the good news is meant to be shared. Am I willing to share this treasure in my life?

Octave of Easter
April 16—April 22

Something to think and pray about each day this week:

Easter Is a Verb

As author Alice Camille states so well, "Easter is truly a verb, a dynamic event pushing upward from the darkness into the light." Christians are Easter people. What that means to me is that we are dynamic: always growing, changing, moving, and engaging. Even those of us who cannot be "in motion" physically—because of necessary employment, family responsibilities, or health issues—can experience the interior "movements" of the soul. Every day the risen Christ invites us to move, to allow the breaking open that happens in a heart that is open to God and to all that divine love brings to us. We sense the inner movement, we listen to the voice of the Spirit, we pay attention to even fleeting emotions and responses that can be, in God's hands, tools for our ongoing creation.

—Vinita Hampton Wright, on her blog, *Days of Deepening Friendship*

The Presence of God
I pause for a moment and think of the love and the grace that God showers on me: I am created in the image and likeness of God; I am God's dwelling place.

Freedom
Lord, you created me to live in freedom. May your Holy Spirit guide me to follow you freely. Instill in my heart a desire to know and love you more each day.

Consciousness
How am I really feeling? Lighthearted? Heavyhearted? I may be very much at peace, happy to be here.
Equally, I may be frustrated, worried, or angry.
I acknowledge how I really am. It is the real me that the Lord loves.

The Word
I read the word of God slowly, a few times over, and I listen to what God is saying to me. (Please turn to the Scripture on the following pages. Inspiration points are there should you need them. When you are ready, return here to continue.)

Conversation
I know with certainty there were times when you carried me, Lord. When it was through your strength I got through the dark times in my life.

Conclusion
I thank God for these moments we have spent together and for any insights I have been given concerning the text.

Sunday 16th April
Easter Sunday of the Resurrection of the Lord
John 20:1–9

Early on the first day of the week, while it was still dark, Mary Magdalene came to the tomb and saw that the stone had been removed from the tomb. So she ran and went to Simon Peter and the other disciple, the one whom Jesus loved, and said to them, "They have taken the Lord out of the tomb, and we do not know where they have laid him." Then Peter and the other disciple set out and went toward the tomb. The two were running together, but the other disciple outran Peter and reached the tomb first. He bent down to look in and saw the linen wrappings lying there, but he did not go in. Then Simon Peter came, following him, and went into the tomb. He saw the linen wrappings lying there, and the cloth that had been on Jesus' head, not lying with the linen wrappings but rolled up in a place by itself. Then the other disciple, who reached the tomb first, also went in, and he saw and believed; for as yet they did not understand the Scripture, that he must rise from the dead.

- Neither Peter nor John come to believe in the Resurrection without enduring confusion and uncertainty. But out of the confusion comes clarity. The empty tomb can only mean that Jesus is truly alive— raised and transformed by the Father. If Jesus is truly risen, then so are we. As we were one with him in his suffering, so are we now one with him in his risen joy. Alleluia!

- Mary went to do her best, to tend to Jesus' mortal remains. She accepted the reality as she saw it but was determined to do what she could to bring dignity and honor. Help us, O God, to do what we can as we remain alert, noticing the movement of your Spirit. May we receive life as you offer it to us—even if in unexpected ways.

Monday 17th April
Matthew 28:8–15

The women left the tomb quickly with fear and great joy, and ran to tell his disciples. Suddenly Jesus met them and said, "Greetings!" And they came to him, took hold of his feet, and worshipped him. Then Jesus said to them, "Do not be afraid; go and tell my brothers to go to Galilee; there they will see me." While they were going, some of the guard went into the city and told the chief priests everything that had happened. After the priests had assembled with the elders, they devised a plan to give a large sum of money to the soldiers, telling them, "You must say, 'His disciples came by night and stole him away while we were asleep.' If this comes to the governor's ears, we will satisfy him and keep you out of trouble." So they took the money and did as they were directed. And this story is still told among the Jews to this day.

• This reading tells of the cover-up orchestrated by the chief priests and elders. Bribery buys the silence of the soldiers, and further bribery is promised to make sure that the governor does not cause trouble. We are familiar with this pattern of corruption, are we not? But Jesus is still risen! Alleluia!

• Galilee was the backwater of Israel, a rural place where the poor and deprived lived. Yet it is the place where Jesus both began and ended his ministry. It is from here that he sends his disciples forth with the message of the Resurrection. Lord, you send me to the "Galilees" of my world, where you are often disguised in the poor, the deprived, the oppressed. Let me be a witness to you, an agent of hope and encouragement to all whom I meet.

Tuesday 18th April
John 20:11–18

Mary stood weeping outside the tomb. As she wept, she bent over to look into the tomb; and she saw two angels in white, sitting where the body of Jesus had been lying, one at the head and the other at the feet. They said to her, "Woman, why are you weeping?" She said to them, "They have taken away my Lord, and I do not know where they have laid him." When she had said this, she turned around and saw Jesus standing there, but she did not know that it was Jesus. Jesus said to her, "Woman, why are you weeping? Whom are you looking for?" Supposing him to be the gardener, she said to him, "Sir, if you have carried him away, tell me where you have laid him, and I will take him away." Jesus said to her, "Mary!" She turned and said to him in Hebrew, "Rabbouni!" (which means Teacher). Jesus said to her, "Do not hold on to me, because I have not yet ascended to the Father. But go to my brothers and say to them, 'I am ascending to my Father and your Father, to my God and your God.'" Mary Magdalene went and announced to the disciples, I have seen the Lord; and she told them that he had said these things to her.

- Do we sometimes think the Lord has been taken away? Prayer and Christian life can be drab, dry, and tiresome. Institutional scandals drain our energy. Jesus' life in us is ever new. We are not to hold on to an "old" Jesus but rather to walk with him as he walks the new journey of life and prayer with us.

- What do I experience in this precious moment of encounter? Mary turned around and saw Jesus. I ask God to give me the strength I need always to be ready to turn around, to look again, that I may see and recognize Jesus' presence in my life.

Wednesday 19th April
Luke 24:13–35

Now on that same day two of them were going to a village called Emmaus, about seven miles from Jerusalem, and talking with each other about all these things that had happened. While they were talking and discussing, Jesus himself came near and went with them, but their eyes were kept from recognizing him. And he said to them, "What are you discussing with each other while you walk along?" They stood still, looking sad. Then one of them, whose name was Cleopas, answered him, "Are you the only stranger in Jerusalem who does not know the things that have taken place there in these days?" He asked them, "What things?" They replied, "The things about Jesus of Nazareth, who was a prophet mighty in deed and word before God and all the people, and how our chief priests and leaders handed him over to be condemned to death and crucified him. But we had hoped that he was the one to redeem Israel. Yes, and besides all this, it is now the third day since these things took place. Moreover, some women of our group astounded us. They were at the tomb early this morning, and when they did not find his body there, they came back and told us that they had indeed seen a vision of angels who said that he was alive. Some of those who were with us went to the tomb and found it just as the women had said; but they did not see him." Then he said to them, "Oh, how foolish you are, and how slow of heart to believe all that the prophets have declared! Was it not necessary that the Messiah should suffer these things and then enter into his glory?" Then beginning with Moses and all the prophets, he interpreted to them the things about himself in all the Scriptures. As they came near the village to which they were going, he walked ahead as if he were going on. But they urged him strongly, saying, "Stay with us, because it is almost evening and the day is now nearly over." So he went in to stay with them. When he was at the table with them, he took bread, blessed and broke it, and gave it to them. Then their eyes were opened, and they recognized him; and he vanished from their sight. They said to each other, "Were not our hearts burning within us while he was talking to us on the road, while he was opening the Scriptures to us?" That same hour they got up and returned to Jerusalem; and they found the eleven and their companions gathered together. They were saying, "The Lord has risen indeed, and he has appeared to Simon!" Then they told what had happened on the road, and how he had been made known to them in the breaking of the bread.

• Join the two disciples on their journey from Jerusalem to Emmaus. Sense their disappointment, despondency, disorientation. Listen as Jesus explains the meaning of the Scriptures to them. Be aware of their hearts burning within them. What a change of mood—from desolation to consolation! Is Jesus warming your heart? Are you seeing anything in a new light?

• Jesus, in times of disillusionment and faded dreams you stand at the door, waiting for me to invite you in. May the experience of your risen presence bring about a transformation in my daily engagement with others.

Thursday 20th April
Luke 24:35–48

Then they told what had happened on the road, and how he had been made known to them in the breaking of the bread. While they were talking about this, Jesus himself stood among them and said to them, "Peace be with you." They were startled and terrified, and thought that they were seeing a ghost. He said to them, "Why are you frightened, and why do doubts arise in your hearts? Look at my hands and my feet; see that it is I myself. Touch me and see; for a ghost does not have flesh and bones as you see that I have." And when he had said this, he showed them his hands and his feet. While in their joy they were disbelieving and still wondering, he said to them, "Have you anything here to eat?" They gave him a piece of broiled fish, and he took it and ate in their presence. Then he said to them, "These are my words that I spoke to you while I was still with you—that everything written about me in the law of Moses, the prophets, and the psalms must be fulfilled." Then he opened their minds to understand the Scriptures, and he said to them, "Thus it is written, that the Messiah is to suffer and to rise from the dead on the third day, and that repentance and forgiveness of sins is to be proclaimed in his name to all nations, beginning from Jerusalem. You are witnesses of these things."

- Lord, you wish me to leave the safety of my private upper room and meet you as you come to me daily in the streets. But first let me be with you in prayer, waiting for the power of your Holy Spirit.

- The Greeks thought that only the soul survived after death. But Luke emphasizes that the risen Jesus is the same as the man who walked our earth. His wounds are still showing. The real Jesus is indeed back with his friends and doing all he can to help them to believe. Help my belief today, Lord.

Friday 21st April

John 21:1–14

After these things Jesus showed himself again to the disciples by the Sea of Tiberias; and he showed himself in this way. Gathered there together were Simon Peter, Thomas called the Twin, Nathanael of Cana in Galilee, the sons of Zebedee, and two others of his disciples. Simon Peter said to them, "I am going fishing." They said to him, "We will go with you." They went out and got into the boat, but that night they caught nothing. Just after daybreak, Jesus stood on the beach; but the disciples did not know that it was Jesus. Jesus said to them, "Children, you have no fish, have you?" They answered him, "No." He said to them, "Cast the net to the right side of the boat, and you will find some." So they cast it, and now they were not able to haul it in because there were so many fish. That disciple whom Jesus loved said to Peter, "It is the Lord!" When Simon Peter heard that it was the Lord, he put on some clothes, for he was naked, and jumped into the lake. But the other disciples came in the boat, dragging the net full of fish, for they were not far from the land, only about a hundred yards off. When they had gone ashore, they saw a charcoal fire there, with fish on it, and bread. Jesus said to them, "Bring some of the fish that you have just caught." So Simon Peter went aboard and hauled the net ashore, full of large fish, a hundred fifty-three of them; and though there were so many, the net was not torn. Jesus said to them, "Come and have breakfast." Now none of the disciples dared to ask him, "Who are you?" because they knew it was the Lord. Jesus came and took the bread and gave it to them, and did the same with the fish. This was now the third time that Jesus appeared to the disciples after he was raised from the dead.

- Peter is not the first to recognize Jesus in this scene, but he is the first to respond. How is it that I need to be open to a voice that calls me beyond myself? I pray that I might hear good news spoken to me by those around me.

- A night of futile fishing leaves empty nets and empty hearts. Jesus takes the initiative and meets them in the early morning light. He invites them to eat: "Breakfast is ready!" There is an abundant table ready: fish, love, warmth, and great joy. Here, fractured relationships are healed.

Saturday 22nd April
Mark 16:9–15

Now after Jesus rose, early on the first day of the week, he appeared first to Mary Magdalene, from whom he had cast out seven demons. She went out and told those who had been with him, while they were mourning and weeping. But when they heard that he was alive and had been seen by her, they would not believe it. After this he appeared in another form to two of them, as they were walking into the country. And they went back and told the rest, but they did not believe them. Later he appeared to the eleven themselves as they were sitting at the table; and he upbraided them for their lack of faith and stubbornness, because they had not believed those who saw him after he had risen. And he said to them, "Go into all the world and proclaim the good news to the whole creation."

- Mark's Gospel highlights the way of discipleship, where the cross and resurrection are intertwined. Jesus takes the initiative, challenging the disciples' incredulity and obstinacy. Jesus, before I ever go searching for you, you already search for me. Help me live in the liberating truth that you are indeed risen!

- As a woman of that time, Mary Magdalene would be an unlikely witness to the Resurrection. I draw inspiration from her as a witness to life, an announcer of truth. The disciples' lack of faith disappointed Jesus, yet he sent them to proclaim the good news. Jesus knows my failures but trusts me.

The Second Week of Easter
April 23—April 29

Something to think and pray about each day this week:

Body and Soul

Jesus' Resurrection affirms the value of the human person and the world in which we live. Jesus was raised as a whole person—body and soul. Jesus did not take on human flesh and then discard it. Jesus retained his whole humanity. Along with the doctrines of the Incarnation and the Eucharist, the Resurrection assures us that God has identified with matter. God has embraced the human condition. A profound unity forever exists between God and the world, between spirit and matter. As Christians, we do not believe simply in the immortality of the soul. We believe in the immortality of the human person. Jesus' Resurrection and ours speak of continuity between this life and the next. Jesus' Resurrection also acknowledges the value of creation. Jesus is with us, death has been destroyed, and human life and activity have lasting value—these are all reasons to rejoice.

—Gerald M. Fagin, SJ, *Putting on the Heart of Christ:*
How the Spiritual Exercises Invite Us to a Virtuous Life

The Presence of God

Jesus, help me to be fully alive to your Holy Presence. Enfold me in your love. Let my heart become one with yours.

Freedom

I will ask God's help,
to be free from my own preoccupations,
to be open to God in this time of prayer,
to come to know, love, and serve God more.

Consciousness

I ask how I am within myself today? Am I particularly tired, stressed, or off form? If any of these characteristics apply, can I try to let go of the concerns that disturb me?

The Word

God speaks to each of us individually. I listen attentively to hear what God is saying to me. Read the text a few times, then listen. (Please turn to the Scripture on the following pages. Inspiration points are there should you need them. When you are ready, return here to continue.)

Conversation

Sometimes I wonder what I might say if I were to meet you in person, Lord.
I think I might say, Thank you, Lord, for always being there for me.

Conclusion

Glory be to the Father, and to the Son, and to the Holy Spirit,
As it was in the beginning, is now and ever shall be,
World without end. Amen.

Sunday 23rd April
Second Sunday of Easter
John 20:19–31

When it was evening on that day, the first day of the week, and the doors of the house where the disciples had met were locked for fear of the Jews, Jesus came and stood among them and said, "Peace be with you." After he said this, he showed them his hands and his side. Then the disciples rejoiced when they saw the Lord. Jesus said to them again, "Peace be with you. As the Father has sent me, so I send you." When he had said this, he breathed on them and said to them, "Receive the Holy Spirit. If you forgive the sins of any, they are forgiven them; if you retain the sins of any, they are retained." But Thomas (who was called the Twin), one of the twelve, was not with them when Jesus came. So the other disciples told him, "We have seen the Lord." But he said to them, "Unless I see the mark of the nails in his hands, and put my finger in the mark of the nails and my hand in his side, I will not believe." A week later his disciples were again in the house, and Thomas was with them. Although the doors were shut, Jesus came and stood among them and said, "Peace be with you." Then he said to Thomas, "Put your finger here and see my hands. Reach out your hand and put it in my side. Do not doubt but believe." Thomas answered him, "My Lord and my God!" Jesus said to him, "Have you believed because you have seen me? Blessed are those who have not seen and yet have come to believe." Now Jesus did many other signs in the presence of his disciples, which are not written in this book. But these are written so that you may come to believe that Jesus is the Messiah, the Son of God, and that through believing you may have life in his name.

- Are the doors of my heart locked? Do I not expect Jesus to show up and visit me? Am I afraid—afraid that my well-ordered ways of thinking and doing things might be turned upside down if I let Jesus in?

- Brave, honest Thomas had gone off to grieve on his own, so he missed that meeting with the Lord. I have suffered in this way when I isolated myself from the community of faith. It is when I am stunned by sorrow that I most need the company of friends and the support of faith.

Monday 24th April
John 3:1–8

Now there was a Pharisee named Nicodemus, a leader of the Jews. He came to Jesus by night and said to him, "Rabbi, we know that you are a teacher who has come from God; for no one can do these signs that you do apart from the presence of God." Jesus answered him, "Very truly, I tell you, no one can see the kingdom of God without being born from above." Nicodemus said to him, "How can anyone be born after having grown old? Can one enter a second time into the mother's womb and be born?" Jesus answered, "Very truly, I tell you, no one can enter the kingdom of God without being born of water and Spirit. What is born of the flesh is flesh, and what is born of the Spirit is spirit. Do not be astonished that I said to you, 'You must be born from above.' The wind blows where it chooses, and you hear the sound of it, but you do not know where it comes from or where it goes. So it is with everyone who is born of the Spirit."

• Nicodemus was a logical and reasonable man, prepared to consider what Jesus said. Yet his mindset hindered him: how could he accomplish a second birth? But Jesus was not suggesting that he do anything! Just as a baby is not born of its own efforts, Jesus was inviting him— and us—to relax, to realize that it is God who brings us to life.

• The Spirit of God is everywhere—let's allow ourselves to be surprised by her! She is the gift of God, and wherever we find joy, peace, compassion, justice, and anything of life, there we find her. Prayer is our opening to this Spirit at prayer time and afterwards.

Tuesday 25th April
Mark 16:15–20

Jesus said to the apostles, "Go into all the world and proclaim the good news to the whole creation. The one who believes and is baptized will be saved; but the one who does not believe will be condemned. And these signs will accompany those who believe: by using my name they will cast out demons; they will speak in new tongues; they will pick up snakes in their hands, and if they drink any deadly thing, it will not hurt them; they will lay their hands on the sick, and they will recover." So then the Lord Jesus, after he had spoken to them, was taken up into heaven and sat down at the right hand of God. And they went out and proclaimed the good news everywhere, while the Lord worked with them and confirmed the message by the signs that accompanied it.

- Resurrection has happened. The Crucified One now walks the earth in the person of his disciples. Lord, send me out each day, to witness to you by my actions. I am to minister to you in the sick, the poor, the hungry, the displaced, and the imprisoned of our world.

- Do I ever refer the good news to myself? The good news about me is that I am massively loved and cared for by God. Creation is at my service. Jesus has died for me. I am promised eternal life. God is with me always, so I need not be afraid. Good news indeed!

Wednesday 26th April
John 3:16–21

Jesus said, "For God so loved the world that he gave his only Son, so that everyone who believes in him may not perish but may have eternal life. Indeed, God did not send the Son into the world to condemn the world, but in order that the world might be saved through him. Those who believe in him are not condemned; but those who do not believe are condemned already, because they have not believed in the name of the only Son of God. And this is the judgment, that the light has come into the world, and people loved darkness rather than light because their deeds were evil. For all who do evil hate the light and do not come to the light, so that their deeds may not be exposed. But those who do what is true come to the light, so that it may be clearly seen that their deeds have been done in God."

- God wants to save the world from all that is evil, bad, sinful. He wants to save us from the worst side of ourselves. He does this by love and compassion, not by correction or rebuke.

- To live the message of John's Gospel requires that one move from the shadows of darkness into the light. Jesus, you are the face of God revealed, a light shining out in our darkened world. I move between the shadow lands of darkness and light. With each daily encounter, may the relationship between us deepen. Let me see as you see, love as you love, and, by my actions, radiate your light to the world.

Thursday 27th April
John 3:31–36

The one who comes from above is above all; the one who is of the earth belongs to the earth and speaks about earthly things. The one who comes from heaven is above all. He testifies to what he has seen and heard, yet no one accepts his testimony. Whoever has accepted his testimony has certified this, that God is true. He whom God has sent speaks the words of God, for he gives the Spirit without measure. The Father loves the Son and has placed all things in his hands. Whoever believes in the Son has eternal life; whoever disobeys the Son will not see life, but must endure God's wrath.

- Giving and receiving—the deepest relationship of love—shines out in this text. The reciprocal love of Father and Son, a love without limits, is poured out on us through the Holy Spirit. May I give to others what I am constantly receiving.

- Lord, you alone can satisfy the longing of my heart and its many contradictions. In this year of faith, confirm my personal faith and commitment to you. May the example of my life invite others to believe in you.

Friday 28th April
John 6:1–15

After this Jesus went to the other side of the Sea of Galilee, also called the Sea of Tiberias. A large crowd kept following him, because they saw the signs that he was doing for the sick. Jesus went up the mountain and sat down there with his disciples. Now the Passover, the festival of the Jews, was near. When he looked up and saw a large crowd coming towards him, Jesus said to Philip, "Where are we to buy bread for these people to eat?" He said this to test him, for he himself knew what he was going to do. Philip answered him, "Six months' wages would not buy enough bread for each of them to get a little." One of his disciples, Andrew, Simon Peter's brother, said to him, "There is a boy here who has five barley loaves and two fish. But what are they among so many people?" Jesus said, "Make the people sit down." Now there was a great deal of grass in the place; so they sat down, about five thousand in all. Then Jesus took the loaves, and when he had given thanks, he distributed them to those who were seated; so also the fish, as much as they wanted. When they were satisfied, he told his disciples, "Gather up the fragments left over, so that nothing may be lost." So they gathered them up, and from the fragments of the five barley loaves, left by those who had eaten, they filled twelve baskets. When the people saw the sign that he had done, they began to say, "This is indeed the prophet who is to come into the world." When Jesus realized that they were about to come and take him by force to make him king, he withdrew again to the mountain by himself.

- In my imagination, I enter this amazing scene. I share Philip's puzzlement; I watch the little boy as he gives up the lunch his mother made for him. I gaze at Jesus as he prays, then as he breaks the bread and the fish. It takes so long to feed everyone, but he is smiling as he works. He fills my empty and grubby hands, too, and I look into his eyes and thank him.

- Where do I place myself in this scene? In the crowd? With Philip and Andrew? With the boy who risks letting his lunch go? Do I offer what little I have? Do I hold out empty hands for bread and fish? Do I help tidy up? Do I catch on to what has happened? Do I go with Jesus as he escapes to the mountain?

Saturday 29th April
John 6:16–21

When evening came, his disciples went down to the sea, got into a boat, and started across the sea to Capernaum. It was now dark, and Jesus had not yet come to them. The sea became rough because a strong wind was blowing. When they had rowed about three or four miles, they saw Jesus walking on the sea and coming near the boat, and they were terrified. But he said to them, "It is I; do not be afraid." Then they wanted to take him into the boat, and immediately the boat reached the land toward which they were going.

- The Sea of Galilee knows sudden changes—from calm surfaces to treacherous waves. Jesus uses this event to challenge the terrified disciples to trust him more. His presence and words turn the tide once again for them. Lord, my life is sometimes plunged into despair by dark events in our church and in our world. Then my faith is tested and I sense your absence. Grant me the grace to hang on in faith.

- Jesus has gone up a mountain to pray while the disciples row across the lake. He does not forget them but from his high ground keeps an eye on their plight. All the time they are struggling with the waves, Jesus has his eyes on them. Lord, I am written in your heart. Even when I forget you in my struggle to survive, you do not forget me.

The Third Week of Easter
April 30—May 6

Something to think and pray about each day this week:

Living Lightly

Your life is an overflowing closet. You know it is. There are sweatshirts folded up in a corner of your mind where your children's birthdays should be stored. That worry about the rust on the car is taking up the space that you had reserved for a slow cup of tea in the morning. I know how you feel. And guess what? There's a way to get stuff back where it belongs: let go of some of it. Living lightly is not just about the stuff we accumulate, and it's not just for people in the second half of life. It's about an attitude of living with fewer burdens and encumbrances, whether you're twenty-one or sixty-five. When done with honest self-awareness, the journey toward living more lightly has moved me to realize that I am blessed by less. Less stuff and worries have opened space to live with more contentment and meaning. Living lightly reminds me that my existence is more than accumulating possessions and status. Ultimately, I am on a spiritual pilgrimage. As I continue to strip away the unnecessary stuff in my closets and mind, I've been able to see more clearly how much is enough and how much is more than enough. It's a delicate dance to balance my own genuine needs with those of others. The spiritual paradox is that the less tightly I cling to my stuff, my way, and my concerns, the happier and more blessed I feel. Once I have enough, less is more.

—Susan V. Vogt, *Blessed by Less*

The Presence of God

"I stand at the door and knock," says the Lord. What a wonderful privilege that the Lord of all creation desires to come to me. I welcome his presence.

Freedom

Saint Ignatius thought that a thick and shapeless tree trunk would never believe that it could become a statue, admired as a miracle of sculpture, and would never submit itself to the chisel of the sculptor, who sees by her genius what she can make of it.
I ask for the grace to let myself be shaped by my loving Creator.

Consciousness

Knowing that God loves me unconditionally, I can afford to be honest about how I am. What are my fears and desires? What do I expect from God? What am I willing to give to God—from my emotions and talents, thoughts and energy? And how do I feel now? I share my feelings openly with the Lord.

The Word

I take my time to read the word of God, slowly, a few times, allowing myself to dwell on anything that strikes me. (Please turn to the Scripture on the following pages. Inspiration points are there should you need them. When you are ready, return here to continue.)

Conversation

Do I notice myself reacting as I pray with the word of God? Do I feel challenged, comforted, angry? Imagining Jesus sitting or standing by me, I speak out my feelings, as one trusted friend to another.

Conclusion

I thank God for these moments we have spent together and for any insights I have been given concerning the text.

Sunday 30th April
Third Sunday of Easter
Luke 24:13–35

Now on that same day two of them were going to a village called Emmaus, about seven miles from Jerusalem, and talking with each other about all these things that had happened. While they were talking and discussing, Jesus himself came near and went with them, but their eyes were kept from recognizing him. And he said to them, "What are you discussing with each other while you walk along?" They stood still, looking sad. Then one of them, whose name was Cleopas, answered him, "Are you the only stranger in Jerusalem who does not know the things that have taken place there in these days?" He asked them, "What things?" They replied, "The things about Jesus of Nazareth, who was a prophet mighty in deed and word before God and all the people, and how our chief priests and leaders handed him over to be condemned to death and crucified him. But we had hoped that he was the one to redeem Israel. Yes, and besides all this, it is now the third day since these things took place. Moreover, some women of our group astounded us. They were at the tomb early this morning, and when they did not find his body there, they came back and told us that they had indeed seen a vision of angels who said that he was alive. Some of those who were with us went to the tomb and found it just as the women had said; but they did not see him." Then he said to them, "Oh, how foolish you are, and how slow of heart to believe all that the prophets have declared! Was it not necessary that the Messiah should suffer these things and then enter into his glory?" Then beginning with Moses and all the prophets, he interpreted to them the things about himself in all the Scriptures. As they came near the village to which they were going, he walked ahead as if he were going on. But they urged him strongly, saying, "Stay with us, because it is almost evening and the day is now nearly over." So he went in to stay with them. When he was at the table with them, he took bread, blessed and broke it, and gave it to them. Then their eyes were opened, and they recognized him; and he vanished from their sight. They said to each other, "Were not our hearts burning within us while he was talking to us on the road, while he was opening the Scriptures to us?" That same hour they got up and returned to Jerusalem; and they found the eleven and their companions gathered together. They were saying, "The Lord has risen indeed, and he has appeared to Simon!" Then they told what had happened on the road, and how he had been made known to them in the breaking of the bread.

• The trudging disciples had turned their back on Jerusalem and were picking over the story as they knew it. So it was that Jesus found them, coming near and walking with them. I let him fall in step with me now. Jesus, find me where I am.

• Draw near, Jesus, and walk with me. Help me recognize how my story comes to life as I listen to yours. Let me hear your good news so that my heart warms.

Monday 1st May
John 6:22–29

The next day the crowd that had stayed on the other side of the lake saw that there had been only one boat there. They also saw that Jesus had not got into the boat with his disciples, but that his disciples had gone away alone. Then some boats from Tiberias came near the place where they had eaten the bread after the Lord had given thanks. So when the crowd saw that neither Jesus nor his disciples were there, they themselves got into the boats and went to Capernaum looking for Jesus. When they found him on the other side of the lake, they said to him, "Rabbi, when did you come here?" Jesus answered them, "Very truly, I tell you, you are looking for me, not because you saw signs, but because you ate your fill of the loaves. Do not work for the food that perishes, but for the food that endures for eternal life, which the Son of Man will give you. For it is on him that God the Father has set his seal." Then they said to him, "What must we do to perform the works of God?" Jesus answered them, "This is the work of God, that you believe in him whom he has sent."

• The crowds search energetically for Jesus. They borrow some boats and row across the lake in search of him. At last they find him and are happy. Jesus, inflame my heart with a strong desire to keep in touch with you. In searching for you, I find happiness.

• The crowd is hungry again and pursues Jesus. They believe he will meet their needs. He tries to deepen their fragile faith in himself. Food for the body is necessary, but the food of eternal life meets a deeper need. Lord,

I can be like the crowd, seeking only to satisfy my immediate hungers. Forgive the times when I have used you to serve my interests.

Tuesday 2nd May
John 6:30–35

The crowd said to Jesus, "What sign are you going to give us then, so that we may see it and believe you? What work are you performing? Our ancestors ate the manna in the wilderness; as it is written, He gave them bread from heaven to eat." Then Jesus said to them, "Very truly, I tell you, it was not Moses who gave you the bread from heaven, but it is my Father who gives you the true bread from heaven. For the bread of God is that which comes down from heaven and gives life to the world." They said to him, "Sir, give us this bread always." Jesus said to them, "I am the bread of life. Whoever comes to me will never be hungry, and whoever believes in me will never be thirsty."

- Help us, Lord, when we are limited by our past. When we know how we have been blessed, help us to stay before you in trust, aware of how little we deserve but ready to receive your grace in new ways.

- Lord, I am still trying to satisfy some need of mine, working for food that cannot last. It is in prayer that I begin to sense a deeper satisfaction and to know that in this bond with you there is something sacred and the chance to live at a deeper level than I have ever done.

Wednesday 3rd May
John 14:6–14

Jesus said to Thomas, "I am the way, and the truth, and the life. No one comes to the Father except through me. If you know me, you will know my Father also. From now on you do know him and have seen him." Philip said to him, "Lord, show us the Father, and we will be satisfied." Jesus said to him, "Have I been with you all this time, Philip, and you still do not know me? Whoever has seen me has seen the Father. How can you say, Show us the Father? Do you not believe that I am in the Father and the Father is in me? The words that I say to you I do not speak on my own; but the Father who dwells in me does his works. Believe me that I am in the Father and the Father is in me; but if you do not, then believe me because of the works themselves. Very truly, I tell you, the one who believes in me will also do the works that I do and, in fact, will do greater works than these, because I am going to the Father. I will do whatever you ask in my name, so that the Father may be glorified in the Son. If in my name you ask me for anything, I will do it."

- We may be tempted, like Thomas, to want specific information about the spiritual life. Yet Jesus makes it clear that we "learn" through our relationship with him. May I lay aside my need for a rational system and allow this relationship to lead and form me.

- Jesus said that a person struggling with faith could look at the simple evidence: the works he did. What evidence of his power and care is here with me now?

Thursday 4th May
John 6:44–51

Jesus said, "No one can come to me unless drawn by the Father who sent me; and I will raise that person up on the last day. It is written in the prophets, 'And they shall all be taught by God.' Everyone who has heard and learned from the Father comes to me. Not that anyone has seen the Father except the one who is from God; he has seen the Father. Very truly, I tell you, whoever believes has eternal life. I am the bread of life. Your ancestors ate the manna in the wilderness, and they died. This is the bread that comes down from heaven, so that one may eat of it and not die. I am the living bread that came down from heaven. Whoever eats of this bread will live forever; and the bread that I will give for the life of the world is my flesh."

- All our practices of prayer—our liturgies, disciplines, and habits—are like school buses: they bring us to where a special kind of learning happens. We need to be present, ready, eager to go to receive truth. Jesus tells us that God wants to be the teacher of each person, and desires to speak heart to heart.

- When you feel drawn to something good, it is God who is drawing you. The drawing may be felt as a tug on the heart or as a good idea. Perhaps it is a kind word that gives courage. God draws me to what is true, to what is life-giving, to what is loving. I am being drawn all the time, and so is everyone else.

Friday 5th May
John 6:52–59

The Jews then disputed among themselves, saying, "How can this man give us his flesh to eat?" So Jesus said to them, "Very truly, I tell you, unless you eat the flesh of the Son of Man and drink his blood, you have no life in you. Those who eat my flesh and drink my blood have eternal life, and I will raise them up on the last day; for my flesh is true food and my blood is true drink. Those who eat my flesh and drink my blood abide in me, and I in them. Just as the living Father sent me, and I live because of the Father, so whoever eats me will live because of me. This is the bread that came down from heaven, not like that which your ancestors ate, and they died. But the one who eats this bread will live forever." He said these things while he was teaching in the synagogue at Capernaum.

- The people who heard Jesus disputed among themselves, setting the human pattern that has endured to this day. My prayer time is not to consider the words of Jesus with my mind but to receive them in my heart. They come from the heart of Jesus and, carrying his life and his love, are addressed to mine.

- The listeners were disputing about "this man." Jesus, I don't understand you either; you are so mysterious! Give me a stronger faith in you so that I may believe what I cannot understand.

Saturday 6th May
John 6:60–69

When many of his disciples heard it, they said, "This teaching is difficult; who can accept it?" But Jesus, being aware that his disciples were complaining about it, said to them, "Does this offend you? Then what if you were to see the Son of Man ascending to where he was before? It is the spirit that gives life; the flesh is useless. The words that I have spoken to you are spirit and life. But among you there are some who do not believe." For Jesus knew from the first who were the ones that did not believe, and who was the one that would betray him. And he said, "For this reason I have told you that no one can come to me unless it is granted by the Father." Because of this many of his disciples turned back and no longer went about with him. So Jesus asked the twelve, "Do you also wish to go away?" Simon Peter answered him, "Lord, to whom can we go? You have the words of eternal life. We have come to believe and know that you are the Holy One of God."

- The message of Jesus was revolutionary and challenged those who heard it. Many, including some of his disciples, chose to walk away. Peter's answer is full of trust. He abandons himself to Christ. In my own life now, how do I respond to Christ's question?

- Lord, to whom can we go? In my fainthearted moments I hear both Jesus' gentle voice, giving me the freedom to choose, and the strength of Peter's reply: You have the words of eternal life. Maybe Peter repeated these words often to himself. It can be a mantra of prayer for us, as can other favorite lines from the Gospels.

The Fourth Week of Easter
May 7—May 13

Something to think and pray about each day this week:

God at Work?

How are we to interpret the alternately serendipitous and disappointing, unexpected and unpredictable, courses of our lives? What is happening when death or financial disaster force us to reconsider what we want from life, when teachers or mentors find and nurture talent we didn't know we had, when we succeed beyond our wildest imaginings, when managers steer our careers in fortuitous directions, when we aren't offered the job we wanted so badly, when friends point out opportunities that we didn't know existed, or when we persist in pursuing a personal passion against all odds of success, only to find that success and fulfillment eventually come? Do such cases merely vindicate human ingenuity, resilience, fortitude, and imagination? Or is God, too, at work in some ineffable way, as Hopkins says, "play[ing] in ten thousand places / Lovely in limbs, and lovely in eyes"?

—Chris Lowney, *Heroic Living*

The Presence of God

To be present is to arrive as one is and open up to the other.
At this instant, as I arrive here, God is present waiting for me.
God always arrives before me, desiring to connect with me
even more than my most intimate friend.
I take a moment and greet my loving God.

Freedom

I am free. When I look at these words in writing, they seem to create in
me a feeling of awe. Yes, a wonderful feeling of freedom. Thank you,
God.

Consciousness

To be conscious about something is to be aware of it.
Dear Lord, help me to remember that you gave me life.
Thank you for the gift of life.
Teach me to slow down, to be still and enjoy the pleasures created for me.
To be aware of the beauty that surrounds me. The marvel of mountains,
the calmness of lakes, the fragility of a flower petal. I need to remember
that all these things come from you.

The Word

The word of God comes to us through the Scriptures. May the Holy Spirit
enlighten my mind and heart to respond to the Gospel teachings. (Please
turn to the Scripture on the following pages. Inspiration points are there
should you need them. When you are ready, return here to continue.)

Conversation

I begin to talk to Jesus about the Scripture I have just read. What part of
it strikes a chord in me? Perhaps the words of a friend—or some story I
have heard recently—will slowly rise to the surface in my consciousness.
If so, does the story throw light on what the Scripture passage may be
trying to say to me?

Conclusion

Glory be to the Father, and to the Son, and to the Holy Spirit,
As it was in the beginning, is now and ever shall be,
World without end. Amen.

Sunday 7th May
Fourth Sunday of Easter
John 10:1–10

Jesus said, "Very truly, I tell you, anyone who does not enter the sheepfold by the gate but climbs in by another way is a thief and a bandit. The one who enters by the gate is the shepherd of the sheep. The gatekeeper opens the gate for him, and the sheep hear his voice. He calls his own sheep by name and leads them out. When he has brought out all his own, he goes ahead of them, and the sheep follow him because they know his voice. They will not follow a stranger, but they will run from him because they do not know the voice of strangers." Jesus used this figure of speech with them, but they did not understand what he was saying to them. So again Jesus said to them, 'Very truly, I tell you, I am the gate for the sheep. All who came before me are thieves and bandits; but the sheep did not listen to them. I am the gate. Whoever enters by me will be saved, and will come in and go out and find pasture. The thief comes only to steal and kill and destroy. I came that they may have life, and have it abundantly."

- Jesus used rich images from daily life to illustrate the depth of his desired relationship with us. He spoke of shepherd and sheep, gatekeeper and gate, pasture and life, recognition and salvation. How do these words relate to my life in this place and time?

- Jesus refers to strangers, thieves and bandits, killing and stealing, running away in fear instead of following, climbing in rather than walking through the open gate. Can I identify the thieves, those intent on destroying me rather than caring for me?

Monday 8th May
John 10:11–18

Jesus said, "I am the good shepherd. The good shepherd lays down his life for the sheep. The hired hand, who is not the shepherd and does not own the sheep, sees the wolf coming and leaves the sheep and runs away—and the wolf snatches them and scatters them. The hired hand runs away because a hired hand does not care for the sheep. I am the good shepherd. I know my own and my own know me, just as the Father knows me and I know the Father. And I lay down my life for the sheep. I have other sheep that do not belong to this fold. I must bring them also, and they will listen to my voice. So there will be one flock, one shepherd. For this reason the Father loves me, because I lay down my life in order to take it up again. No one takes it from me, but I lay it down of my own accord. I have power to lay it down, and I have power to take it up again. I have received this command from my Father."

• Jesus calls us to humility and trust, cautioning us against those who work only for what they can get and warning against whatever might snatch or scatter us. The shepherd keeps the sheep in view, regarding them and seeing beyond them. I ask God for the humility I need, that I might listen for the voice of the Good Shepherd, allowing him to lead me and trusting that he is leading others, too—even if in ways I don't understand.

• We know leaders who want influence or money, who value their own reputation and life above that of their followers, and who can be bought. Such leaders are a sad mistake, and we live to regret giving them power. Lord, help us, your followers, discern well and know when we are being led astray by faulty leaders.

Tuesday 9th May
John 10:22–30

It was the feast of the Dedication at Jerusalem; it was winter, and Jesus was walking in the temple, in the portico of Solomon. So the Jews gathered around him and said to him, "How long will you keep us in suspense? If you are the Christ, tell us plainly." Jesus answered them, "I told you, and you do not believe. The works that I do in my Father's name, they bear witness to me; but you do not believe, because you do not belong to my sheep. My sheep hear my voice, and I know them, and they follow me; and I give them eternal life, and they shall never perish, and no one shall snatch them out of my hand. My Father, who has given them to me, is greater than all, and no one is able to snatch them out of the Father's hand. I and the Father are one."

• Perhaps I have sometimes felt like these people, wishing for a plain sign from God. Yet Jesus chooses to speak in parables instead of forcing assent through logic or argument. Do I offer to others, even those who differ from me, the freedom that Jesus offers us all?

- The festival of Dedication was a celebration of light. But the people in this scene remain in the dark, blind to the mystery of Jesus. I, too, have my blind spots; the truth may be confronting me on some issue, but I close my eyes to it. Jesus, if I am to be your true disciple, I need to listen to your words.

Wednesday 10th May
John 12:44–50

Jesus cried aloud, "Whoever believes in me believes not in me but in him who sent me. And whoever sees me sees him who sent me. I have come as light into the world, so that everyone who believes in me should not remain in the darkness. I do not judge anyone who hears my words and does not keep them, for I came not to judge the world, but to save the world. The one who rejects me and does not receive my word has a judge; on the last day the word that I have spoken will serve as judge, for I have not spoken on my own, but the Father who sent me has himself given me a commandment about what to say and what to speak. And I know that his commandment is eternal life. What I speak, therefore, I speak just as the Father has told me."

- Jesus says clearly that he has not come to judge us but to save us. It is for us to hear and respond. Don't let me complicate things, Lord, by overthinking and endless debating. Help me listen with my whole self—mind and heart.

- What light shines on my life because of Jesus? What would be different if I had not witnessed this light?

Thursday 11th May
John 13:16–20

Jesus said to his disciples, "Very truly, I tell you, servants are not greater than their master, nor are messengers greater than the one who sent them. If you know these things, you are blessed if you do them. I am not speaking of all of you; I know whom I have chosen. But it is to fulfill the Scripture, 'The one who ate my bread has lifted his heel against me.' I tell you this now, before it occurs, so that when it does occur, you may believe that I am he. Very truly, I tell you, whoever receives one whom I send receives me; and whoever receives me receives him who sent me."

- Saint Ignatius reminds us that love is shown more in deeds than in words. I ask God for the help I need to allow the words in my mind and heart become evident in my feet and hands, that I might recognize where God wants me to be and do what God wants me to do.

- I consider what it means to be servant or messenger. I am known, chosen, trusted, and sent. Jesus allows that there is a difference between knowing and doing. I take this time to let my knowing deepen, to become part of me.

Friday 12th May
John 14:1–6

Jesus said to the disciples, "Do not let your hearts be troubled. Believe in God, believe also in me. In my Father's house there are many dwelling places. If it were not so, would I have told you that I go to prepare a place for you? And if I go and prepare a place for you, I will come again and will take you to myself, so that where I am, there you may be also. And you know the way to the place where I am going." Thomas said to him, "Lord, we do not know where you are going. How can we know the way?" Jesus said to him, "I am the way, and the truth, and the life. No one comes to the Father except through me."

- In his farewell message, Jesus speaks to the disciples encouragement, kindness, and promise. There are no maps, no compasses—only Jesus. He promises to be the true guide, the gateway into loving communion with the Father. Jesus, inclusion is the nature of God. No one is blocked entry to your dwelling place. Inspired by you, may I be more open, more tolerant, more appreciative of difference. Let me trust that, in the end, all the rooms of God's house will be full.

- Though all sorts of things go wrong for us, we are not abandoned. We are destined for a blessed future, because he will come again and take us to himself. Lord, I often wonder what way to go in life. May I always turn to you for guidance, and whatever way I choose, may I try to live out of your commandment to love.

Saturday 13th May

John 14:7–14

Jesus said to Thomas, "If you know me, you will know my Father also. From now on you do know him and have seen him." Philip said to him, "Lord, show us the Father, and we will be satisfied." Jesus said to him, "Have I been with you all this time, Philip, and you still do not know me? Whoever has seen me has seen the Father. How can you say, Show us the Father? Do you not believe that I am in the Father and the Father is in me? The words that I say to you I do not speak on my own; but the Father who dwells in me does his works. Believe me that I am in the Father and the Father is in me; but if you do not, then believe me because of the works themselves. Very truly, I tell you, the one who believes in me will also do the works that I do and, in fact, will do greater works than these, because I am going to the Father. I will do whatever you ask in my name, so that the Father may be glorified in the Son. If in my name you ask me for anything, I will do it."

- Jesus reveals the depth of relationship between Father and Son. To know the Son is to know the Father. For John, "knowing" is an affair of the heart, a felt knowledge born of mutual love. It is not simply head knowledge. I ask to know God more deeply.

- Jesus, you call me to be audacious—I am to do even greater works than you do. But your central work is the giving of your life. Prepare me to give of my very self.

The Fifth Week of Easter
May 14—May 20

Something to think and pray about each day this week:

In the Ordinary

I'll admit that I tend to be a bit cavalier about things like very old ages, 50th wedding anniversaries, or new babies. It's not that I don't care, but I just don't get caught up in the ooh-ing and ahh-ing. These events are just part of life, right? Babies are born every day. People live long enough to celebrate 50th anniversaries and 90-something birthdays. What I've come to realize is that those moments I've so easily dismissed are the miracles of everyday life!

Yes, birth and aging are as ordinary as can be, but God shows up in the ordinary. We ought to celebrate the awesome ability for a human being to have lived and experienced a century! We ought to praise God for the miracle of forming an amazingly and extremely complex conscious organism in just nine months' time! Despite the fact that these things happen all the time they still carry a miraculous character that captivates us—or should.

—Andy Otto on *dotMagis*, the blog of IgnatianSpirituality.com

The Presence of God

Be still and know that I am God. Lord, may your Spirit guide me to seek your loving presence more and more. For it is there I find rest and refreshment from this busy world.

Freedom

By God's grace I was born to live in freedom. Free to enjoy the pleasures he created for me. Dear Lord, grant that I may live as you intended, with complete confidence in your loving care.

Consciousness

In God's loving presence I unwind the past day,
starting from now and looking back, moment by moment.
I gather in all the goodness and light, in gratitude.
I attend to the shadows and what they say to me,
seeking healing, courage, forgiveness.

The Word

The word of God comes to us through the Scriptures. May the Holy Spirit enlighten my mind and heart to respond to the Gospel teachings. (Please turn to the Scripture on the following pages. Inspiration points are there should you need them. When you are ready, return here to continue.)

Conversation

Jesus, you always welcomed little children when you walked on this earth. Teach me to have a childlike trust in you. To live in the knowledge that you will never abandon me.

Conclusion

Glory be to the Father, and to the Son, and to the Holy Spirit,
As it was in the beginning, is now and ever shall be,
World without end. Amen.

Sunday 14th May
Fifth Sunday of Easter
John 14:1–12

Jesus said to his disciples, "Do not let your hearts be troubled. Believe in God, believe also in me. In my Father's house there are many dwelling places. If it were not so, would I have told you that I go to prepare a place for you? And if I go and prepare a place for you, I will come again and will take you to myself, so that where I am, there you may be also. And you know the way to the place where I am going." Thomas said to him, "Lord, we do not know where you are going. How can we know the way?" Jesus said to him, "I am the way, and the truth, and the life. No one comes to the Father except through me. If you know me, you will know my Father also. From now on you do know him and have seen him." Philip said to him, "Lord, show us the Father, and we will be satisfied." Jesus said to him, "Have I been with you all this time, Philip, and you still do not know me? Whoever has seen me has seen the Father. How can you say, Show us the Father? Do you not believe that I am in the Father and the Father is in me? The words that I say to you I do not speak on my own; but the Father who dwells in me does his works. Believe me that I am in the Father and the Father is in me; but if you do not, then believe me because of the works themselves. Very truly I tell you, the one who believes in me will also do the works that I do and, in fact, will do greater works than these, because I am going to the Father."

- Jesus sees how the disciples do not understand him and asks for their trust, inviting them not to let their hearts be troubled. Jesus looks on me with the same compassion, recognizing my hesitation, my doubts, my questions. He says to me, "Peace!" reminding me that I have a place in his heart now, a place there forever.

- Philip says, "We will be satisfied"; it sounds like a prayer that begins, "All I want is. . . ." Help me, Lord, to seek your will and not my own.

Monday 15th May
John 14:21–26

Jesus said, "They who have my commandments and keep them are those who love me; and those who love me will be loved by my Father, and I will love them and reveal myself to them." Judas (not Iscariot) said to him, "Lord, how is it that you will reveal yourself to us, and not to the world?" Jesus answered him, "Those who love me will keep my word, and my Father will love them, and we will come to them and make our home with them. Whoever does not love me does not keep my words; and the word that you hear is not mine, but is from the Father who sent me. I have said these things to you while I am still with you. But the Advocate, the Holy Spirit, whom the Father will send in my name, will teach you everything, and remind you of all that I have said to you."

- Lord, I often feel my life is shapeless and going nowhere. Thank you for the gift of the great Spirit of God, who is by my side, defending me, consoling me and teaching me the ways of love. "Come, Holy Spirit, enkindle in me the fire of your love."

- I imagine the Father and the Son deciding to come to me. Why do they do this? What do they think and say about me as they travel? What gifts do they choose for me? What do they find when they arrive? I am the focus of a great love.

Tuesday 16th May
John 14:27–31a

Jesus said to his disciples, "Peace I leave with you; my peace I give to you. I do not give to you as the world gives. Do not let your hearts be troubled, and do not let them be afraid. You heard me say to you, I am going away, and I am coming to you. If you loved me, you would rejoice that I am going to the Father, because the Father is greater than I. And now I have told you this before it occurs, so that when it does occur, you may believe. I will no longer talk much with you, for the ruler of this world is coming. He has no power over me; but I do as the Father has commanded me, so that the world may know that I love the Father." . . .

- Throughout the Old and New Testament there are echoes of the words "Do not be afraid" and "Do not let your hearts be troubled." The evil forces of this world have no power over Jesus and need have no power over us as his disciples. That is why we need not be afraid.

- The peace that Jesus promises is not an escape from trouble but rather the courage to face it calmly. As he spoke these words of peace, he was walking out to Gethsemane and his passion. Lord, that is the peace I seek: to be able to face sorrow and pain without the overwhelming fear that all is lost.

Wednesday 17th May

John 15:1–8

Jesus said, "I am the true vine, and my Father is the vine-grower. He removes every branch in me that bears no fruit. Every branch that bears fruit he prunes to make it bear more fruit. You have already been cleansed by the word that I have spoken to you. Abide in me as I abide in you. Just as the branch cannot bear fruit by itself unless it abides in the vine, neither can you unless you abide in me. I am the vine, you are the branches. Those who abide in me and I in them bear much fruit, because apart from me you can do nothing. Whoever does not abide in me is thrown away like a branch and withers; such branches are gathered, thrown into the fire, and burned. If you abide in me, and my words abide in you, ask for whatever you wish, and it will be done for you. My Father is glorified by this, that you bear much fruit and become my disciples."

- The term "to abide" was music to the Hebrews, who had been nomads and exiles. They longed for a place in which they could rest permanently. Jesus offers, not a country, but his very self, for this abiding. Relationship, not place, is what matters. I thank God that even though my life is always changing, Jesus is my home, my permanent resting place.

- How do I abide in the Lord? Above all by prayer, raising my heart and mind to God each morning. There is a worldwide community that prays along with me, as we all abide in Jesus and draw strength from him.

Thursday 18th May

John 15:9–11

Jesus said to his disciples, "As the Father has loved me, so I have loved you; abide in my love. If you keep my commandments, you will abide in my love, just as I have kept my Father's commandments and abide in his love. I have said these things to you so that my joy may be in you, and that your joy may be complete."

- It's simple: Jesus wants me to be happy! I realize that what is in question is not superficial but is a happiness that comes from joy of being in the right place—in right relationship with God, with others, and with myself. Help me, Lord, to abide.

- If we could grasp God's unconditional love for us, life would be radically a journey of joy. Joy can be present in the midst of hardship. Jesus' joy is profound and deep, even in his passion. It is the joy of being loved by the Father. My joy must spring from a deep down awareness that I am massively loved by God. Lord, I do not know why you should care that my joy may be complete. But you do, so let me give time now to savor this and to praise and thank you.

Friday 19th May
John 15:12–17

Jesus said to his disciples, "This is my commandment, that you love one another as I have loved you. No one has greater love than this, to lay down one's life for one's friends. You are my friends if you do what I command you. I do not call you servants any longer, because the servant does not know what the master is doing; but I have called you friends, because I have made known to you everything that I have heard from my Father. You did not choose me but I chose you. And I appointed you to go and bear fruit, fruit that will last, so that the Father will give you whatever you ask him in my name. I am giving you these commands so that you may love one another."

- Lord, you are inviting me, choosing me, to be your intimate friend, to go out in your name, and to make an impact on this precious world, and bear lasting fruit. Is there any reason I should hold back?

- My well-being is intertwined with the well-being of every other human being. Jesus understood this and thus said again and again how we must care for one another. I try to imagine my life connected to others, here and everywhere.

Saturday 20th May
John 15:18–21

Jesus said to his disciples, "If the world hates you, be aware that it hated me before it hated you. If you belonged to the world, the world would love you as its own. Because you do not belong to the world, but I have chosen you out of the world—therefore the world hates you. Remember the word that I said to you, 'Servants are not greater than their master.' If they persecuted me, they will persecute you; if they kept my word, they will keep yours also. But they will do all these things to you on account of my name, because they do not know him who sent me."

- Jesus wants a world in which love, friendship and inclusion prevail. But we find ourselves in a world of domination, corruption, revenge, and exclusion. To have the courage to make right choices, we must be firmly grounded in the friendship and support of Jesus. He doesn't promise that we will be successful when we stand for the truth, but we are to be available, faithful, and loving. The struggle to witness to the Gospel will deepen the companionship between Jesus and ourselves. We are in this together.

- This talk about hatred is distasteful stuff, Lord, politically incorrect. But I have to admit that it rings true. It happens that good Christians are slandered and hated, for whatever reason. Then I need to remember how you were hated, and kept your peace, and did not let your heart flame up in resentment.

May 21—May 27

Something to think and pray about each day this week:

Symbols in the Sand

I was in County Donegal in Ireland one summer, facilitating a retreat in a lovely little house beside a long and almost deserted beach that skirted a sea loch. We had been looking at the problems of letting things go, and I suggested to those on retreat that if there was something they wanted to let go of—perhaps some fear or anxiety or resentment—they might like to go down to the shore at low tide and draw some symbol of their preoccupation in the sand, and then the next morning go back to the beach and notice how, while they had slept, the advancing and receding tides had washed away their symbol.

It felt only right to do this exercise myself, and so that evening I made a sign in the sand that represented a situation I was anxious about. As I made my symbol, I realized that it was helping me clarify exactly what it was I was so angry about and so afraid of. Drawing in the sand had, that night, the same effect as speaking out my concerns to a wise friend. It was also a way of turning my anxieties into prayer.

—Margaret Silf, *The Other Side of Chaos*

The Presence of God
I pause for a moment and think of the love and the grace that God showers on me: I am created in the image and likeness of God; I am God's dwelling place.

Freedom
Lord, you created me to live in freedom. May your Holy Spirit guide me to follow you freely. Instill in my heart a desire to know and love you more each day.

Consciousness
How am I really feeling? Lighthearted? Heavyhearted? I may be very much at peace, happy to be here.
Equally, I may be frustrated, worried, or angry.
I acknowledge how I really am. It is the real me that the Lord loves.

The Word
I read the word of God slowly, a few times over, and I listen to what God is saying to me. (Please turn to the Scripture on the following pages. Inspiration points are there should you need them. When you are ready, return here to continue.)

Conversation
I know with certainty there were times when you carried me, Lord. When it was through your strength I got through the dark times in my life.

Conclusion
I thank God for these moments we have spent together and for any insights I have been given concerning the text.

Sunday 21st May
Sixth Sunday of Easter
John 14:15–21

Jesus said to his disciples, "If you love me, you will keep my commandments. And I will ask the Father, and he will give you another Advocate, to be with you forever. This is the Spirit of truth, whom the world cannot receive, because it neither sees him nor knows him. You know him, because he abides with you, and he will be in you. I will not leave you orphaned; I am coming to you. In a little while the world will no longer see me, but you will see me; because I live, you also will live. On that day you will know that I am in my Father, and you in me, and I in you. They who have my commandments and keep them are those who love me; and those who love me will be loved by my Father, and I will love them and reveal myself to them."

- I know, Lord, that the same Holy Spirit joins me to you as joined you to your father. That Spirit dwells in me, an abiding presence whose voice can easily be drowned by my everyday plans and concerns. To be open to the Spirit, I must quiet first my body, then my heart.

- Jesus speaks about being still alive even after his death. Mostly we find Jesus to be alive for us in the love of others. There is an energy of love that is connected to the energy of God, for God is love. I do not need to rely on my own resources but turn to God who promises to help me, ready to send the Holy Spirit.

Monday 22nd May
John 15:26—16:4a

Jesus said to the disciples, "When the Advocate comes, whom I will send to you from the Father, the Spirit of truth who comes from the Father, he will testify on my behalf. You also are to testify because you have been with me from the beginning. I have said these things to you to keep you from stumbling. They will put you out of the synagogues. Indeed, an hour is coming when those who kill you will think that by doing so they are offering worship to God. And they will do this because they have not known the Father or me. But I have said these things to you so that when their hour comes you may remember that I told you about them. I did not say these things to you from the beginning, because I was with you."

- Terrible things have been done in God's name. But God's way is love, and Jesus assures us that those who do such things are misled. We ask to know him more closely so that we will not make the same mistakes.

- There's an atmosphere in these chapters of John's Gospel that Jesus wants to be with us, that he likes being with us, and cares about his friendships with us. Prayer is first of all God's invitation to us to be present before we take action. We pray because God is God, because God exists, and because God is love. Prayer time is "handing over time"—handing over cares, joys, and sorrows into the care of the loving God.

Tuesday 23rd May

John 16:5–11

Jesus said, "Now I am going to him who sent me; yet none of you asks me, 'Where are you going?' But because I have said these things to you, sorrow has filled your hearts. Nevertheless, I tell you the truth: it is to your advantage that I go away, for if I do not go away, the Advocate will not come to you; but if I go, I will send him to you. And when he comes, he will prove the world wrong about sin and righteousness and judgment: about sin, because they do not believe in me; about righteousness, because I am going to the Father and you will see me no longer; about judgment, because the ruler of this world has been condemned."

- These words of Jesus at the Last Supper reflect some of the heavy sorrow of that meal, darkened by the disciples' awareness that they are losing Jesus. What he says to them applies to us also: Jesus remains with us through his Spirit, the Paraclete, dwelling in us and linking us to the Father as he linked Jesus to the Father.

- I am not alone. The Holy Spirit can help me in everything, no matter how weak and helpless I feel. Bidden or unbidden, the Spirit is present everywhere, challenging false values so that truth and goodness may prevail. I am meant to be a spokesperson for the Spirit. Can the Spirit count on me?

Wednesday 24th May
John 16:12–15

Jesus said, "I still have many things to say to you, but you cannot bear them now. When the Spirit of truth comes, he will guide you into all the truth; for he will not speak on his own, but will speak whatever he hears, and he will declare to you the things that are to come. He will glorify me, because he will take what is mine and declare it to you. All that the Father has is mine. For this reason I said that he will take what is mine and declare it to you."

- Jesus presents the Trinity in terms of a divine relationship, a community of love. It is to be the model of all human society. Saint Ignatius spoke of the Trinity in terms of three notes that combine to make one musical chord—each makes a profound contribution to the whole. This may or may not help us to understand the Trinity. But what is more important is that the three divine Persons understand and love us!

- Jesus is sensitive to his followers' limited understanding. By telling them he has more to tell them, he is, in a gentle way, preparing them! I ask his wisdom to know when it is good to speak and when it is better to wait and be silent. Jesus knows how anxious we can be both to let go of the past and to trust what the future will bring. Can I speak to him about my anxieties?

Thursday 25th May
The Ascension of the Lord
Matthew 28:16–20

Now the eleven disciples went to Galilee, to the mountain to which Jesus had directed them. When they saw him, they worshiped him; but some doubted. And Jesus came and said to them, "All authority in heaven and on earth has been given to me. Go therefore and make disciples of all nations, baptizing them in the name of the Father and of the Son and of the Holy Spirit, and teaching them to obey everything that I have commanded you. And remember, I am with you always, to the end of the age."

- Lord, you were talking to eleven men who had little education, money, or influence, in a despised province of the Roman Empire. But they obeyed you because they knew you were with them. Today, we are sometimes too well educated. It is harder than ever to make the Gospel heard. Yet your word goes out to all nations, and you are still with us.

- I put myself in the skin of one of the eleven disciples, still fearful of those who have arrested and crucified my master, sensing how forlorn I will be without his presence, and as the text says, doubtful. I hear Jesus' commission: Go and teach all nations. My heart sinks. Where do I start? Then I hear his promise: I am with you always.

Friday 26th May
John 16:20–23

Jesus said to his disciples, "Very truly, I tell you, you will weep and mourn, but the world will rejoice; you will have pain, but your pain will turn into joy. When a woman is in labor, she has pain, because her hour has come. But when her child is born, she no longer remembers the anguish because of the joy of having brought a human being into the world. So you have pain now; but I will see you again, and your hearts will rejoice, and no one will take your joy from you. On that day you will ask nothing of me. Very truly, I tell you, if you ask anything of the Father in my name, he will give it to you."

- Childbirth was a traditional biblical metaphor for the sufferings that were to herald the age of the Messiah. Giving birth to a renewed world will always entail suffering. Jesus, I ask you now to help me remain close to you with a passionate heart and to accept patiently whatever you want of me. And make me a joyous person!

- Problems can be a path toward growth, especially in the context of love. They may also be a cul-de-sac, blocking any future development and joy. With Jesus we walk always with the "Alleluia" on our lips and in our hearts. I pray for a deep appreciation of God's goodness, and for trust.

Saturday 27th May
John 16:23b–28

Jesus said to his disciples, "Very truly, I tell you, if you ask anything of the Father in my name, he will give it to you. Until now you have not asked for anything in my name. Ask and you will receive, so that your joy may be complete. I have said these things to you in figures of speech. The hour is coming when I will no longer speak to you in figures, but will tell you plainly of the Father. On that day you will ask in my name. I do not say to you that I will ask the Father on your behalf; for the Father himself loves you, because you have loved me and have believed that I came from God. I came from the Father and have come into the world; again, I am leaving the world and am going to the Father."

- As Jesus is joined to the Father through the Holy Spirit, so are we, because Jesus is our brother. We pray, and sometimes prayer is answered very directly. Even when this appears not to happen, no prayer is wasted. We are gifted with the Spirit of Jesus, alive in our lives and in our love. We ask always in his name, knowing that in his name God will always hear us, inspire us, direct us, and love us.

- A request for something "in Jesus' name" asks for something that will help bring about God's reign on earth. So I pray, "Thy kingdom come. Thy will be done on earth." While God's kingdom is not of this world, in the sense of sharing this world's values, it is certainly present wherever people live the Beatitudes and practice what Jesus teaches.

Something to think and pray about each day this week:

Seeing Beauty

Now that it's firmly Spring, I find myself thinking immediately of the beauty of God's creation—not just natural beauty, but also all the beautiful things that humanity offers. I have friends who, no matter their age or circumstances, who bring beauty into my life. Architecture, secular and sacred, speaks loudly to me, but so do art and music. God's beauty is everywhere—in an old man holding his granddaughter's hand as they prepare to cross the street, in the tender ministrations of a nurse as she bathes a patient, in a woman rushing to a second job to keep her family afloat. Why can't I see this all the time?

—Paul Brian Campbell, SJ, on his blog *People for Others*

The Presence of God
Jesus, help me to be fully alive to your Holy Presence. Enfold me in your love. Let my heart become one with yours.

Freedom
I will ask God's help,
to be free from my own preoccupations,
to be open to God in this time of prayer,
to come to know, love, and serve God more.

Consciousness
I ask how I am within myself today? Am I particularly tired, stressed, or off form? If any of these characteristics apply, can I try to let go of the concerns that disturb me?

The Word
God speaks to each of us individually. I listen attentively to hear what God is saying to me. Read the text a few times, then listen. (Please turn to the Scripture on the following pages. Inspiration points are there should you need them. When you are ready, return here to continue.)

Conversation
Sometimes I wonder what I might say if I were to meet you in person, Lord.
I think I might say, Thank you, Lord, for always being there for me.

Conclusion
Glory be to the Father, and to the Son, and to the Holy Spirit,
As it was in the beginning, is now and ever shall be,
World without end. Amen.

Sunday 28th May
Seventh Sunday of Easter
John 17:1–11a

Jesus looked up to heaven and said, "Father, the hour has come; glorify your Son so that the Son may glorify you, since you have given him authority over all people, to give eternal life to all whom you have given him. And this is eternal life, that they may know you, the only true God, and Jesus Christ whom you have sent. I glorified you on earth by finishing the work that you gave me to do. So now, Father, glorify me in your own presence with the glory that I had in your presence before the world existed. I have made your name known to those whom you gave me from the world. They were yours, and you gave them to me, and they have kept your word. Now they know that everything you have given me is from you; for the words that you gave to me I have given to them, and they have received them and know in truth that I came from you; and they have believed that you sent me. I am asking on their behalf; I am not asking on behalf of the world, but on behalf of those whom you gave me, because they are yours. All mine are yours, and yours are mine; and I have been glorified in them. And now I am no longer in the world, but they are in the world, and I am coming to you. Holy Father, protect them in your name that you have given me, so that they may be one, as we are one."

- To be enveloped by intimacy with God is to experience something of what eternal life will be like. God, protect me and those I love. Keep me in the hollow of your hand, and draw me ever more deeply into your friendship.

- As I grow in knowledge of God, I begin to taste the eternal life Jesus promises. I thank God for the light I have, for the quiet revelations, and for the personal inspirations that have been given to me.

Monday 29th May
John 16:29–33

Jesus' disciples said, "Yes, now you are speaking plainly, not in any figure of speech! Now we know that you know all things, and do not need to have anyone question you; by this we believe that you came from God." Jesus answered them, "Do you now believe? The hour is coming, indeed it has come, when you will be scattered, each one to his home, and you will leave me alone. Yet I am not alone because the Father is with me. I have said this to you, so that in me you may have peace. In the world you face persecution. But take courage; I have conquered the world!"

- The disciples proclaim their faith in Jesus. But these same disciples will scatter when he is arrested and crucified. Yet he never despairs of them—or of me. When I face opposition and rejection, it is hard to keep faith. In such moments, Father, give me your courage and peace. You are always watching out for me in my struggles.

- There is a slightly manic tinge about the disciples' speech. Jesus looks into their hearts and brings them back to the grim realities that he and they face. He knows how they will fail—you will leave me alone—and he loves them as they are, promises them peace, and urges them to courage. Lord, you have no illusions about my fallible heart but you promise peace to me, too.

Tuesday 30th May
John 17:1–11a

After Jesus had spoken these words, he looked up to heaven and said, "Father, the hour has come; glorify your Son so that the Son may glorify you, since you have given him authority over all people, to give eternal life to all whom you have given him. And this is eternal life, that they may know you, the only true God, and Jesus Christ whom you have sent. I glorified you on earth by finishing the work that you gave me to do. So now, Father, glorify me in your own presence with the glory that I had in your presence before the world existed. I have made your name known to those whom you gave me from the world. They were yours, and you gave them to me, and they have kept your word. Now they know that everything you have given me is from you; for the words that you gave to me I have given to them, and they have received them and know in truth that I came from you; and they have believed that you sent me. I am asking on their behalf; I am not asking on behalf of the world, but on behalf of those whom you gave me, because they are yours. All mine are yours, and yours are mine; and I have been glorified in them. And now I am no longer in the world, but they are in the world, and I am coming to you. Holy Father, protect them in your name that you have given me, so that they may be one, as we are one."

- I have to work at this, Lord. To know the only true God is beyond my imagination. Do we, in our glorified bodies, leave behind our senses of smell, taste, touch, hearing, vision, that delight us now and seem to be harbingers of better things to come? Somehow the knowledge of the one true God must bring all these joys to a new level.

- Eternal life is not just for the future; it is a gift partly given now in our faith. To be in touch with Jesus is to be in touch with a rich and full eternal life. Something is given that will last forever: the mysterious life of God. We touch that life in prayer. It is like living water, or new sight.

Wednesday 31st May
Visitation of the Blessed Virgin Mary
Luke 1:39–56

In those days Mary set out and went with haste to a Judean town in the hill country, where she entered the house of Zechariah and greeted Elizabeth. When Elizabeth heard Mary's greeting, the child leapt in her womb. And Elizabeth was filled with the Holy Spirit and exclaimed with a loud cry, "Blessed are you among women, and blessed is the fruit of your womb. And why has this happened to me, that the mother of my Lord comes to me? For as soon as I heard the sound of your greeting, the child in my womb leapt for joy. And blessed is she who believed that there would be a fulfillment of what was spoken to her by the Lord." And Mary said,

> "My soul magnifies the Lord,
> and my spirit rejoices in God my Saviour,
> for he has looked with favor on the lowliness of his servant.
> Surely, from now on all generations will call me blessed;
> for the Mighty One has done great things for me,
> and holy is his name.
> His mercy is for those who fear him
> from generation to generation.
> He has shown strength with his arm;
> he has scattered the proud in the thoughts of their hearts.
> He has brought down the powerful from their thrones,
> and lifted up the lowly;

he has filled the hungry with good things,
and sent the rich away empty.
He has helped his servant Israel,
in remembrance of his mercy,
according to the promise he made to our ancestors,
to Abraham and to his descendants forever."

And Mary remained with her for about three months and then returned to her home.

- There is no false humility in Mary's prayer; rather, there's the true humility of knowing that all that is being accomplished in her is done by God. She accepts the greatness of her mission fully, joyfully, and expectantly. Lord, help me to do your will joyfully and fearlessly. I want to answer your call with an exultant Yes! secure in the knowledge that, as I move into the unknown, my journey will be made radiant by your transfiguring presence.

- Father, give me an intimate knowledge of the many gifts I have received. Filled with gratitude, may I use these gifts in the service of your beloved poor.

Thursday 1st June
John 17:20–26

Jesus prayed, "I ask not only on behalf of these, but also on behalf of those who will believe in me through their word, that they may all be one. As you, Father, are in me and I am in you, may they also be in us, so that the world may believe that you have sent me. The glory that you have given me I have given them, so that they may be one, as we are one, I in them and you in me, that they may become completely one, so that the world may know that you have sent me and have loved them even as you have loved me. Father, I desire that those also, whom you have given me, may be with me where I am, to see my glory, which you have given me because you loved me before the foundation of the world. Righteous Father, the world does not know you, but I know you; and these know that you have sent me. I made your name known to them, and I will make it known, so that the love with which you have loved me may be in them, and I in them."

- In opening ourselves to prayer, we are opening ourselves to Jesus praying for us. I sit and silently allow his prayer for me to take over my heart. I am one of those who, through the words handed down by the disciples, now believe in Jesus. Here Jesus speaks of me, he prays for me, that I may be one with him and with his Father.

- What Jesus asks for us is what he sought for himself: unity with God. As I am invited into this relationship, I consider what it might cost me and I ask for the freedom I need. Jesus wants his disciples to live in such a way that the work of God is evident in them. I think of how I live, and I name the help I need.

Friday 2nd June
John 21:15–19

When they had finished breakfast, Jesus said to Simon Peter, "Simon son of John, do you love me more than these?" He said to him, "Yes, Lord; you know that I love you." Jesus said to him, "Feed my lambs." A second time he said to him, "Simon son of John, do you love me?" He said to him, "Yes, Lord; you know that I love you." Jesus said to him, "Tend my sheep." He said to him the third time, "Simon son of John, do you love me?" Peter felt hurt because he said to him the third time, "Do you love me?" And he said to him, "Lord, you know everything; you know that I love you." Jesus said to him, "Feed my sheep. Very truly, I tell you, when you were younger, you used to fasten your own belt and to go wherever you wished. But when you grow old, you will stretch out your hands, and someone else will fasten a belt around you and take you where you do not wish to go." (He said this to indicate the kind of death by which he would glorify God.) After this he said to him, "Follow me."

- Peter must have wondered, *Where do I stand now?* But Jesus shows him amazing courtesy and kindness, and all doubts are dispelled. Peter becomes a new creation: a fisherman-turned-shepherd.

- Guided by Saint Ignatius, I might ask, "What have I done for Christ? What am I doing for Christ? What will I do?" Peter realizes that he is being given increasing responsibility for the flock. How graciously do I accept growing responsibility?

Saturday 3rd June
John 21:20–25

Peter turned and saw the disciple whom Jesus loved following them; he was the one who had reclined next to Jesus at the supper and had said, "Lord, who is it that is going to betray you?" When Peter saw him, he said to Jesus, "Lord, what about him?" Jesus said to him, "If it is my will that he remain until I come, what is that to you? Follow me!" So the rumor spread in the community that this disciple would not die. Yet Jesus did not say to him that he would not die, but, "If it is my will that he remain until I come, what is that to you?" This is the disciple who is testifying to these things and has written them, and we know that his testimony is true. But there are also many other things that Jesus did; if every one of them were written down, I suppose that the world itself could not contain the books that would be written.

- "What about him?" asked Peter. Is there a hint here of sibling rivalry, jealous curiosity? There is reproach in Jesus' comment: "What is that to you?" Lord, will I ever outgrow this sense of rivalry, wanting to be the center of attention? Let your love flow through me in an unselfish way.

- Before God, I consider the works of Jesus in my life, giving thanks for both the hidden and the evident ways in which I have come to life. I think of myself as a Gospel, a testament to God's loving presence and action.

June 4—June 10

Something to think and pray about each day this week:

Enthused in the Spirit

As recorded in Acts of the Apostles, chapter 2, the apostles proclaimed the Gospel for the first time on that day. When all was said and done, 3,000 people had been added to the church. That must have been some proclamation! What accounts for its power? The crowds who gathered to hear the apostles weren't "wowed" by healings or miracles or impressed by soaring rhetoric. Rather, what captured their imagination was the total lack of inhibition displayed by the apostles; so much so that the crowds commented that perhaps these followers of Jesus had been drinking too much wine. And in truth, the apostles were preaching while intoxicated—not with "spirits" but with the Holy Spirit. The crowds saw a group of men who should have been terrified to set foot in public instead taking to the streets filled with uninhibited joy and enthusiasm for Jesus Christ. It was this dramatic and observable transformation in the behavior of a small group of former fishermen and tax collectors that caught the attention of thousands and led them to "sign on" that very day.

—Joe Paprocki, *Under the Influence of Jesus*

The Presence of God

"I stand at the door and knock," says the Lord. What a wonderful privilege that the Lord of all creation desires to come to me. I welcome his presence.

Freedom

Saint Ignatius thought that a thick and shapeless tree trunk would never believe that it could become a statue, admired as a miracle of sculpture, and would never submit itself to the chisel of the sculptor, who sees by her genius what she can make of it.
I ask for the grace to let myself be shaped by my loving Creator.

Consciousness

Knowing that God loves me unconditionally, I can afford to be honest about how I am. What are my fears and desires? What do I expect from God? What am I willing to give to God—from my emotions and talents, thoughts and energy? And how do I feel now? I share my feelings openly with the Lord.

The Word

I take my time to read the word of God, slowly, a few times, allowing myself to dwell on anything that strikes me. (Please turn to the Scripture on the following pages. Inspiration points are there should you need them. When you are ready, return here to continue.)

Conversation

Do I notice myself reacting as I pray with the word of God? Do I feel challenged, comforted, angry? Imagining Jesus sitting or standing by me, I speak out my feelings, as one trusted friend to another.

Conclusion

I thank God for these moments we have spent together and for any insights I have been given concerning the text.

Sunday 4th June
Pentecost Sunday
John 20:19–23

When it was evening on that day, the first day of the week, and the doors of the house where the disciples had met were locked for fear of the Jews, Jesus came and stood among them and said, "Peace be with you." After he said this, he showed them his hands and his side. Then the disciples rejoiced when they saw the Lord. Jesus said to them again, "Peace be with you. As the Father has sent me, so I send you." When he had said this, he breathed on them and said to them, "Receive the Holy Spirit. If you forgive the sins of any, they are forgiven them; if you retain the sins of any, they are retained."

• In the book of Genesis, God breathes on human beings to bring them life. Now Jesus breathes his spirit into his disciples to give them new life. They will have power over sin, which otherwise deadens the human heart. Holy Spirit, I welcome you now into my small heart. Let today be "the first day of the week" for me, which means the first day of my renewed creation. Let us celebrate this together.

• I listen to Jesus speak to me: "Peace be with you." I bring before him those aspects of my life most in need of peace and hear him say again, "Peace be with you." Jesus speaks of peace but shows his hands and his feet. He reminds me that there is a cost to being a presence of peace in the world.

Monday 5th June
Mark 12:1–12

Jesus began to speak to them in parables. "A man planted a vineyard, put a fence around it, dug a pit for the wine press, and built a watchtower; then he leased it to tenants and went to another country. When the season came, he sent a slave to the tenants to collect from them his share of the produce of the vineyard. But they seized him, and beat him, and sent him away empty-handed. And again he sent another slave to them; this one they beat over the head and insulted. Then he sent another, and that one they killed. And so it was with many others; some they beat, and others they killed. He had still one other, a beloved son. Finally he sent him to them, saying, 'They will respect my son.' But those tenants said to one another, 'This is the heir; come, let us kill him, and the inheritance will be ours.' So they seized him, killed him, and threw him out of the vineyard. What then will the owner of the vineyard do? He will come and destroy the tenants and give the vineyard to others. Have you not read this Scripture:

'The stone that the builders rejected
has become the cornerstone;
this was the Lord's doing,
and it is amazing in our eyes'?"

When they realized that he had told this parable against them, they wanted to arrest him, but they feared the crowd. So they left him and went away.

- Many prophets were ill-treated or killed because they disturbed people. Jesus, the beloved Son, would suffer the same fate. How do I see my prophetic role? Do I feel silenced by an unfriendly environment, or do I have the courage to be prophetic by my life, word, and example?

- Jesus reminds us that there are many ways in which God's messages arrive. We easily develop habits that enable us to dismiss or ignore these messages. I carefully review my concerns at these times to see where God may be approaching me in ways I do not expect to or notice.

Tuesday 6th June
Mark 12:13–17

Then they sent to Jesus some Pharisees and some Herodians to trap him in what he said. And they came and said to him, "Teacher, we know that you are sincere, and show deference to no one; for you do not regard people with partiality, but teach the way of God in accordance with truth. Is it lawful to pay taxes to the emperor, or not? Should we pay them, or should we not?" But knowing their hypocrisy, he said to them, "Why are you putting me to the test? Bring me a denarius and let me see it." And they brought one. Then he said to them, "Whose head is this, and whose title?" They answered, "The emperor's." Jesus said to them, "Give to the emperor the things that are the emperor's, and to God the things that are God's." And they were utterly amazed at him.

- The Pharisees and Herodians benefited from being under Roman rule, and Jesus as much as told them they owe something in return. But life and truth and religion are more than political. As the emperor was seen as almost divine, Jesus asserted that only God is divine and only to God is worship due.

- Jesus advised us to pray that we would not be put to the test or led into temptation. Jesus made decisions from the wisdom of his relationship with the Father. Although the approach of the Pharisees was flattering and courteous, Jesus recognized that he was being tested. I pray that I may have the presence of mind not to be distracted by empty conversations.

Wednesday 7th June
Mark 12:18–27

Some Sadducees, who say there is no resurrection, came to Jesus and asked him a question, saying, "Teacher, Moses wrote for us that 'if a man's brother dies, leaving a wife but no child, the man shall marry the widow and raise up children for his brother.' There were seven brothers; the first married and, when he died, left no children; and the second married her and died, leaving no children; and the third likewise; none of the seven left children. Last of all the woman herself died. In the resurrection whose wife will she be? For the seven had married her." Jesus said to them, "Is not this the reason you are wrong, that you know neither the Scriptures nor the power of God? For when they rise from the dead, they neither marry nor are given in marriage, but are like angels in heaven. And as for the dead being raised, have you not read in the book of Moses, in the story about the bush, how God said to him, 'I am the God of Abraham, the God of Isaac, and the God of Jacob'? He is God not of the dead, but of the living; you are quite wrong."

- Jesus invokes the story of Moses at the burning bush to underline that the God revealed there is God of the living, not of the dead. How strong is my belief in the resurrection? What difference does this belief make to the way I live here and now?

- The strange questions lead to a good answer about God: God is the God of life, of living beings. We are to leave what comes after this life to God, acknowledging that answers will not be easily forthcoming. Many faith questions have a place in prayer. We grapple with big religious questions but know that they get some sort of a context at the feet of Jesus or at the cross.

Thursday 8th June
Mark 12:28–34

One of the scribes came near and heard them disputing with one another, and seeing that Jesus answered them well, he asked him, "Which commandment is the first of all?" Jesus answered, "The first is, 'Hear, O Israel: the Lord our God, the Lord is one; you shall love the Lord your God with all your heart, and with all your soul, and with all your mind, and with all your strength.' The second is this, 'You shall love your neighbor as yourself.' There is no other commandment greater than these." Then the scribe said to him, "You are right, Teacher; you have truly said that 'he is one, and besides him there is no other'; and 'to love him with all the heart, and with all the understanding, and with all the strength,' and 'to love one's neighbor as oneself,'—this is much more important than all whole burnt offerings and sacrifices." When Jesus saw that he answered wisely, he said to him, "You are not far from the kingdom of God." After that no one dared to ask him any question.

- Jesus teaches that adherence to religious rituals is less important than love of God and love of neighbor. But do I sometimes find religious practices easier than engaging with others?

- The Jewish lawyers were blamed for multiplying regulations, but they also liked to seek out the essentials of the law, to give the whole of their religion in one sound bite. Jesus takes the lawyer's question seriously and points to an interior religion, one of the heart, not of rule-keeping or ritual. What question might I bring to Jesus today in my prayer?

Friday 9th June
Mark 12:35–37

While Jesus was teaching in the temple, he said, "How can the scribes say that the Messiah is the son of David? David himself, by the Holy Spirit, declared, 'The Lord said to my Lord, "Sit at my right hand, until I put your enemies under your feet."' David himself calls him Lord; so how can he be his son?" And the large crowd was listening to him with delight.

- When the scribes teach that the Messiah is the son of David, they seem to imply that he is inferior to David. Jesus argues that Psalm 110 (used during the coronation of a king) shows that the opposite is the case. In its opening verse, David (its presumed author) writes that the Lord

(God) speaks to my lord (the king). My lord, or the Messiah, is therefore superior to David. There is even a hint of divine status, or at least of a divine relationship, in what follows: Sit at my right hand. Does this episode deepen your understanding of who Jesus is?

• Who is Jesus for me? How would I introduce him to someone else? All titles are inadequate for him. Above all, he is the Son of God. Spending time with him is a means to knowing him more fully. I express gratitude for the ongoing invitation to form a deeper relationship with him.

Saturday 10th June
Mark 12:38–44

As Jesus taught, he said, "Beware of the scribes, who like to walk around in long robes, and to be greeted with respect in the marketplaces, and to have the best seats in the synagogues and places of honor at banquets! They devour widows' houses and for the sake of appearance say long prayers. They will receive the greater condemnation." He sat down opposite the treasury, and watched the crowd putting money into the treasury. Many rich people put in large sums. A poor widow came and put in two small copper coins, which are worth a penny. Then he called his disciples and said to them, "Truly I tell you, this poor widow has put in more than all those who are contributing to the treasury. For all of them have contributed out of their abundance; but she out of her poverty has put in everything she had, all she had to live on."

• Jesus contrasts the widow's generosity with the disposition of the rich, who made large offerings out of their abundance. Implicitly he may be criticizing the religious authorities for the pressure they put on people to part with what they cannot afford. Do I appreciate the qualities that can be found in the widows (and other poor) of my world?

• Everything you say, Lord, touches my conscience. You warn me against coveting a posh car (the equivalent of long robes) or a high public profile. You remind me how women have always been imposed upon by religious charlatans. You who lived a hidden life for nine-tenths of your years on earth are a model of how to walk humbly before our God.

The Tenth Week of Ordinary Time
June 11—June 17

Something to think and pray about each day this week:

Prayers for a Workday

God my Creator, thanks for giving me work to do. When the project gets twisted up or when you think it will never end, or when the hours seem twice as long as they are, send up a prayer of thanks. You have work, and that's huge. You are employed. It's not a perfect job and it may not be a very good job, but all you must deal with is this day, and you are working. Remind me, Holy Spirit, when my attitude veers off course. I can fume at others who make life hard, or at the job itself because it's a drudge or full of stress. But so much of that is outside my control. What I can focus on is myself. Am I in too big a hurry? Am I taking on stress that isn't even mine? Am I allowing a horrible commute to color the rest of the day? Am I allowing this person to push my buttons? Is my ego working overtime? Walk with me, Jesus, and help me walk with my coworkers. Pope Francis has stressed that the church must go outside itself to where people actually live and that priests and bishops must be out among the people, laboring beside them. When we walk alongside our colleagues— through whatever kind of day we have—we are following Jesus, and Jesus is walking there too.

—Vinita Hampton Wright, on her blog, *Days of Deepening Friendship*

The Presence of God
To be present is to arrive as one is and open up to the other.
At this instant, as I arrive here, God is present waiting for me.
God always arrives before me, desiring to connect with me
even more than my most intimate friend.
I take a moment and greet my loving God.

Freedom
I am free. When I look at these words in writing, they seem to create in me a feeling of awe. Yes, a wonderful feeling of freedom. Thank you, God.

Consciousness
To be conscious about something is to be aware of it.
Dear Lord, help me to remember that you gave me life.
Thank you for the gift of life.
Teach me to slow down, to be still and enjoy the pleasures created for me.
To be aware of the beauty that surrounds me. The marvel of mountains, the calmness of lakes, the fragility of a flower petal. I need to remember that all these things come from you.

The Word
The word of God comes to us through the Scriptures. May the Holy Spirit enlighten my mind and heart to respond to the Gospel teachings. (Please turn to the Scripture on the following pages. Inspiration points are there should you need them. When you are ready, return here to continue.)

Conversation
I begin to talk to Jesus about the piece of Scripture I have just read. What part of it strikes a chord in me? Perhaps the words of a friend—or some story I have heard recently—will slowly rise to the surface in my consciousness. If so, does the story throw light on what the Scripture passage may be trying to say to me?

Conclusion
Glory be to the Father, and to the Son, and to the Holy Spirit,
As it was in the beginning, is now and ever shall be,
World without end. Amen.

Sunday 11th June
The Most Holy Trinity
John 3:16–18

Jesus said, "For God so loved the world that he gave his only Son, so that everyone who believes in him may not perish but may have eternal life. Indeed, God did not send the Son into the world to condemn the world, but in order that the world might be saved through him. Those who believe in him are not condemned; but those who do not believe are condemned already, because they have not believed in the name of the only Son of God."

- "God so loved the world that he gave his only Son"! This is the heart of the good news, and I must be eternally grateful for it. There are no strings or stings attached to God's loving. Nor must there be any strings or stings in the quality of my loving.

- We believe that God intervened in human history and gave his only Son to show that his attitude to us is that of a loving parent. Prayer may be compared to a time of opening ourselves to the light of God, like sunning ourselves in the warmth of the sun, the gentle and bright light that illuminates us completely.

Monday 12th June
(Tenth Week in Ordinary Time)
Matthew 5:1–12

When Jesus saw the crowds, he went up the mountain; and after he sat down, his disciples came to him. Then he began to speak, and taught them, saying:

"Blessed are the poor in spirit, for theirs is the kingdom of heaven.
Blessed are those who mourn, for they will be comforted.
Blessed are the meek, for they will inherit the earth.
Blessed are those who hunger and thirst for righteousness, for they will be filled.
Blessed are the merciful, for they will receive mercy.
Blessed are the pure in heart, for they will see God.
Blessed are the peacemakers, for they will be called children of God.

Blessed are those who are persecuted for righteousness' sake, for theirs
is the kingdom of heaven.

Blessed are you when people revile you and persecute you and utter
all kinds of evil against you falsely on my account. Rejoice and be
glad, for your reward is great in heaven, for in the same way they
persecuted the prophets who were before you."

- Today, and always, Jesus is "sitting down" in the Sacred Space of my
heart. I listen to him and his words of life. Which beatitude do I find
most affirming? Which gives me most encouragement for my life journey right now? Which of these Beatitudes challenges me the most?

- The Beatitudes touch paradox, indicating that we find life where we
might least expect it. The beatitudes can be understood rightly in the
life and example of Jesus, who lived simply, showed mercy and compassion, and hungered for the Father's will.

Tuesday 13th June

Matthew 5:13–16

Jesus said to the crowds, "You are the salt of the earth; but if salt has lost
its taste, how can its saltiness be restored? It is no longer good for anything, but is thrown out and trampled under foot. You are the light of the
world. A city built on a hill cannot be hid. No one after lighting a lamp
puts it under the bushel basket, but on the lampstand, and it gives light to
all in the house. In the same way, let your light shine before others, so that
they may see your good works and give glory to your Father in heaven."

- We often think of lighting as something decorative, an enhancement
of our living spaces. Jesus refers to light more as something that reveals
life and truth. I talk to God about the sort of light I am and listen to
know what sort of light God wants me to be.

- Sometimes we are put in the spotlight; briefly we are the light of the
world, and we can pray that when we are in such focus we are worthy
of our Christian vocation. Most of the time we are more like salt, or
leaven, working for good but unseen. Lord, what do you ask of me, to
be light or salt, to shine in public or to work invisibly?

Wednesday 14th June
Matthew 5:17–19

Jesus said to the crowds, "Do not think that I have come to abolish the law or the prophets; I have come not to abolish but to fulfill. For truly I tell you, until heaven and earth pass away, not one letter, not one stroke of a letter, will pass from the law until all is accomplished. Therefore, whoever breaks one of the least of these commandments, and teaches others to do the same, will be called least in the kingdom of heaven; but whoever does them and teaches them will be called great in the kingdom of heaven."

- The historical words of the prophets are endorsed by Jesus. The word of God endures forever, and salvation is for all who heed the prophetic warnings. Jesus fulfills the law by living as God desires; he crowns the law by putting love above all.

- Jesus loves his Jewish religion. Also, he understands the heart of it. He wants to fulfill it by loving his Father perfectly and by loving all God's people, even as far as dying for them. I pray to be a good disciple by living like that. Have I grasped the heart of my religion?

Thursday 15th June
Matthew 5:20–26

Jesus said to the crowds, "For I tell you, unless your righteousness exceeds that of the scribes and Pharisees, you will never enter the kingdom of heaven. You have heard that it was said to those of ancient times, 'You shall not murder; and whoever murders shall be liable to judgment.' But I say to you that if you are angry with a brother or sister, you will be liable to judgment; and if you insult a brother or sister, you will be liable to the council; and if you say, 'You fool,' you will be liable to the hell of fire. So when you are offering your gift at the altar, if you remember that your brother or sister has something against you, leave your gift there before the altar and go; first be reconciled to your brother or sister, and then come and offer your gift. Come to terms quickly with your accuser while you are on the way to court with him, or your accuser may hand you over to the judge, and the judge to the guard, and you will be thrown into prison. Truly I tell you, you will never get out until you have paid the last penny."

- The standards operating in the kingdom of heaven are high! Jesus does not dismiss Old Testament teaching but goes to the root of things. We can be smug and content with our conventional good behavior. However, Jesus says to us, "But what about your anger? What about insulting someone? Do you despise anyone, ever?"

- Events that seem to be of little significance when they occur may be seeds of something of great importance later on. They can lead to major changes, adjustments, and turning points in life. Decisive moments can be influenced by what seemed small. We pray to see where God may be leading us in the little things.

Friday 16th June
Matthew 5:27–32

Jesus said to the crowds, "You have heard that it was said, 'You shall not commit adultery.' But I say to you that everyone who looks at a woman with lust has already committed adultery with her in his heart. If your right eye causes you to sin, tear it out and throw it away; it is better for you to lose one of your members than for your whole body to be thrown into hell. And if your right hand causes you to sin, cut it off and throw it away; it is better for you to lose one of your members than for your whole body to go into hell. It was also said, 'Whoever divorces his wife, let him give her a certificate of divorce.' But I say to you that anyone who divorces his wife, except on the ground of unchastity, causes her to commit adultery; and whoever marries a divorced woman commits adultery."

- It is not uncommon for people to take issue with these words of Jesus, thinking he speaks too harshly, too violently; we can get stuck in the words, forgetting the call to action. We might take some time in prayer to go beyond his words, to seek out what is in his heart.

- Lord, what is the core that you're getting at with these strict statements? What do you want me to hear today?

Saturday 17th June
Matthew 5:33–37

Jesus said to the crowds, "Again, you have heard that it was said to those of ancient times, 'You shall not swear falsely, but carry out the vows you have made to the Lord.' But I say to you, Do not swear at all, either by heaven, for it is the throne of God, or by the earth, for it is his footstool, or by Jerusalem, for it is the city of the great King. And do not swear by your head, for you cannot make one hair white or black. Let your word be 'Yes, Yes' or 'No, No'; anything more than this comes from the evil one."

- Jesus again takes a teaching from the Jewish tradition and nuances it further. His argument ends with a call to values that are highly rated today (even if not always practiced): simplicity in our relationships, honesty in our communication with each other, transparency in our words. How do I find myself responding to this call?

- My actions show the sincerity of my words. I ask God's help to live as I profess. I know that I have made promises in the past and admit that I may not always have fulfilled these promises. I place myself before God who loves me, recognizes my desire to do good, and forgives me.

The Eleventh Week of Ordinary Time
June 18—June 24

Something to think and pray about each day this week:

The Centrality of Jesus

Pope Francis offers us an entirely different path for renewal, especially in the Church. For him, renewal is not about tinkering with structures or doing a new thing. Rather, it means reclaiming the centrality of Jesus Christ. And that, in turn, depends entirely on a new spirit and a new heart. The renewal that Pope Francis shows us is the conversion of heart that happens by walking with Jesus, by being in close contact with him. This is why he constantly insists that we read a passage of the Gospels day-by-day and reflect and pray on it, whether we are on public transport or at home. That is walking with Jesus. When we make that kind of day-by-day commitment to walk with Jesus, we begin to live in a world of grace, depending on more than our human efforts. When Jesus walks with us and is our guide, Pope Francis tells us, we will keep discovering the deepest truth that makes us free and gives us life. The grace is already given to us to be uncovered, discovered, and embraced.

—Blase J. Cupich, Archbishop of Chicago, in the introduction to
Walking with Jesus by Pope Francis

The Presence of God
Be still and know that I am God. Lord, may your Spirit guide me to seek your loving presence more and more. For it is there I find rest and refreshment from this busy world.

Freedom
By God's grace I was born to live in freedom. Free to enjoy the pleasures he created for me. Dear Lord, grant that I may live as you intended, with complete confidence in your loving care.

Consciousness
In God's loving presence I unwind the past day,
starting from now and looking back, moment by moment.
I gather in all the goodness and light, in gratitude.
I attend to the shadows and what they say to me,
seeking healing, courage, forgiveness.

The Word
The word of God comes to us through the Scriptures. May the Holy Spirit enlighten my mind and heart to respond to the Gospel teachings. (Please turn to the Scripture on the following pages. Inspiration points are there should you need them. When you are ready, return here to continue.)

Conversation
Jesus, you always welcomed little children when you walked on this earth. Teach me to have a childlike trust in you. To live in the knowledge that you will never abandon me.

Conclusion
Glory be to the Father, and to the Son, and to the Holy Spirit,
As it was in the beginning, is now and ever shall be,
World without end. Amen.

Sunday 18th June
The Most Holy Body and Blood of Christ
John 6:51–58

Jesus said, "I am the living bread that came down from heaven. Whoever eats of this bread will live forever; and the bread that I will give for the life of the world is my flesh." The Jews then disputed among themselves, saying, "How can this man give us his flesh to eat?" So Jesus said to them, "Very truly, I tell you, unless you eat the flesh of the Son of Man and drink his blood, you have no life in you. Those who eat my flesh and drink my blood have eternal life, and I will raise them up on the last day; for my flesh is true food and my blood is true drink. Those who eat my flesh and drink my blood abide in me, and I in them. Just as the living Father sent me, and I live because of the Father, so whoever eats me will live because of me. This is the bread that came down from heaven, not like that which your ancestors ate, and they died. But the one who eats this bread will live forever."

- In Hebrew, the expression "flesh and blood" means the whole being. The reality of Christ's presence at the Eucharist is beyond our comprehension. We are asked not to understand it but to experience it.

- Jesus leads me to appreciate the closeness to which he calls me. *Eat, live,* and *abide* are words that belong to the home. Jesus invites me to bring anything in my life that is unsettled or out of place, that it may find its home in him.

Monday 19th June
(Eleventh Week in Ordinary Time)
Matthew 5:38–42

Jesus said to the crowds, "You have heard that it was said, 'An eye for an eye and a tooth for a tooth.' But I say to you, Do not resist an evildoer. But if anyone strikes you on the right cheek, turn the other also; and if anyone wants to sue you and take your coat, give your cloak as well; and if anyone forces you to go one mile, go also the second mile. Give to everyone who begs from you, and do not refuse anyone who wants to borrow from you."

- The radical nature of Jesus' teaching compels us to engage in a positive manner with all those we encounter. The settling of old scores diminishes both parties. Jesus instead is generous when unfair demands are made on him. He simply loves everyone. From today I will try to ignore insult and injury. I will thus become a little bit more like my Lord.

- There are times when we let go of some hurt or grievance and try to help someone who has upset us. We don't always see the good effect of this and may feel let down or even stupid when we do this. At such times, Lord, help us persevere in kindness.

Tuesday 20th June
Matthew 5:43–48

Jesus said to the crowds, "You have heard that it was said, 'You shall love your neighbor and hate your enemy.' But I say to you, Love your enemies and pray for those who persecute you, so that you may be children of your Father in heaven; for he makes his sun rise on the evil and on the good, and sends rain on the righteous and on the unrighteous. For if you love those who love you, what reward do you have? Do not even the tax collectors do the same? And if you greet only your brothers and sisters, what more are you doing than others? Do not even the Gentiles do the same? Be perfect, therefore, as your heavenly Father is perfect."

- We are to open our hearts even to those who hate us. This is not hopeless idealism but a wise strategy for overcoming the persecutor. Aggression is changed into a strategy for winning through the wisdom of love.

- Prayer and love can go together. To pray for another person opens our heart to him or her. It is one of the ways of forgiveness and a step on paths to healing. We can come to see the love of God, which is poured on all, by looking at another person.

Wednesday 21st June
Matthew 6:1–6, 16–18

Jesus said to the crowds, "Beware of practicing your piety before others in order to be seen by them; for then you have no reward from your Father in heaven. So whenever you give alms, do not sound a trumpet before you, as the hypocrites do in the synagogues and in the streets, so that they may be praised by others. Truly I tell you, they have received their reward. But when you give alms, do not let your left hand know what your right hand is doing, so that your alms may be done in secret; and your Father who sees in secret will reward you. And whenever you pray, do not be like the hypocrites; for they love to stand and pray in the synagogues and at the street corners, so that they may be seen by others. Truly I tell you, they have received their reward. But whenever you pray, go into your room and shut the door and pray to your Father who is in secret; and your Father who sees in secret will reward you. . . . And whenever you fast, do not look dismal, like the hypocrites, for they disfigure their faces so as to show others that they are fasting. Truly I tell you, they have received their reward. But when you fast, put oil on your head and wash your face, so that your fasting may be seen not by others but by your Father who is in secret; and your Father who sees in secret will reward you."

• It is remarkable how strongly Jesus feels about hypocrisy. He hammers home his disapproval through a series of examples: Hypocrisy can undermine the virtue in almsgiving, in prayer, and in fasting. This list is not exhaustive. Maybe you can add to it. Ask Jesus to sensitize you to any hypocrisy that may have crept into your own life.

• Do I sometimes set out to get praise and admiration? We are asked to carry out almsgiving, prayer, and fasting in secret. Whatever is done with sincere love will last eternally. I ask for a heart that is free, that enables me to live with sincere love.

Thursday 22nd June
Matthew 6:7–15

Jesus said, "When you are praying, do not heap up empty phrases as the Gentiles do; for they think that they will be heard because of their many words. Do not be like them, for your Father knows what you need before you ask him. Pray then in this way: Our Father in heaven, hallowed be your name. Your kingdom come. Your will be done, on earth as it is in heaven. Give us this day our daily bread. And forgive us our debts, as we also have forgiven our debtors. And do not bring us to the time of trial, but rescue us from the evil one. For if you forgive others their trespasses, your heavenly Father will also forgive you; but if you do not forgive others, neither will your Father forgive your trespasses."

- Listening to God and letting God work is the heart of prayer, though we can spend much time wanting God to listen to us. Empty phrases, hollow words, and one-sided conversations do not give life. It is the action of God that is most important, not words or great ideas.

- Prayer is a call to conversion. The Father's will was a guiding light to Jesus. His relationship with Abba was at the heart of his prayer of thanksgiving. In our relationship with God we ask that God's will be done in us, while acknowledging our weakness and our capacity to lose direction.

Friday 23rd June
The Most Sacred Heart of Jesus
Matthew 11:25–30

At that time Jesus said, "I thank you, Father, Lord of heaven and earth, because you have hidden these things from the wise and the intelligent and have revealed them to infants; yes, Father, for such was your gracious will. All things have been handed over to me by my Father; and no one knows the Son except the Father, and no one knows the Father except the Son and anyone to whom the Son chooses to reveal him. Come to me, all you that are weary and are carrying heavy burdens, and I will give you rest. Take my yoke upon you, and learn from me; for I am gentle and humble in heart, and you will find rest for your souls. For my yoke is easy, and my burden is light."

- A child can receive the message that eludes the scholar; we may receive a sudden and unexpected insight even when our best efforts at making sense fail. Our time of prayer helps us stand back and work less. Instead of struggling to understand, I accept that I am understood, cherished, and loved.

- I reflect on the burdens I am carrying. I bring them to Jesus. What difference does it make when he takes my burdens on his shoulders? Do I find rest? I ask for the grace to be aware that I am never alone in my weariness, for he is there.

Saturday 24th June
Nativity of Saint John the Baptist
Luke 1:57–66, 80

Now the time came for Elizabeth to give birth, and she bore a son. Her neighbors and relatives heard that the Lord had shown his great mercy to her, and they rejoiced with her. On the eighth day they came to circumcise the child, and they were going to name him Zechariah after his father. But his mother said, "No; he is to be called John." They said to her, "None of your relatives has this name." Then they began motioning to his father to find out what name he wanted to give him. He asked for a writing tablet and wrote, "His name is John." And all of them were amazed. Immediately his mouth was opened and his tongue freed, and he began to speak, praising God. Fear came over all their neighbors, and all these things were talked about throughout the entire hill country of Judea. All who heard them pondered them and said, "What then will this child become?" For, indeed, the hand of the Lord was with him. . . . The child grew and became strong in spirit, and he was in the wilderness until the day he appeared publicly to Israel.

• Praise, amazement, and joy are hallmarks of a life rooted in you, Lord. Fill me with these gifts. Enable me to trace your grace in my life and to lift up my voice in joyful thanksgiving.

• Perhaps, with every child, God moves the world in a new direction. How do I stay open to the God of surprises, to the Spirit who moves at will? Is my comfort zone too well defended for me to be surprised by grace?

The Twelfth Week of Ordinary Time
June 25—July 1

Something to think and pray about each day this week:

The Act of Walking

Jesus is walking ahead of us. He is always before us. He goes ahead of us and leads the way. . . . This is the source of our confidence and our joy: to be his disciples, to remain with him, to walk behind him, to follow him. . . . [T]o walk is [. . .] an action, an action of Jesus that is ongoing: "Jesus was walking . . ." This is something striking about the Gospels: Jesus is often walking, and he teaches his disciples along the way. This is important. Jesus did not come to teach a philosophy, an ideology . . . but rather "a way," a journey to be undertaken with him, and we learn the way as we go, by walking. Yes, [. . .] this is our joy: to walk with Jesus. And this is not easy, or comfortable, because the way Jesus chooses is the way of the cross. As they journey together, he speaks to his disciples about what will happen in Jerusalem: he foretells his passion, death, and resurrection. And they are "shocked" and "full of fear." They were shocked, certainly, because for them going up to Jerusalem meant sharing in the triumph of the Messiah, in his victory—we see this in the request made by James and John [to sit on either side of him in his kingdom]. But they were also full of fear for what was about to happen to Jesus, and for what they themselves might have to endure. Unlike the disciples in those days, we know that Jesus has won, and that we need not fear the cross; indeed, the cross is our hope.

—Pope Francis, *Walking with Jesus*

The Presence of God
I pause for a moment and think of the love and the grace that God showers on me: I am created in the image and likeness of God; I am God's dwelling place.

Freedom
Lord, you created me to live in freedom. May your Holy Spirit guide me to follow you freely. Instill in my heart a desire to know and love you more each day.

Consciousness
How am I really feeling? Lighthearted? Heavyhearted? I may be very much at peace, happy to be here.
Equally, I may be frustrated, worried, or angry.
I acknowledge how I really am. It is the real me that the Lord loves.

The Word
I read the word of God slowly, a few times over, and I listen to what God is saying to me. (Please turn to the Scripture on the following pages. Inspiration points are there should you need them. When you are ready, return here to continue.)

Conversation
I know with certainty there were times when you carried me, Lord. When it was through your strength I got through the dark times in my life.

Conclusion
I thank God for these moments we have spent together and for any insights I have been given concerning the text.

Sunday 25th June
Twelfth Sunday in Ordinary Time
Matthew 10:26–33

Jesus said to the disciples, "So have no fear of them; for nothing is covered up that will not be uncovered, and nothing secret that will not become known. What I say to you in the dark, tell in the light; and what you hear whispered, proclaim from the housetops. Do not fear those who kill the body but cannot kill the soul; rather fear him who can destroy both soul and body in hell. Are not two sparrows sold for a penny? Yet not one of them will fall to the ground unperceived by your Father. And even the hairs of your head are all counted. So do not be afraid; you are of more value than many sparrows. Everyone therefore who acknowledges me before others, I also will acknowledge before my Father in heaven; but whoever denies me before others, I also will deny before my Father in heaven."

- Father God, you have created me in your image and likeness; every hair on my head you have counted. You know all my concerns and accompany me on all life's journeys. Help me sense your presence and resist fearfulness.

- For the Christian, the role model is Jesus Christ, who reveals to us what God is like. Lord Jesus, may I prove to be a true disciple of yours by listening attentively to your word and by caring for the poor, the weak, and the needy.

Monday 26th June
Matthew 7:1–5

Jesus said to the crowds, "Do not judge, so that you may not be judged. For with the judgment you make you will be judged, and the measure you give will be the measure you get. Why do you see the speck in your neighbor's eye, but do not notice the log in your own eye? Or how can you say to your neighbor, 'Let me take the speck out of your eye,' while the log is in your own eye? You hypocrite, first take the log out of your own eye, and then you will see clearly to take the speck out of your neighbor's eye."

- Becoming obsessed with a small failing in another person can distract us from being aware of a much greater shortcoming in ourselves. Pray for an enlightened self-knowledge and a nonjudgmental attitude (generosity of spirit) towards others.

- Our relationship to God, which we share with everyone, can be an entry into the world of love in which all, even those we find hard to relate to, are loved by God. As I ask God to look upon me lovingly and to judge me favorably, I try to do the same for others. I pray for forgiveness and ask God's help to be more forgiving myself.

Tuesday 27th June
Matthew 7:6, 12–14

Jesus said to the crowds, "Do not give what is holy to dogs; and do not throw your pearls before swine, or they will trample them under foot and turn and maul you. In everything do to others as you would have them do to you; for this is the law and the prophets. Enter through the narrow gate; for the gate is wide and the road is easy that leads to destruction, and there are many who take it. For the gate is narrow and the road is hard that leads to life, and there are few who find it."

- It is easy to drift, to follow the broad and easy route, but that does not lead to life. Jesus is the way to life, and he is the entry point. "Very truly, I tell you, I am the gate for the sheep . . . Whoever enters by me will be saved and will come in and go out and find pasture" (John 10:7–9). Lord, help me to be a good follower of you.

- "Pearls before swine"—the phrase seems harsh, yet it reflects life experience. All communication must be geared to the listener's ability to take it in. Good news may not make sense to listeners whose world is far removed from such messages.

Wednesday 28th June
Matthew 7:15–20

Jesus told the crowds, "Beware of false prophets, who come to you in sheep's clothing but inwardly are ravenous wolves. You will know them by their fruits. Are grapes gathered from thorns, or figs from thistles? In the same way, every good tree bears good fruit, but the bad tree bears bad fruit. A good tree cannot bear bad fruit, nor can a bad tree bear good fruit. Every tree that does not bear good fruit is cut down and thrown into the fire. Thus you will know them by their fruits."

- Jesus has extraordinary clarity about what can be going on in the human heart. I can often see the bad spirit working in the heart of another, but what about my own heart? I imagine myself as a fruit tree. What sort will it be? Lord, let me bear good fruit at harvesttime!

- As I turn away from false prophets and seek guidance of those who may truly help me, I ask the Spirit for guidance. I think of the fruits I have prayed for in the past or pray for now. I ask God to help me appreciate where these fruits may be budding, present, or already given away.

Thursday 29th June
Saints Peter and Paul, Apostles
Matthew 16:13–19

Now when Jesus came into the district of Caesarea Philippi, he asked his disciples, "Who do people say that the Son of Man is?" And they said, "Some say John the Baptist, but others Elijah, and still others Jeremiah or one of the prophets." He said to them, "But who do you say that I am?" Simon Peter answered, "You are the Messiah, the Son of the living God." And Jesus answered him, "Blessed are you, Simon son of Jonah! For flesh and blood has not revealed this to you, but my Father in heaven. And I tell you, you are Peter, and on this rock I will build my church, and the gates of Hades will not prevail against it. I will give you the keys of the kingdom of heaven, and whatever you bind on earth will be bound in heaven, and whatever you loose on earth will be loosed in heaven."

- Let me imagine myself in that setting, under the cliff face in Caesarea Philippi, as Jesus asks his momentous question: "Who do you say that I am?" Suddenly the dimensions of his mission expand. He is handing over to us (the ecclesia, or people of God) the task of continuing his mission.

- Jesus' personal question brought the discussion about him to a new level, like the movement from what do you want? (John 1:38) to whom do you want? (John 18:4). Peter responded in a personal way, seeing Jesus as Messiah and the Son of the living God. Time spent with Jesus forms our understanding of him.

Friday 30th June
Matthew 8:1–4

When Jesus had come down from the mountain, great crowds followed him; and there was a leper who came to him and knelt before him, saying, "Lord, if you choose, you can make me clean." He stretched out his hand and touched him, saying, "I do choose. Be made clean!" Immediately his leprosy was cleansed. Then Jesus said to him, "See that you say nothing to anyone; but go, show yourself to the priest, and offer the gift that Moses commanded, as a testimony to them."

- Note that leprosy (an unspecified skin disease) isolated the sufferer from contact with other Jews. So Jesus' healing of the leper enabled him to rejoin the Jewish community. When has Jesus' healing of you restored you to community?

- Lord, let me taste the drama of this eager leper. He was breaking the law, which forbade him to come closer than fifty feet to a non-leper or to exchange greetings with others. When this man's faith broke through legal limitations, Jesus not only spoke with him but also touched him. Jesus cannot bear to see us isolated.

Saturday 1st July
Matthew 8:5–17

When Jesus entered Capernaum, a centurion came to him, appealing to him and saying, "Lord, my servant is lying at home paralyzed, in terrible distress." And he said to him, "I will come and cure him." The centurion answered, "Lord, I am not worthy to have you come under my roof; but only speak the word, and my servant will be healed. For I also am a man under authority, with soldiers under me; and I say to one, 'Go,' and he goes, and to another, 'Come,' and he comes, and to my slave, 'Do this,' and the slave does it." When Jesus heard him, he was amazed and said to those who followed him, "Truly I tell you, in no one in Israel have I found such faith. I tell you, many will come from east and west and will eat with Abraham and Isaac and Jacob in the kingdom of heaven, while the heirs of the kingdom will be thrown into the outer darkness, where there will be weeping and gnashing of teeth." And to the centurion Jesus said, "Go; let it be done for you according to your faith." And the servant was healed in that hour. When Jesus entered Peter's house, he saw his mother-in-law lying in bed with a fever; he touched her hand, and the fever left her, and she got up and began to serve him. That evening they brought to him many who were possessed with demons; and he cast out the spirits with a word, and cured all who were sick. This was to fulfill what had been spoken through the prophet Isaiah, "He took our infirmities and bore our diseases."

- Can we capture the attitude of the centurion, a Roman officer, commander in an occupying force, who with the utmost politeness asks this Jewish teacher for help? His sensitivity (he felt an observant Jew might be reluctant to enter the house of a Gentile) and humility so astonished early Christians that they incorporated his words into the liturgy of the Eucharist: *Lord, I am not worthy to receive you under my roof.*

- Lord, I can receive you in Holy Communion day by day. May I welcome you with the same reverence as the Roman centurion, and with the same expectation that you will bring healing.

The Thirteenth Week of Ordinary Time
July 2—July 8

Something to think and pray about each day this week:

The Way to Life

It is always a joyful experience for us to read and reflect on the Beatitudes! Jesus proclaimed them in his first great sermon, preached on the shore of the Sea of Galilee. There was a very large crowd, so Jesus went up on the mountain to teach his disciples. That is why it is known as "the Sermon on the Mount." In the Bible, the mountain is regarded as a place where God reveals himself. Jesus, by preaching on the mount, reveals himself to be a divine teacher, a new Moses. What does he tell us? He shows us the way to life, the way that he himself has taken. Jesus himself *is* the way, and he proposes this way as *the path to true happiness*. Throughout his life, from his birth in the stable in Bethlehem until his death on the cross and his resurrection, Jesus embodied the Beatitudes. All the promises of God's kingdom were fulfilled in him. In proclaiming the Beatitudes, Jesus asks us to follow him and to travel with him along the path of love, the path that alone leads to eternal life. It is not an easy journey, yet the Lord promises us his grace, and he never abandons us. We face so many challenges in life: poverty, distress, humiliation, the struggle for justice, persecutions, the difficulty of daily conversion, the effort to remain faithful to our call to holiness, and many others. But if we open the door to Jesus and allow him to be part of our lives, if we share our joys and sorrows with him, then we will experience the peace and joy that only God, who is infinite love, can give.

—Pope Francis, *Walking with Jesus*

The Presence of God
Jesus, help me to be fully alive to your Holy Presence. Enfold me in your love. Let my heart become one with yours.

Freedom
I will ask God's help,
to be free from my own preoccupations,
to be open to God in this time of prayer,
to come to know, love, and serve God more.

Consciousness
I ask how I am within myself today? Am I particularly tired, stressed, or off form? If any of these characteristics apply, can I try to let go of the concerns that disturb me?

The Word
God speaks to each of us individually. I listen attentively to hear what God is saying to me. Read the text a few times, then listen. (Please turn to the Scripture on the following pages. Inspiration points are there should you need them. When you are ready, return here to continue.)

Conversation
Sometimes I wonder what I might say if I were to meet you in person, Lord.
I think I might say, Thank you, Lord, for always being there for me.

Conclusion
Glory be to the Father, and to the Son, and to the Holy Spirit,
As it was in the beginning, is now and ever shall be,
World without end. Amen.

Sunday 2nd July
Thirteenth Sunday in Ordinary Time
Matthew 10:37–42

Jesus said to his disciples, "Whoever loves father or mother more than me is not worthy of me; and whoever loves son or daughter more than me is not worthy of me; and whoever does not take up the cross and follow me is not worthy of me. Those who find their life will lose it, and those who lose their life for my sake will find it. Whoever welcomes you welcomes me, and whoever welcomes me welcomes the one who sent me. Whoever welcomes a prophet in the name of a prophet will receive a prophet's reward; and whoever welcomes a righteous person in the name of a righteous person will receive the reward of the righteous; and whoever gives even a cup of cold water to one of these little ones in the name of a disciple—truly I tell you, none of these will lose their reward."

- Jesus acknowledges virtue in a person who welcomes righteousness. He recognizes support even in people who are not well acquainted with him yet. I hope to have this generous spirit toward others.

- We can grasp at life or hold it lightly. Grasping just makes us anxious and greedy; holding life lightly builds up our trust and hope.

Monday 3rd July
John 20:24–29

But Thomas (who was called the Twin), one of the twelve, was not with them when Jesus came. So the other disciples told him, "We have seen the Lord." But he said to them, "Unless I see the mark of the nails in his hands, and put my finger in the mark of the nails and my hand in his side, I will not believe." A week later his disciples were again in the house, and Thomas was with them. Although the doors were shut, Jesus came and stood among them and said, "Peace be with you." Then he said to Thomas, "Put your finger here and see my hands. Reach out your hand and put it in my side. Do not doubt but believe." Thomas answered him, "My Lord and my God!" Jesus said to him, "Have you believed because you have seen me? Blessed are those who have not seen and yet have come to believe."

- We might well be grateful to Thomas for expressing and representing some of our own doubts. Jesus rebukes Thomas for his lack of faith but does not dismiss him. In fact, the encounter becomes an occasion for a profound and personal profession of faith by Thomas: "My Lord and my God!" Jesus can bring something good from my doubts.

- People sometimes worry when they question the church's teaching, but it is healthy to examine what we believe in order to come to an adult understanding of our faith. Believers are to be thinkers, and doubting can be an honest step in our struggle to believe.

Tuesday 4th July
Matthew 8:23–27

And when Jesus got into the boat, his disciples followed him. A windstorm arose on the sea, so great that the boat was being swamped by the waves; but he was asleep. And they went and woke him up, saying, "Lord, save us! We are perishing!" And he said to them, "Why are you afraid, you of little faith?" Then he got up and rebuked the winds and the sea; and there was a dead calm. They were amazed, saying, "What sort of man is this, that even the winds and the sea obey him?"

- In this story we can experience the drama, fear, relief. Does being in the boat with a sleeping Jesus resonate in any way with situations in my own life? Have there been times of turbulence when Jesus (God) seemed uninterested, uncaring? If so, was my faith weakened or strengthened by having this experience?

- We may feel that Jesus is asleep, not near us. He woke at the moment he was really needed and calmed the waters. In prayer he calms us, too, maybe not immediately but he does stretch out his hand to us when we face anxiety, darkness, and despair. The Lord of wind and sea, the one in whom all was created, can create calm and confidence in every part of life.

Wednesday 5th July
Matthew 8:28–34

When Jesus came to the other side, to the country of the Gadarenes, two demoniacs coming out of the tombs met him. They were so fierce that no one could pass that way. Suddenly they shouted, "What have you to do

with us, Son of God? Have you come here to torment us before the time?"
Now a large herd of swine was feeding at some distance from them. The
demons begged him, "If you cast us out, send us into the herd of swine."
And he said to them, "Go!" So they came out and entered the swine;
and suddenly, the whole herd rushed down the steep bank into the lake
and perished in the water. The swineherds ran off, and on going into the
town, they told the whole story about what had happened to the demoniacs. Then the whole town came out to meet Jesus; and when they saw
him, they begged him to leave their neighborhood.

• Lord, with you close beside me, I need not fear the forces of darkness
  in the world. You deliver me from all evil and do everything to ensure
  that goodness triumphs. Help me trust your divine power and become
  attentive to the ways you communicate the message of light.

• The real sign here is not the stampede of pigs but Jesus' power over
  evil. Because the townspeople cannot cope with divine power, they ask
  Jesus to leave. But he has won a fundamental victory over evil and has
  established the reign of God. So we can pray "Thy kingdom come"
  and "Deliver us from evil" with complete confidence.

Thursday 6th July
Matthew 9:1–8

And after getting into a boat he crossed the sea and came to his own
town. And just then some people were carrying a paralyzed man lying
on a bed. When Jesus saw their faith, he said to the paralytic, "Take
heart, son; your sins are forgiven." Then some of the scribes said to themselves, "This man is blaspheming." But Jesus, perceiving their thoughts,
said, "Why do you think evil in your hearts? For which is easier, to say,
'Your sins are forgiven,' or to say, 'Stand up and walk'? But so that you
may know that the Son of Man has authority on earth to forgive sins—"
he then said to the paralytic—"Stand up, take your bed and go to your
home." And he stood up and went to his home. When the crowds saw it,
they were filled with awe, and they glorified God, who had given such
authority to human beings.

• The healing of the paralyzed man shows the power of Jesus to forgive
  sins. Jesus wants to renew every person with the gift of his healing

grace just as he did for the paralytic. I can bring to Jesus the areas of my life that need healing.

- Here are two things that sometimes bother me, Lord: a conscience that accuses me and a paralytic weariness that keeps me from doing what I should. When you saw the paralytic laid before you, you looked first to his peace of soul. So much joy is hidden in those words: *Take heart; your sins are forgiven.* When I know I am OK with God, I find the energy and strength to get on my feet and walk. Touch me in the same way, Lord.

Friday 7th July
Matthew 9:9–13

As Jesus was walking along, he saw a man called Matthew sitting at the tax booth; and he said to him, "Follow me." And he got up and followed him. And as he sat at dinner in the house, many tax collectors and sinners came and were sitting with him and his disciples. When the Pharisees saw this, they said to his disciples, "Why does your teacher eat with tax collectors and sinners?" But when he heard this, he said, "Those who are well have no need of a physician, but those who are sick. Go and learn what this means, 'I desire mercy, not sacrifice.' For I have come to call not the righteous but sinners."

- Matthew the tax collector serves a system that encourages greed and exploits the poor. The Jews regard tax collectors as wicked people who violate God's law. Yet when Matthew gets up to follow Jesus, he pledges solemnly to be kind and just in his dealings. There is hope for us all! We can be converted as he was.

- No matter how I see myself, Jesus sees me as a friend. Matthew throws a big party and invites all those rejected by the religious establishment. Jesus enjoys sharing meals; he never says, "I won't sit down with that person!" Here we have a model of the Eucharist: communion with Christ and with one another—and no one on the "unwanted" list.

Saturday 8th July
Matthew 9:14–17

The disciples of John came to Jesus, saying, "Why do we and the Pharisees fast often, but your disciples do not fast?" And Jesus said to them, "The wedding guests cannot mourn as long as the bridegroom is with them, can they? The days will come when the bridegroom is taken away from them, and then they will fast. No one sews a piece of unshrunk cloth on an old cloak, for the patch pulls away from the cloak, and a worse tear is made. Neither is new wine put into old wineskins; otherwise, the skins burst, and the wine is spilled, and the skins are destroyed; but new wine is put into fresh wineskins, and so both are preserved."

• Using the example of wineskins, Jesus indicates how the existing Jewish traditions could be enhanced in light of his preaching about the kingdom of God. Jesus, may I more readily see the ways through which your teaching offers me new life.

• Jesus uses wedding imagery to let us know how intimate his relationship is with us. It's a time to be joyful. The bridegroom's absence will be brief—Jesus will die—but he will return to be close to us always, bringing love, joy, and peace. Lord, help me respond joyously to your friendship with me.

The Fourteenth Week of Ordinary Time
July 9—July 15

Something to think and pray about each day this week:

The How of God's Revelation

I suspect that more often than I want to admit, I walk through my day too busy harrumphing about this and that, too careful of what I look at, to let myself be surprised by God in unexpected places. Like the morning I put a cup of tea on the counter to steep and ran down to throw a load of wash in the dryer. Fifteen minutes later the tea was forgotten, oversteeped and bitter. I resigned myself to facing the morning traffic without caffeine. But when I went to fish my keys from the bin on the counter, there was a perfectly steaming cup of tea in a travel mug waiting for me. Made by a child who'd never tried to make tea before. I still delight in this small miracle of infused knowledge, seeing in my mind's eye God standing at the kitchen door, an amused look on His face, holding out a cup of tea, handle first, as I dash by. "You want to try it; trust me." For all that I hope to seek and know "God in all things," for all that I profess God immanent and invincible—the *how* of God's revelation in my life continually surprises me with its gentle humor and unassuming immediacy. At every time and in every place, God will do anything to draw close to us.

—Michelle Francl-Donnay on *dotMagis*,
the blog of IgnatianSpirituality.com

The Presence of God

"I stand at the door and knock," says the Lord. What a wonderful privilege that the Lord of all creation desires to come to me. I welcome his presence.

Freedom

Saint Ignatius thought that a thick and shapeless tree trunk would never believe that it could become a statue, admired as a miracle of sculpture, and would never submit itself to the chisel of the sculptor, who sees by her genius what she can make of it.
I ask for the grace to let myself be shaped by my loving Creator.

Consciousness

Knowing that God loves me unconditionally, I can afford to be honest about how I am. What are my fears and desires? What do I expect from God? What am I willing to give to God—from my emotions and talents, thoughts and energy? And how do I feel now? I share my feelings openly with the Lord.

The Word

I take my time to read the word of God, slowly, a few times, allowing myself to dwell on anything that strikes me. (Please turn to the Scripture on the following pages. Inspiration points are there should you need them. When you are ready, return here to continue.)

Conversation

Do I notice myself reacting as I pray with the word of God? Do I feel challenged, comforted, angry? Imagining Jesus sitting or standing by me, I speak out my feelings, as one trusted friend to another.

Conclusion

I thank God for these moments we have spent together and for any insights I have been given concerning the text.

Sunday 9th July
Fourteenth Sunday in Ordinary Time
Matthew 11:25–30

At that time Jesus said, "I thank you, Father, Lord of heaven and earth, because you have hidden these things from the wise and the intelligent and have revealed them to infants; yes, Father, for such was your gracious will. All things have been handed over to me by my Father; and no one knows the Son except the Father, and no one knows the Father except the Son and anyone to whom the Son chooses to reveal him. Come to me, all you that are weary and are carrying heavy burdens, and I will give you rest. Take my yoke upon you, and learn from me; for I am gentle and humble in heart, and you will find rest for your souls. For my yoke is easy, and my burden is light."

• Jesus is inviting those who are not in the comfort zone, who feel oppressed by anxiety and uncertainty. Lord, I do not ask that you bring my life completely under control; to be mortal is to face uncomfortable realities. I beg you to be my uncomfortable comfort zone.

• In this passage of Scripture, Jesus offers us a lifeline. "Come to me . . ." he says. Sounds simple, doesn't it? And yet we find it difficult to believe that reaching out to Jesus can make a difference. Lord, you invite us to take your hand and walk with you; how stubborn we can be sometimes. Help us receive your whispered invitation and respond with faith.

Monday 10th July
Matthew 9:18–26

While Jesus was saying these things to them, suddenly a leader of the synagogue came in and knelt before him, saying, "My daughter has just died; but come and lay your hand on her, and she will live." And Jesus got up and followed him, with his disciples. Then suddenly a woman who had been suffering from hemorrhages for twelve years came up behind him and touched the fringe of his cloak, for she said to herself, "If I only touch his cloak, I will be made well." Jesus turned, and seeing her he said, "Take heart, daughter; your faith has made you well." And instantly the woman was made well. When Jesus came to the leader's house and saw the flute players and the crowd making a commotion, he said, "Go away;

for the girl is not dead but sleeping." And they laughed at him. But when the crowd had been put outside, he went in and took her by the hand, and the girl got up. And the report of this spread throughout that district.

- Jesus heals the woman with the hemorrhages because her reaching out to touch the hem of his garment is the supreme act of faith. There is no limit to the healing and renewal Jesus can accomplish in my life. Do I believe that he can heal me?

- Jesus is open to the needs of a child, to the prayer of a humble woman. I lower my gaze and become humbler to see if I might see what Jesus sees. Help me, Lord, not to seek many great things but to pay attention to what is really important.

Tuesday 11th July
Matthew 9:32–38

A demoniac who was mute was brought to him. And when the demon had been cast out, the one who had been mute spoke; and the crowds were amazed and said, "Never has anything like this been seen in Israel." But the Pharisees said, "By the ruler of the demons he casts out the demons." Then Jesus went about all the cities and villages, teaching in their synagogues, and proclaiming the good news of the kingdom, and curing every disease and every sickness. When he saw the crowds, he had compassion for them, because they were harassed and helpless, like sheep without a shepherd. Then he said to his disciples, "The harvest is plentiful, but the laborers are few; therefore ask the Lord of the harvest to send out laborers into his harvest."

- Jesus saw people searching for meaning, for the truth he spoke. He knows that sometimes we look in the wrong places for meaning. We look for fullness and get caught in superficiality. We look for faith and hope and get caught in trivialities.

- Jesus cured every disease and sickness. I bring all aspects of my life to prayer, knowing that God wants to bring healing. I may recall times when I have been too busy or stressed. I picture Jesus looking with compassion on me then, keeping alive in his heart God's desire for me that I have lost sight of. I linger in Jesus' compassionate gaze.

Wednesday 12th July
Matthew 10:1–7

Jesus summoned his twelve disciples and gave them authority over unclean spirits, to cast them out, and to cure every disease and every sickness. These are the names of the twelve apostles: first, Simon, also known as Peter, and his brother Andrew; James son of Zebedee, and his brother John; Philip and Bartholomew; Thomas and Matthew the tax collector; James son of Alphaeus, and Thaddaeus; Simon the Cananaean, and Judas Iscariot, the one who betrayed him. These twelve Jesus sent out with the following instructions: "Go nowhere among the Gentiles, and enter no town of the Samaritans, but go rather to the lost sheep of the house of Israel. As you go, proclaim the good news, 'The kingdom of heaven has come near.'"

- Jesus sends out his disciples with the clear instruction to "proclaim the good news" of the kingdom of heaven. He sends them on a mission of teaching and healing to proclaim the message of God's saving love to those who are in most need of hearing it. Help me, Lord, to understand how my faith can have a missionary dimension.

- How can I bring this reign of God alive in today's world? In places where evil can easily reign, God's reign arrives through people such as the apostles—and me. I pray that I may accept the trust Jesus places in me.

Thursday 13th July
Matthew 10:7–15

Jesus said to his disciples, "As you go, proclaim the good news, 'The kingdom of heaven has come near.' Cure the sick, raise the dead, cleanse the lepers, cast out demons. You received without payment; give without payment. Take no gold, or silver, or copper in your belts, no bag for your journey, or two tunics, or sandals, or a staff; for laborers deserve their food. Whatever town or village you enter, find out who in it is worthy, and stay there until you leave. As you enter the house, greet it. If the house is worthy, let your peace come upon it; but if it is not worthy, let your peace return to you. If anyone will not welcome you or listen to your words, shake off the dust from your feet as you leave that house or town. Truly I tell you, it will be more tolerable for the land of Sodom and Gomorrah on the day of judgment than for that town.

- Jesus imparts a radical message to his disciples as he sends them out on mission. They are to cast out demons and cleanse lepers just as he did. They must take nothing for the journey, not even spare shoes and clothing. This is a rallying call by Jesus to his closest followers to trust completely in the providence and love of God.

- Lord, I pray that I may cling less to material things and more to your providential presence, which is alive and active in every moment of my day and every decision I make. Help me place all my hope and trust in you—for your love and generosity are never outdone.

Friday 14th July
Matthew 10:16–23

Jesus said to the twelve, "See, I am sending you out like sheep into the midst of wolves; so be wise as serpents and innocent as doves. Beware of them, for they will hand you over to councils and flog you in their synagogues; and you will be dragged before governors and kings because of me, as a testimony to them and the Gentiles. When they hand you over, do not worry about how you are to speak or what you are to say; for what you are to say will be given to you at that time; for it is not you who speak, but the Spirit of your Father speaking through you. Brother will betray brother to death, and a father his child, and children will rise against parents and have them put to death; and you will be hated by all because of my name. But the one who endures to the end will be saved. When they persecute you in one town, flee to the next; for truly I tell you, you will not have gone through all the towns of Israel before the Son of Man comes."

- Lord, send forth your Holy Spirit when I feel weighed down by struggles and persecutions. Help me trust in the power of your Spirit, the very life of God within me that guides me into the ways of truth and love.

- Lord, you do not try to seduce us, as advertisers do, with promises of pleasure and success. If we are true to you, we will meet opposition and worse. Freedom from criticism belongs only to the bland and spineless, those who say and do nothing and keep their heads low.

Saturday 15th July
Matthew 10:24–33

Jesus said to the twelve, "A disciple is not above the teacher, nor a slave above the master; it is enough for the disciple to be like the teacher, and the slave like the master. If they have called the master of the house Beelzebul, how much more will they malign those of his household! So have no fear of them; for nothing is covered up that will not be uncovered, and nothing secret that will not become known. What I say to you in the dark, tell in the light; and what you hear whispered, proclaim from the housetops. Do not fear those who kill the body but cannot kill the soul; rather fear him who can destroy both soul and body in hell. Are not two sparrows sold for a penny? Yet not one of them will fall to the ground unperceived by your Father. And even the hairs of your head are all counted. So do not be afraid; you are of more value than many sparrows. Everyone therefore who acknowledges me before others, I also will acknowledge before my Father in heaven; but whoever denies me before others, I also will deny before my Father in heaven."

- The attentive care of God the Father extends even to the sparrows, and we are of more value than many sparrows. Father God, you have created me in your image and likeness; every hair on my head you have counted. You know all my concerns and accompany me on all life's journeys. Help my awareness of your supporting presence.

- The underlying message of these various sayings of Jesus is encouragement. When events go against us, we are to remain confident, trusting in God's care. We are not to be deterred in the face of opposition. We read here of God's sovereignty over all creation. So whatever happens, I am not to be afraid. All will be well for me.

The Fifteenth Week of Ordinary Time
July 16—July 22

Something to think and pray about each day this week:

Listen and Feel

Every human experience has a religious dimension. All of life is suffused with God's presence. So remind yourself that God is present as you begin your period of prayer. Do not worry about distractions. If something keeps intruding during your prayer, spend some time talking with God about it. Be flexible, because God's Spirit blows where it will. Prayer can open your mind and widen your vision. Be open to new ways of seeing God, people, and yourself. As you open yourself to the Spirit of God, different emotions might be evoked, such as sadness from tender memories or joy from a celebration recalled. Our emotions are messages from God that can tell us much about our spiritual quest. Also, prayer strengthens our will to act. Through prayer, God can touch our will and empower us to live according to what we know is true. The great mystics and saints realized that they had to use all their resources to know God better. Indeed, God speaks to us continually and touches us constantly. We must learn to listen and feel with all the means that God has given us. Come to prayer with an open mind, heart, and will.

—Jacqueline Bergan and Marie Schwan, CSJ,
Praying with Ignatius of Loyola

The Presence of God

To be present is to arrive as one is and open up to the other.
At this instant, as I arrive here, God is present waiting for me.
God always arrives before me, desiring to connect with me
even more than my most intimate friend.
I take a moment and greet my loving God.

Freedom

I am free. When I look at these words in writing, they seem to create in me a feeling of awe. Yes, a wonderful feeling of freedom. Thank you, God.

Consciousness

To be conscious about something is to be aware of it.
Dear Lord, help me to remember that you gave me life.
Thank you for the gift of life.
Teach me to slow down, to be still and enjoy the pleasures created for me.
To be aware of the beauty that surrounds me. The marvel of mountains, the calmness of lakes, the fragility of a flower petal. I need to remember that all these things come from you.

The Word

The word of God comes to us through the Scriptures. May the Holy Spirit enlighten my mind and heart to respond to the Gospel teachings. (Please turn to the Scripture on the following pages. Inspiration points are there should you need them. When you are ready, return here to continue.)

Conversation

I begin to talk to Jesus about the piece of Scripture I have just read. What part of it strikes a chord in me? Perhaps the words of a friend—or some story I have heard recently—will slowly rise to the surface in my consciousness. If so, does the story throw light on what the Scripture passage may be trying to say to me?

Conclusion

Glory be to the Father, and to the Son, and to the Holy Spirit,
As it was in the beginning, is now and ever shall be,
World without end. Amen.

Sunday 16th July
Fifteenth Sunday in Ordinary Time
Matthew 13:1–9

Jesus went out of the house and sat beside the lake. Such great crowds gathered around him that he got into a boat and sat there, while the whole crowd stood on the beach. And he told them many things in parables, saying: "Listen! A sower went out to sow. And as he sowed, some seeds fell on the path, and the birds came and ate them up. Other seeds fell on rocky ground, where they did not have much soil, and they sprang up quickly, since they had no depth of soil. But when the sun rose, they were scorched; and since they had no root, they withered away. Other seeds fell among thorns, and the thorns grew up and choked them. Other seeds fell on good soil and brought forth grain, some a hundredfold, some sixty, some thirty. Let anyone with ears listen!"

- The different kinds of ground on which the seed falls represent the different ways in which we receive God's word. The degree of receptivity depends on the individual and the particular circumstances of his or her life. The parable provides hope and encouragement, in that the sower succeeds ultimately in producing a crop from the seed that fell on good soil.

- Such crowds gathered to see and hear Jesus that he had to preach from a boat. They were hungry for spiritual nourishment and for leadership. Lord Jesus, I pray for the church and for all believers today. Make of us a community of disciples, all seeking you.

Monday 17th July
Matthew 10:34—11:1

Jesus said, "Do not think that I have come to bring peace to the earth; I have not come to bring peace, but a sword. For I have come to set a man against his father, and a daughter against her mother, and a daughter-in-law against her mother-in-law; and one's foes will be members of one's own household. Whoever loves father or mother more than me is not worthy of me; and whoever loves son or daughter more than me is not worthy of me; and whoever does not take up the cross and follow me is not worthy of me. Those who find their life will lose it, and those who lose their life for my sake will find it. Whoever welcomes you welcomes me, and whoever welcomes me welcomes the one who sent me. Whoever welcomes a prophet in the name of a prophet will receive a prophet's reward; and whoever welcomes a righteous person in the name of a righteous person will receive the reward of the righteous; and whoever gives even a cup of cold water to one of these little ones in the name of a disciple—truly I tell you, none of these will lose their reward." Now when Jesus had finished instructing his twelve disciples, he went on from there to teach and proclaim his message in their cities.

• I pray that Jesus will give me the courage I need to stand with him despite losing things I hold dear. While Jesus warns us about the cost of discipleship, he also promises that even the small efforts we make in following him will have their reward. He knows my weakness, so he asks me to take baby steps—even to give a cup of water to someone.

• Isn't it strange that we save our life by losing it? It's only when energies go into the good of others, rather than just for our own good, that we can preserve and enhance our life.

Tuesday 18th July
Matthew 11:20–24

Then Jesus began to reproach the cities in which most of his deeds of power had been done, because they did not repent. "Woe to you, Chorazin! Woe to you, Bethsaida! For if the deeds of power done in you had been done in Tyre and Sidon, they would have repented long ago in sackcloth and ashes. But I tell you, on the day of judgment it will be more tolerable for Tyre and Sidon than for you. And you, Capernaum, will you be exalted to heaven? No, you will be brought down to Hades. For if the deeds of power done in you had been done in Sodom, it would have remained until this day. But I tell you that on the day of judgment it will be more tolerable for the land of Sodom than for you."

• Jesus taught about the kingdom of God and proclaimed a message of healing and conversion, but his teaching and powerful deeds were not always accepted. Can I identify ways in which Jesus' teaching is actively having an effect in my life?

• Cities have always flattered themselves! It is easy to be proud of being first, biggest, or best. All this counts for little in Jesus' scale of things. Jesus rebukes the people of Chorazin, Bethsaida, and Capernaum for not being open to the fruits of his mission and thus missing what God offers them.

Wednesday 19th July
Matthew 11:25–27

At that time Jesus said, "I thank you, Father, Lord of heaven and earth, because you have hidden these things from the wise and the intelligent and have revealed them to infants; yes, Father, for such was your gracious will. All things have been handed over to me by my Father; and no one knows the Son except the Father, and no one knows the Father except the Son and anyone to whom the Son chooses to reveal him."

- Jesus wants to show us the Father's love. He wants to bless us and reveal the Father's love as we draw closer to him. Can I open my heart more fully to receive the gift of God's love just like the simplicity of a little child longing for the loving embrace of a parent?

- A curtain is drawn back here to show the unique personal relationship between Jesus and his Father. The distinctive and intimate name "Abba, Father" appears five times here. This is the common domestic name in Aramaic (Jesus' native language) by which a child would call his/her natural father. For presuming this unique and intimate relationship, the scribes and Pharisees condemned Jesus to death on a cross. The Son has privileged access to the Father. It is not an exclusive or closed relationship, however, because Jesus invites others to participate in it. Lord Jesus, help each of us to experience that we, too, are truly beloved sons and daughters of our heavenly Father.

Thursday 20th July
Matthew 11:28–30

Jesus said, "Come to me, all you that are weary and are carrying heavy burdens, and I will give you rest. Take my yoke upon you, and learn from me; for I am gentle and humble in heart, and you will find rest for your souls. For my yoke is easy, and my burden is light."

- We can speak with Jesus as we would with any friend, sharing our joys, struggles, hopes, and fears. He never grows tired of listening to us and constantly renews us with the gift of his love. What do I want to share with him now in this time of prayer?

- The yoke was originally a term for Roman oppression of the Jews. People felt crushed by Rome's demands. Jesus promises that if I join him, he will not be oppressive. I ask to feel the lightness and energy that he offers me.

Friday 21st July
Matthew 12:1–8

At that time Jesus went through the grainfields on the Sabbath; his disciples were hungry, and they began to pluck heads of grain and to eat. When the Pharisees saw it, they said to him, "Look, your disciples are doing what is not lawful to do on the Sabbath." He said to them, "Have you not read what David did when he and his companions were hungry? He entered the house of God and ate the bread of the Presence, which it was not lawful for him or his companions to eat, but only for the priests. Or have you not read in the law that on the Sabbath the priests in the temple break the Sabbath and yet are guiltless? I tell you, something greater than the temple is here. But if you had known what this means, 'I desire mercy and not sacrifice,' you would not have condemned the guiltless. For the Son of Man is lord of the sabbath."

- The well-intentioned Pharisees could not stop themselves finding fault with others; paying careful attention to the details, they forgot the bigger picture. I look at life with the eye of Jesus, praying for a greater ability to understand and forgive the shortcomings of others—and my own.

- The Bible gave a simple command: to keep the Sabbath holy. The rabbis went on to classify 39 sorts of work that were not permitted on the Sabbath. Jesus draws them back to the simplicity of God's command. Lord, forgive my foolish judgments when I throw rules at people who in your eyes are doing what is innocent and natural.

Saturday 22nd July
Saint Mary Magdalene
John 20:1–2, 11–18

Early on the first day of the week, while it was still dark, Mary Magdalene came to the tomb and saw that the stone had been removed from the tomb. So she ran and went to Simon Peter and the other disciple, the one whom Jesus loved, and said to them, "They have taken the Lord out of the tomb, and we do not know where they have laid him." . . . But Mary stood weeping outside the tomb. As she wept, she bent over to look into the tomb; and she saw two angels in white, sitting where the body of Jesus had been lying, one at the head and the other at the feet. They said to her, "Woman, why are you weeping?" She said to them, "They have taken away my Lord, and I do not know where they have laid him." When she had said this, she turned around and saw Jesus standing there, but she did not know that it was Jesus. Jesus said to her, "Woman, why are you weeping? For whom are you looking?" Supposing him to be the gardener, she said to him, "Sir, if you have carried him away, tell me where you have laid him, and I will take him away." Jesus said to her, "Mary!" She turned and said to him in Hebrew, "Rabbouni!" (which means Teacher). Jesus said to her, "Do not hold on to me, because I have not yet ascended to the Father. But go to my brothers and say to them, 'I am ascending to my Father and your Father, to my God and your God.'" Mary Magdalene went and announced to the disciples, "I have seen the Lord"; and she told them that he had said these things to her.

- "Why are you weeping?" Jesus continues to ask these sorts of probing, caring questions. Today, why am I sad? What do I miss, or what worries me?

- How does the grace of the Resurrection affect me? I pray that I may welcome with joy the message of the risen Jesus, believing in the power of his presence in my life.

The Sixteenth Week of Ordinary Time
July 23—July 29

Something to think and pray about each day this week:

Past, Present, Future

While it's easy to think about the Examen as being oriented to the past, this prayer helps us to pay attention to where God is in the past, present, and future. The prayer begins with God in the present: God is with me, here and now as I pray. God is in the past, throughout the day that I have been reviewing. And I can trust that God will also be in my future and pray out of that sensibility. In this way, the Examen always ends with hope. Why should we hope, even in the midst of personal struggles and difficulties? Why not succumb to despair when we cannot see our own way out of pain and suffering? One great reason for hope for the future is recalling how God has been with us in the past. We cannot see into the future and know exactly how God will bring good out of difficulty. However, we can remember when and where God has brought good out of past suffering. This is the centerpiece of the Gospels and the heart of the Christian story: the transformation of the suffering and death of Jesus into the Resurrection and new life. It's also how God continues to act in our own lives.

—Marina McCoy on *dotMagis*, the blog of IgnatianSpirituality.com

The Presence of God

Be still and know that I am God. Lord, may your Spirit guide me to seek your loving presence more and more. For it is there I find rest and refreshment from this busy world.

Freedom

By God's grace I was born to live in freedom. Free to enjoy the pleasures he created for me. Dear Lord, grant that I may live as you intended, with complete confidence in your loving care.

Consciousness

In God's loving presence I unwind the past day,
starting from now and looking back, moment by moment.
I gather in all the goodness and light, in gratitude.
I attend to the shadows and what they say to me,
seeking healing, courage, forgiveness.

The Word

The word of God comes to us through the Scriptures. May the Holy Spirit enlighten my mind and heart to respond to the Gospel teachings. (Please turn to the Scripture on the following pages. Inspiration points are there should you need them. When you are ready, return here to continue.)

Conversation

Jesus, you always welcomed little children when you walked on this earth. Teach me to have a childlike trust in you. To live in the knowledge that you will never abandon me.

Conclusion

Glory be to the Father, and to the Son, and to the Holy Spirit,
As it was in the beginning, is now and ever shall be,
World without end. Amen.

Sunday 23rd July
Sixteenth Sunday in Ordinary Time
Matthew 13:24–30

Jesus put before them another parable: "The kingdom of heaven may be compared to someone who sowed good seed in his field; but while everybody was asleep, an enemy came and sowed weeds among the wheat, and then went away. So when the plants came up and bore grain, then the weeds appeared as well. And the slaves of the householder came and said to him, 'Master, did you not sow good seed in your field? Where, then, did these weeds come from?' He answered, 'An enemy has done this.' The slaves said to him, 'Then do you want us to go and gather them?' But he replied, 'No; for in gathering the weeds you would uproot the wheat along with them. Let both of them grow together until the harvest; and at harvest time I will tell the reapers, Collect the weeds first and bind them in bundles to be burned, but gather the wheat into my barn.'"

- The weeds are a species of wild wheat, sometimes known as "false wheat." Only at harvesttime can the farmer distinguish the real from the false. Jesus is saying that good and bad are mixed together in this world and indeed in each of us. We must be patient with others and with ourselves.

- Jesus does not condone or encourage what is not of God; yet he seems able to acknowledge that different motivations and spirits are at work. How might I let this spirit of Jesus shape my life? Perhaps I can look back on events in my life that seemed barren or weedy and see now that God was at work.

Monday 24th July
Matthew 12:38–42

Some of the scribes and Pharisees said to Jesus, "Teacher, we wish to see a sign from you." But he answered them, "An evil and adulterous generation asks for a sign, but no sign will be given to it except the sign of the prophet Jonah. For just as Jonah was three days and three nights in the belly of the sea monster, so for three days and three nights the Son of Man will be in the heart of the earth. The people of Nineveh will rise up at the judgment with this generation and condemn it, because they repented at the proclamation of Jonah, and see, something greater than Jonah is here! The queen of the South will rise up at the judgment with this generation and condemn it, because she came from the ends of the earth to listen to the wisdom of Solomon, and see, something greater than Solomon is here!"

- Signs from God sometimes seem desirable—and even reasonable to expect. Jesus reminds me that I may be looking in the wrong direction. I pray that I may see and appreciate where God is already at work in the events and relationships of my life.

- My prayer time can train the eye of my heart to recognize God at work. As I become more familiar with and trusting in God's Spirit, I need less proof and am able to rely on what I have learned. God trusts me. I learn to trust God's Spirit in me.

Tuesday 25th July
Matthew 20:20–28

The mother of the sons of Zebedee came to him with her sons, and kneeling before him, she asked a favor of him. And he said to her, "What do you want?" She said to him, "Declare that these two sons of mine will sit, one at your right hand and one at your left, in your kingdom." But Jesus answered, "You do not know what you are asking. Are you able to drink the cup that I am about to drink?" They said to him, "We are able." He said to them, "You will indeed drink my cup, but to sit at my right hand and at my left, this is not mine to grant, but it is for those for whom it has been prepared by my Father." When the ten heard it, they were angry with the two brothers. But Jesus called them to him and said, "You know that the rulers of the Gentiles lord it over them, and their great ones are tyrants over them. It will not be so among you; but whoever wishes to be great among you must be your servant, and whoever wishes to be first among you must be your slave; just as the Son of Man came not to be served but to serve, and to give his life a ransom for many."

- Jesus is sensitive; he defends the two brothers against the other apostles. Then he broadens everyone's perspective. "You all want to be great? Fine! You will indeed become great—by serving others." And so it was. In my prayer, I let him ask me about my quality of service. This is what measures my closeness to him.

- The honesty of this mother's approach enabled Jesus to answer her situation directly. I follow her example, speaking to Jesus clearly and frankly, listening for his clear and frank answer.

Wednesday 26th July
Matthew 13:1–9

That same day Jesus went out of the house and sat beside the lake. Such great crowds gathered around him that he got into a boat and sat there, while the whole crowd stood on the beach. And he told them many things in parables, saying: "Listen! A sower went out to sow. And as he sowed, some seeds fell on the path, and the birds came and ate them up. Other seeds fell on rocky ground, where they did not have much soil, and they sprang up quickly, since they had no depth of soil. But when the sun rose, they were scorched; and since they had no root, they withered away. Other seeds fell among thorns, and the thorns grew up and choked them. Other seeds fell on good soil and brought forth grain, some a hundredfold, some sixty, some thirty. Let anyone with ears listen!"

- Not all of Jesus' words bear fruit. Knowing this did not stop him from speaking; he continued to proclaim the good news, truth, and life to any who would listen. I pray for the strength to continue speaking and acting—even in the absence of evident encouraging results.

- Truth is not determined by a majority but is scattered abroad, being recognized and valued by some. I ask God to help me hear Jesus' word for me and take it to heart.

Thursday 27th July
Matthew 13:10–17

Then the disciples came and asked him, "Why do you speak to them in parables?" He answered, "To you it has been given to know the secrets of the kingdom of heaven, but to them it has not been given. For to those who have, more will be given, and they will have an abundance; but from those who have nothing, even what they have will be taken away. The reason I speak to them in parables is that seeing they do not perceive, and hearing they do not listen, nor do they understand. With them indeed is fulfilled the prophecy of Isaiah that says:

'You will indeed listen, but never understand,
and you will indeed look, but never perceive.
For this people's heart has grown dull,
and their ears are hard of hearing,
and they have shut their eyes;
so that they might not look with their eyes,
and listen with their ears,
and understand with their heart and turn—
and I would heal them.'

But blessed are your eyes, for they see, and your ears, for they hear. Truly I tell you, many prophets and righteous people longed to see what you see, but did not see it, and to hear what you hear, but did not hear it."

- Some people find faith easy; others find it impossible. I thank Jesus that I do see and hear. I ask to cultivate this gift by becoming more open to God in my prayer.

- The events of Jesus' ministry seem to go over the heads of some by-standers. Parables will highlight some of the truths of life and of God, and people who may miss the obvious will get the message. Every story Jesus tells will throw some light on God, the world, and the self. These clues can be a good starting point to praying the parables.

Friday 28th July
Matthew 13:18–23

Jesus said to the crowds, "Hear then the parable of the sower. When anyone hears the word of the kingdom and does not understand it, the evil one comes and snatches away what is sown in the heart; this is what was sown on the path. As for what was sown on rocky ground, this is the one who hears the word and immediately receives it with joy; yet such a person has no root, but endures only for a while, and when trouble or persecution arises on account of the word, that person immediately falls away. As for what was sown among thorns, this is the one who hears the word, but the cares of the world and the lure of wealth choke the word, and it yields nothing. But as for what was sown on good soil, this is the one who hears the word and understands it, who indeed bears fruit and yields, in one case a hundredfold, in another sixty, and in another thirty."

- I allow my imagination to dwell with the scene Jesus presents, picturing the growth and identifying what threatens growth. I take care not to allow the weeds and barrenness to dominate but accept that God pictures a flourishing harvest and never gives up that hope for me.

- Jesus speaks of the word of God as something organic and growing. Let me think back to seeds that have grown in my heart: probably happenings rather than preachers' words. I saw a kindness, a courageous stance, an example of honesty that cost the honest person dearly. That was the seed. It stayed with me, and was active in my heart.

Saturday 29th July
John 11:19–27

Many of the Jews had come to Martha and Mary to console them about their brother. When Martha heard that Jesus was coming, she went and met him, while Mary stayed at home. Martha said to Jesus, "Lord, if you had been here, my brother would not have died. But even now I know that God will give you whatever you ask of him." Jesus said to her, "Your brother will rise again." Martha said to him, "I know that he will rise again in the resurrection on the last day." Jesus said to her, "I am the resurrection and the life. Those who believe in me, even though they die, will live, and everyone who lives and believes in me will never die. Do you believe this?" She said to him, "Yes, Lord, I believe that you are the Messiah, the Son of God, the one coming into the world."

- Martha's faith in Jesus is absolute. She believes that her brother Lazarus will rise again in the resurrection on the last day. She acknowledges Jesus as "the Messiah, the Son of God." Faith in the resurrection helps us live with an attitude of hope, sharing in the joy of the victory of the risen Christ over sin and death.

- Remember the words of the poet John Donne: Death be not proud, though some have called thee / Mighty and dreadful, for thou art not so, / For those whom thou think'st thou dost overthrow, / Die not, poor Death, nor yet canst thou kill me . . . / One short sleep past, we wake eternally, / And death shall be no more; / Death, thou shalt die.

The Seventeenth Week of Ordinary Time
July 30—August 5

Something to think and pray about each day this week:

Honesty and Freedom

Honesty is an integral part of humility, which means saying yes to our humanness, accepting both the agony and the ecstasy of our creature-hood. We are of the earth—*humus*—and are called to embrace the totality of who we are. To accept our limitations and fulfill our potential takes courage. Humility—accepting the truth—requires honesty. Honesty and humility demand surrender or a letting go of our desire for control, security, esteem, and approval. Honesty and humility call us to reflect, as St. Ignatius did, on the patterns of our life that deflect us from the way of Christ. Thus, the examination of conscience became integral to the spirituality of Ignatius. He encouraged those who came to him for direction and confession to persist in a thorough examination of their soul. This examination of conscience that Ignatius developed and expanded as the examen of consciousness is basic and foundational for authentic inner healing. Ignatius identified and named his sinfulness on the way to aligning his intention with the intention of God present within him. Only God's love and grace made this possible. This same love and grace are available to us. With confidence in God's help, we can look forward to the freedom brought by God's forgiveness and by honesty with ourselves.

—Jacqueline Bergan and Marie Schwan, CSJ,
Praying with Ignatius of Loyola

The Presence of God

I pause for a moment and think of the love and the grace that God showers on me: I am created in the image and likeness of God; I am God's dwelling place.

Freedom

Lord, you created me to live in freedom. May your Holy Spirit guide me to follow you freely. Instill in my heart a desire to know and love you more each day.

Consciousness

How am I really feeling? Lighthearted? Heavyhearted? I may be very much at peace, happy to be here.

Equally, I may be frustrated, worried, or angry.

I acknowledge how I really am. It is the real me that the Lord loves.

The Word

I read the word of God slowly, a few times over, and I listen to what God is saying to me. (Please turn to the Scripture on the following pages. Inspiration points are there should you need them. When you are ready, return here to continue.)

Conversation

I know with certainty there were times when you carried me, Lord. When it was through your strength I got through the dark times in my life.

Conclusion

I thank God for these moments we have spent together and for any insights I have been given concerning the text.

Sunday 30th July
Seventeenth Sunday in Ordinary Time
Matthew 13:44–52

Jesus said to the crowds, "The kingdom of heaven is like treasure hidden in a field, which someone found and hid; then in his joy he goes and sells all that he has and buys that field. Again, the kingdom of heaven is like a merchant in search of fine pearls; on finding one pearl of great value, he went and sold all that he had and bought it. Again, the kingdom of heaven is like a net that was thrown into the sea and caught fish of every kind; when it was full, they drew it ashore, sat down, and put the good into baskets but threw out the bad. So it will be at the end of the age. The angels will come out and separate the evil from the righteous and throw them into the furnace of fire, where there will be weeping and gnashing of teeth. Have you understood all this?" They answered, "Yes." And he said to them, "Therefore every scribe who has been trained for the kingdom of heaven is like the master of a household who brings out of his treasure what is new and what is old."

- The parable is not inviting you to think about somebody else—some random trespasser. Jesus is inviting you to recognize where your heart is. For whom or for what would you go without everything else?

- Think about this hidden treasure. It inspires, enlivens, and opens horizons of new plans and dreams. Not everyone should be told about it immediately, but the excitement it brings cannot always be hidden. I thank God for what gives meaning to my life. Perhaps God looks at me and sees a hidden treasure, wondering when I might discover it.

Monday 31st July
Matthew 13:31–35

Jesus put before them another parable: "The kingdom of heaven is like a mustard seed that someone took and sowed in his field; it is the smallest of all the seeds, but when it has grown it is the greatest of shrubs and becomes a tree, so that the birds of the air come and make nests in its branches." He told them another parable: "The kingdom of heaven is like yeast that a woman took and mixed in with three measures of flour until all of it was leavened." Jesus told the crowds all these things in parables;

without a parable he told them nothing. This was to fulfill what had been spoken through the prophet: "I will open my mouth to speak in parables."

- Notice how Jesus spoke about small things, how he found significance in what might easily be overlooked. Let Jesus look at your life—even at your humble tasks—to see if he might not lead you to wisdom, insight, and truth.

- These are the most comforting of parables, because they show the kingdom of heaven as organic, with its own life force: growing by trickling increment beyond all our expectations, inviting all sorts of birds onto its branches, and growing secretly like yeast in a loaf.

Tuesday 1st August
Matthew 13:36–43

Then Jesus left the crowds and went into the house. And his disciples approached him, saying, "Explain to us the parable of the weeds of the field." He answered, "The one who sows the good seed is the Son of Man; the field is the world, and the good seed are the children of the kingdom; the weeds are the children of the evil one, and the enemy who sowed them is the devil; the harvest is the end of the age, and the reapers are angels. Just as the weeds are collected and burned up with fire, so will it be at the end of the age. The Son of Man will send his angels, and they will collect out of his kingdom all causes of sin and all evildoers, and they will throw them into the furnace of fire, where there will be weeping and gnashing of teeth. Then the righteous will shine like the sun in the kingdom of their Father. Let anyone with ears listen!"

- Jesus uses the image of the field to explain the presence of both good and evil in the world and to illustrate how these forces are manifested at the end of time. I give thanks for the fruits of my faith and the goodness Jesus works in my life. I offer to him any weaknesses that may block me from flourishing as a child of God.

- The good seed is sown in the world as it is. There is no need to wait until things are better; I can do whatever good I can do right now. Like a seed growing toward the light, I allow myself to dwell in the presence of God, who loves me. I still any voices that are not for my growth, wanting only to respond to the word that God speaks to me.

Wednesday 2nd August
Matthew 13:44–46

Jesus said to his disciples, "The kingdom of heaven is like treasure hidden in a field, which someone found and hid; then in his joy he goes and sells all that he has and buys that field. Again, the kingdom of heaven is like a merchant in search of fine pearls; on finding one pearl of great value, he went and sold all that he had and bought it."

- The kingdom is a treasure as precious as the finest of pearls. It should be our greatest and most important possession. It means that my values are the values of God. Is that how I see it? Would anyone know by observing my life?

- What Jesus describes could easily have happened then in Palestine. Ordinary people used the ground as the safest place to keep their most treasured possessions. There were caches of coins buried all over the country, forgotten when the owner died. Lord, you talk of the joy of discovery. That is the sign that I have found your treasure, a deep happiness in knowing you.

Thursday 3rd August
Matthew 13:47–53

Jesus said, "Again, the kingdom of heaven is like a net that was thrown into the sea and caught fish of every kind; when it was full, they drew it ashore, sat down, and put the good into baskets but threw out the bad. So it will be at the end of the age. The angels will come out and separate the evil from the righteous and throw them into the furnace of fire, where there will be weeping and gnashing of teeth. Have you understood all this?" They answered, "Yes." And he said to them, "Therefore every scribe who has been trained for the kingdom of heaven is like the master of a household who brings out of his treasure what is new and what is old." When Jesus had finished these parables, he left that place.

- Putting the good fish into baskets and dispensing with the bad was part of the fisherman's daily job. When describing the kingdom of heaven, Jesus was speaking to them in language they could relate to. I pray, Lord, that with your grace I may nurture the goodness in my life so that my ways may reflect your ways and I can contribute to the building of your kingdom of justice, peace, and love.

- Will judgment be a final division of good and bad? The early church held the hope that somehow, by the goodness of God, we will all be saved. I must work and pray for this.

Friday 4th August
Matthew 13:54–58

Jesus came to his hometown and began to teach the people in their synagogue, so that they were astounded and said, "Where did this man get this wisdom and these deeds of power? Is not this the carpenter's son? Is not his mother called Mary? And are not his brothers James and Joseph and Simon and Judas? And are not all his sisters with us? Where then did this man get all this?" And they took offense at him. But Jesus said to them, "Prophets are not without honor except in their own country and in their own house." And he did not do many deeds of power there, because of their unbelief.

- There was a moment when the light broke through, when the people realized the power of Jesus' wisdom and actions. Then the clouds came over and they thought, *If he were so special, we would not have missed it.* Sometimes we have moments of recognition when we see how blessed we are, but so easily do we return to our usual complaints.

- The people of Jesus' hometown were not ready to hear wisdom from one of their own. It may be that I am sometimes deaf to the wisdom that is around me, paying more attention to voices from far away.

Saturday 5th August
Matthew 14:1–12

At that time Herod the ruler heard reports about Jesus; and he said to his servants, "This is John the Baptist; he has been raised from the dead, and for this reason these powers are at work in him." For Herod had arrested John, bound him, and put him in prison on account of Herodias, his brother Philip's wife, because John had been telling him, "It is not lawful for you to have her." Though Herod wanted to put him to death, he feared the crowd, because they regarded him as a prophet. But when Herod's birthday came, the daughter of Herodias danced before the company, and she pleased Herod so much that he promised on oath to grant her whatever she might ask. Prompted by her mother, she said, "Give me the head of John the Baptist here on a platter." The king was grieved, yet out of regard for his oaths and for the guests, he commanded it to be given; he sent and had John beheaded in the prison. The head was brought on a platter and given to the girl, who brought it to her mother. His disciples came and took the body and buried it; then they went and told Jesus.

- John's death led his disciples to Jesus. When all seemed lost, they risked their lives in a final act of love to reclaim John's body, and then they went and told Jesus. Let us realize that chaos and destruction often lead us into the next good thing.

- The vanity of Herod brought him into terrible situations. I think of how well I am able to back down, to change my mind, to admit that I am wrong. I ask God for the help I need.

The Eighteenth Week of Ordinary Time
August 6—August 12

Something to think and pray about each day this week:

Profound Experiences of God

Let us look at the Transfiguration (Mark 9:2–8) with its obvious reference to the baptism of Jesus in the Jordan (Mark 1:9). At the baptism we read: "And just as [Jesus] was coming up out of the water, he saw the heavens torn apart and the Spirit descending like a dove on him. And a voice came from heaven, 'You are my Son, the Beloved; with you I am well pleased'" (Mark 1:10–11). How did Jesus feel as he heard these words, he the Jew of the first commandment? We can ask him to reveal this to us. Now at the Transfiguration Jesus has another profound experience of God. At least one can read the scene this way even if some commentators see the scene as a postresurrection appearance translated to the public life. Jesus has just predicted the Passion for the first time; he can sense the hatred and venom beginning to surround him. At this critical juncture he once again hears similar words, "This is my Son, the Beloved; listen to him" (Mark 9:7). What a comfort these words must have been to him. After all, it is the leaders of God's religion who are out to kill Jesus. Could he have had doubts about the course he was on? I know people who have cried with joy that Jesus heard such words of warmth and love and reassurance from God in this dark hour. And they have felt that the memory of this experience sustained him in the Garden of Gethsemane. How does the scene strike you? What is Jesus like for you?

—William A. Barry, SJ, *Seek My Face*

The Presence of God
Jesus, help me to be fully alive to your Holy Presence. Enfold me in your love. Let my heart become one with yours.

Freedom
I will ask God's help,
to be free from my own preoccupations,
to be open to God in this time of prayer,
to come to know, love, and serve God more.

Consciousness
I ask how I am within myself today? Am I particularly tired, stressed, or off form? If any of these characteristics apply, can I try to let go of the concerns that disturb me?

The Word
God speaks to each of us individually. I listen attentively to hear what God is saying to me. Read the text a few times, then listen. (Please turn to the Scripture on the following pages. Inspiration points are there should you need them. When you are ready, return here to continue.)

Conversation
Sometimes I wonder what I might say if I were to meet you in person, Lord.
I think I might say, Thank you, Lord, for always being there for me.

Conclusion
Glory be to the Father, and to the Son, and to the Holy Spirit,
As it was in the beginning, is now and ever shall be,
World without end. Amen.

Sunday 6th August
The Transfiguration of the Lord
Matthew 17:1–9

Six days later, Jesus took with him Peter and James and his brother John and led them up a high mountain, by themselves. And he was transfigured before them, and his face shone like the sun, and his clothes became dazzling white. Suddenly there appeared to them Moses and Elijah, talking with him. Then Peter said to Jesus, "Lord, it is good for us to be here; if you wish, I will make three dwellings here, one for you, one for Moses, and one for Elijah." While he was still speaking, suddenly a bright cloud overshadowed them, and from the cloud a voice said, "This is my Son, the Beloved; with him I am well pleased; listen to him!" When the disciples heard this, they fell to the ground and were overcome by fear. But Jesus came and touched them, saying, "Get up and do not be afraid." And when they looked up, they saw no one except Jesus himself alone. As they were coming down the mountain, Jesus ordered them, "Tell no one about the vision until after the Son of Man has been raised from the dead."

- Transfiguration is about Jesus and about us. When we are with him, we are with the divine. When he is with us, he is with the human. His love, grace, sacraments, peace, and compassion can transfigure us. May I be present in prayer to this light.

- The voice from the cloud had a simple message for Jesus and for us. Jesus saw that there was a time for silence and a time to speak. I ask God to help me to know which is appropriate—and when. I may draw strength from considering how I have been able to show restraint in the past.

Monday 7th August
Matthew 14:13–21

Now when Jesus heard of the death of John the Baptist, he withdrew from there in a boat to a deserted place by himself. But when the crowds heard it, they followed him on foot from the towns. When he went ashore, he saw a great crowd; and he had compassion for them and cured their sick. When it was evening, the disciples came to him and said, "This is a deserted place, and the hour is now late; send the crowds away so that they may go into the villages and buy food for themselves." Jesus said to them, "They need not go away; you give them something to eat." They replied, "We have nothing here but five loaves and two fish." And he said, "Bring them here to me." Then he ordered the crowds to sit down on the grass. Taking the five loaves and the two fish, he looked up to heaven, and blessed and broke the loaves, and gave them to the disciples, and the disciples gave them to the crowds. And all ate and were filled; and they took up what was left over of the broken pieces, twelve baskets full. And those who ate were about five thousand men, besides women and children.

- Jesus does not produce food out of nowhere. He takes the little that the apostles have and multiplies it a thousandfold. I am reminded that Jesus can provide spiritual nourishment beyond my imagining. There is a mysterious disproportion between what I give and what the Lord makes of it.

- When Jesus had heard the news about John the Baptist's execution, he needed time alone, despite the expectations of the crowds. If I have ever heard myself say that I am too busy to pray, I think of what moves Jesus and ask that God's spirit guide and direct me, too.

Tuesday 8th August
Matthew 14:22–36

Jesus made the disciples get into the boat and go on ahead to the other side, while he dismissed the crowds. And after he had dismissed the crowds, he went up the mountain by himself to pray. When evening came, he was there alone, but by this time the boat, battered by the waves, was far from the land, for the wind was against them. And early in the morning he came walking towards them on the lake. But when the disciples saw him walking on the lake, they were terrified, saying, "It is a ghost!" And they cried out in fear. But immediately Jesus spoke to them and said, "Take heart, it is I; do not be afraid." Peter answered him, "Lord, if it is you, command me to come to you on the water." He said, "Come." So Peter got out of the boat, started walking on the water, and came towards Jesus. But when he noticed the strong wind, he became frightened, and beginning to sink, he cried out, "Lord, save me!" Jesus immediately reached out his hand and caught him, saying to him, "You of little faith, why did you doubt?" When they got into the boat, the wind ceased. And those in the boat worshipped him, saying, "Truly you are the Son of God." When they had crossed over, they came to land at Gennesaret. After the people of that place recognized him, they sent word throughout the region and brought all who were sick to him, and begged him that they might touch even the fringe of his cloak; and all who touched it were healed.

- The apostles, despite living side by side with Jesus and seeing the wonders he worked, failed to believe that he could save them from the ferocity of the storm. So many storms batter our own lives—sin and temptation, anxiety, fear, and despair—and yet Jesus is no farther away from us than he was from the disciples in that small boat.

- When we're in the storm, we bring our troubles to Jesus. We sit with him in prayer and let him know how we are and just allow his calm to come over us. Our prayer gives us the courage and strength to deal with the storms in our lives.

Wednesday 9th August
Matthew 15:21–28

Jesus left that place and went away to the district of Tyre and Sidon. Just then a Canaanite woman from that region came out and started shouting, "Have mercy on me, Lord, Son of David; my daughter is tormented by a demon." But he did not answer her at all. And his disciples came and urged him, saying, "Send her away, for she keeps shouting after us." He answered, "I was sent only to the lost sheep of the house of Israel." But she came and knelt before him, saying, "Lord, help me." He answered, "It is not fair to take the children's food and throw it to the dogs." She said, "Yes, Lord, yet even the dogs eat the crumbs that fall from their masters' table." Then Jesus answered her, "Woman, great is your faith! Let it be done for you as you wish." And her daughter was healed instantly.

- Matthew introduces us to a mother who will do anything to attain her daughter's healing and who will persist in interceding with Jesus for her child. She comes looking for something not for herself, but for another. How powerful is the prayer of intercession! Jesus, Lord of all, hear our prayers of intercession for those we love.

- The Canaanite woman acknowledges Jesus as Son of David, a Messianic title. She kneels before him and calls him "Lord." She refuses to take offense at a seemingly rude insult. She knows the power and the mercy of this man. She believes in him. Her request is granted. What can I let this woman teach me?

Thursday 10th August
John 12:24–26

Jesus said "Very truly, I tell you, unless a grain of wheat falls into the earth and dies, it remains just a single grain; but if it dies, it bears much fruit. Those who love their life lose it, and those who hate their life in this world will keep it for eternal life. Whoever serves me must follow me, and where I am, there will my servant be also. Whoever serves me, the Father will honor."

- Without the right conditions, a grain will lie dormant and never bear fruit. The grain needs sun, rain, nutrients before it can begin to grow. Is my faith life dormant? Or am I nourishing it so that it will yield an abundant harvest? What needs to die in me that I may live more fully?

- The image Jesus presents is simple yet strong. He does not speak of "passing away" or "falling asleep" but of death and loss. Faith in Jesus strengthens me to look beyond death to the beginning of new life. Jesus speaks to me as friend and calls me into his family.

Friday 11th August
Matthew 16:24–28

Jesus told his disciples, "If any want to become my followers, let them deny themselves and take up their cross and follow me. For those who want to save their life will lose it, and those who lose their life for my sake will find it. For what will it profit them if they gain the whole world but forfeit their life? Or what will they give in return for their life? For the Son of Man is to come with his angels in the glory of his Father, and then he will repay everyone for what has been done. Truly I tell you, there are some standing here who will not taste death before they see the Son of Man coming in his kingdom."

- This passage brings us to the heart of the paradox of discipleship. To win, we must lose. To gain, we must give up. To live forever, we must die. We are not called on to go out looking for a cross, simply not to run from it when it comes.

- Comfort becomes a priority when the world is a rough place. Perhaps we need to be careful not to cushion ourselves too much, careful not to forget that the cross is always within sight of the Christian. We may not want to make life difficult for ourselves, but our prayer acknowledges the pain that is experienced by others in which Jesus still suffers.

Saturday 12th August
Matthew 17:14–20

When they came to the crowd, a man came to him, knelt before him, and said, "Lord, have mercy on my son, for he is an epileptic and he suffers terribly; he often falls into the fire and often into the water. And I brought him to your disciples, but they could not cure him." Jesus answered, "You faithless and perverse generation, how much longer must I be with you? How much longer must I put up with you? Bring him here to me." And Jesus rebuked the demon, and it came out of him, and the boy was cured instantly. Then the disciples came to Jesus privately and said, "Why could we not cast it out?" He said to them, "Because of your little faith. For truly I tell you, if you have faith the size of a mustard seed, you will say to this mountain, 'Move from here to there,' and it will move; and nothing will be impossible for you."

- We, too, often ask Jesus, *why? Why can we not accomplish your work in our lives?* In this reading, Jesus himself supplies the answer: because of your little faith. Lord, grant us the faith that will move mountains— mountains of inertia and apathy, of fear and anxiety, of selfishness and despair.

- Jesus has no doubt that if we had enough faith we could move mountains. In other words, if my relationship with the Father were as strong as Jesus', the power of God could flow freely through me and achieve great things. Do I want this?

The Nineteenth Week of Ordinary Time
August 13—August 19

Something to think and pray about each day this week:

Understanding Intercession

I finally (in my late 50s) came to understand what intercession is all about. I got a phone call one morning telling me that a member of my community was seriously ill in the hospital. I rushed to his bedside and there found his mother (a retired nurse) and his father (a retired surgeon) at his bedside. As we waited for my friend to go into surgery, his mother explained to me that her son (who had been staying with his parents) was so sick by 4:00 in the morning that they had to bring him to the hospital. His mother said, "I was so worried. I wanted to talk to an expert and I knew Dr. XX was the man to talk to. But it was 4:00 a.m. and I knew he wouldn't answer his phone, so I called his mother and asked her to have him phone me because I knew he'd answer her call. And he did. And he got back to me at once!" And, all of a sudden, I understood why it is good to pray to Our Lady and the saints to intercede for us.

—Paul Brian Campbell, SJ, on his blog *People for Others*

The Presence of God

"I stand at the door and knock," says the Lord. What a wonderful privilege that the Lord of all creation desires to come to me. I welcome his presence.

Freedom

Saint Ignatius thought that a thick and shapeless tree trunk would never believe that it could become a statue, admired as a miracle of sculpture, and would never submit itself to the chisel of the sculptor,
who sees by her genius what she can make of it.
I ask for the grace to let myself be shaped by my loving Creator.

Consciousness

Knowing that God loves me unconditionally, I can afford to be honest about how I am. What are my fears and desires? What do I expect from God? What am I willing to give to God—from my emotions and talents, thoughts and energy? And how do I feel now? I share my feelings openly with the Lord.

The Word

I take my time to read the word of God, slowly, a few times, allowing myself to dwell on anything that strikes me. (Please turn to the Scripture on the following pages. Inspiration points are there should you need them. When you are ready, return here to continue.)

Conversation

Do I notice myself reacting as I pray with the word of God? Do I feel challenged, comforted, angry? Imagining Jesus sitting or standing by me, I speak out my feelings, as one trusted friend to another.

Conclusion

I thank God for these moments we have spent together and for any insights I have been given concerning the text.

Sunday 13th August
Nineteenth Sunday in Ordinary Time
Matthew 14:22–33

Jesus made the disciples get into the boat and go on ahead to the other side, while he dismissed the crowds. And after he had dismissed the crowds, he went up the mountain by himself to pray. When evening came, he was there alone, but by this time the boat, battered by the waves, was far from the land, for the wind was against them. And early in the morning he came walking toward them on the sea. But when the disciples saw him walking on the sea, they were terrified, saying, "It is a ghost!" And they cried out in fear. But immediately Jesus spoke to them and said, "Take heart, it is I; do not be afraid." Peter answered him, "Lord, if it is you, command me to come to you on the water." He said, "Come." So Peter got out of the boat, started walking on the water, and came toward Jesus. But when he noticed the strong wind, he became frightened, and beginning to sink, he cried out, "Lord, save me!" Jesus immediately reached out his hand and caught him, saying to him, "You of little faith, why did you doubt?" When they got into the boat, the wind ceased. And those in the boat worshiped him, saying, "Truly you are the Son of God."

- I pray for a deeper trust as I hear his words: "Take heart, it is I; do not be afraid." I can rely too much on myself and, like Peter, lose sight of where I am going. Help me, Jesus, to keep my eyes fixed on you and to trust that you reach out to me.

- I'm fascinated by that first step of Peter as he climbed over the side of the boat. He was looking at Jesus, not at the water. His mind was charged with Jesus' invitation: *Come.* So often the way out of depression, fear, or anxiety is not a thought or a consideration but a physical step. I take a risk and find myself strong enough to walk forward, keeping my eyes on the Lord.

Monday 14th August
Matthew 17:22–27

As they were gathering in Galilee, Jesus said to them, "The Son of Man is going to be betrayed into human hands, and they will kill him, and on the third day he will be raised." And they were greatly distressed. When they reached Capernaum, the collectors of the temple tax came to Peter and said, "Does your teacher not pay the temple tax?" He said, "Yes, he does." And when he came home, Jesus spoke of it first, asking, "What do you think, Simon? From whom do kings of the earth take toll or tribute? From their children or from others?" When Peter said, "From others," Jesus said to him, "Then the children are free. However, so that we do not give offense to them, go to the lake and cast a hook; take the first fish that comes up; and when you open its mouth, you will find a coin; take that and give it to them for you and me."

- The disciples were unable to cope with news of Jesus' sufferings. Suffering disorients us—we cannot understand it fully, so we need to stay close to Jesus, else we will become lost. He brings meaning from it at a profound level that we cannot grasp, except in faith.

- The disciples just couldn't grasp that Jesus would die a terrible death, but then rise again. Only afterwards do we understand many things. This is why it is important to cultivate reflectiveness, else we miss the Lord's delicate touch in daily events.

Tuesday 15th August
The Assumption of the Blessed Virgin Mary
Luke 1:39–56

In those days Mary set out and went with haste to a Judean town in the hill country, where she entered the house of Zechariah and greeted Elizabeth. When Elizabeth heard Mary's greeting, the child leapt in her womb. And Elizabeth was filled with the Holy Spirit and exclaimed with a loud cry, "Blessed are you among women, and blessed is the fruit of your womb. And why has this happened to me, that the mother of my Lord comes to me? For as soon as I heard the sound of your greeting, the child in my womb leapt for joy. And blessed is she who believed that there would be a fulfillment of what was spoken to her by the Lord." And Mary said,

> "My soul magnifies the Lord,
> and my spirit rejoices in God my Saviour,
> for he has looked with favor on the lowliness of his servant.
> Surely, from now on all generations will call me blessed;
> for the Mighty One has done great things for me,
> and holy is his name.

His mercy is for those who fear him
from generation to generation.
He has shown strength with his arm;
he has scattered the proud in the thoughts of their hearts.
He has brought down the powerful from their thrones,
and lifted up the lowly;
he has filled the hungry with good things,
and sent the rich away empty.
He has helped his servant Israel,
in remembrance of his mercy,
according to the promise he made to our ancestors,
to Abraham and to his descendants forever."

And Mary remained with her for about three months and then returned to her home.

- Mary realized that she was blessed, that great things had happened in her life. She saw the source of them and gave thanks to God. She inspires me and helps me appreciate goodness and give thanks to God, its source.

- As well as acknowledging God's goodness, I lay before God my thirst for justice, peace, and equality. I look forward to the day when God will satisfy the hungry.

Wednesday 16th August
Matthew 18:15–20

"If another member of the church sins against you, go and point out the fault when the two of you are alone. If the member listens to you, you have regained that one. But if you are not listened to, take one or two others along with you, so that every word may be confirmed by the evidence of two or three witnesses. If the member refuses to listen to them, tell it to the church; and if the offender refuses to listen even to the church, let such a one be to you as a Gentile and a tax-collector. Truly I tell you, whatever you bind on earth will be bound in heaven, and whatever you loose on earth will be loosed in heaven. Again, truly I tell you, if two of you agree on earth about anything you ask, it will be done for you by my Father in heaven. For where two or three are gathered in my name, I am there among them."

- Perhaps Jesus does not mean that the agreement disciples might reach is a guarantee of God's miraculous intervention but sees that the miracle lies in two people being fully of one mind and heart. When people trust one another and believe in God, the reign of God is brought into being.

- If I am upset with somebody, then the first person for me to approach is that person, with respect and kindness, whether it is a relation or an acquaintance, a parish priest or an official. So many people start by running to authority. Whatever I do when I am upset, Lord, let me do it in charity.

Thursday 17th August
Matthew 18:21—19:1

Then Peter came and said to him, "Lord, if another member of the church sins against me, how often should I forgive? As many as seven times?" Jesus said to him, "Not seven times, but, I tell you, seventy-seven times. For this reason the kingdom of heaven may be compared to a king who wished to settle accounts with his slaves. When he began the reckoning, one who owed him ten thousand talents was brought to him; and, as he could not pay, his lord ordered him to be sold, together with his wife and children and all his possessions, and payment to be made. So the slave fell on his knees before him, saying, 'Have patience with me, and I will pay you everything.' And out of pity for him, the lord of that slave released him and forgave him the debt. But that same slave, as he went out, came upon one of his fellow slaves who owed him a hundred denarii; and seizing him by the throat, he said, 'Pay what you owe.' Then his fellow slave fell down and pleaded with him, 'Have patience with me, and I will pay you.' But he refused; then he went and threw him into prison until he should pay the debt. When his fellow slaves saw what had happened, they were greatly distressed, and they went and reported to their lord all that had taken place. Then his lord summoned him and said to him, 'You wicked slave! I forgave you all that debt because you pleaded with me. Should you not have had mercy on your fellow slave, as I had mercy on you?' And in anger his lord handed him over to be tortured until he should pay his entire debt. So my heavenly Father will also do to every one of you, if you do not forgive your brother or sister from your heart."

When Jesus had finished saying these things, he left Galilee and went to the region of Judea beyond the Jordan.

- Forgiveness can be very hard. C. S. Lewis wrote, "Everyone says forgiveness is a lovely idea, until there is something to forgive." When we fail to forgive, we are shackled to the evil that has been done to us. We cannot move forward.

- If I must be prepared to forgive seventy-seven times, then I must also be ready to ask for forgiveness—and believe I am forgiven—seventy-seven times. Forgiveness comes slowly; we can begin by praying for someone who hurt us badly. "Forgive us our sins, as we (try to) forgive those who sin against us."

Friday 18th August
Matthew 19:3–12

Some Pharisees came to him, and to test him they asked, "Is it lawful for a man to divorce his wife for any cause?" He answered, "Have you not read that the one who made them at the beginning made them male and female and said, 'For this reason a man shall leave his father and mother and be joined to his wife, and the two shall become one flesh?' So they are no longer two, but one flesh. Therefore what God has joined together, let no one separate." They said to him, "Why then did Moses command us to give a certificate of dismissal and to divorce her?" He said to them, "It was because you were so hard-hearted that Moses allowed you to divorce your wives, but at the beginning it was not so. And I say to you, whoever divorces his wife, except for unchastity, and marries another commits adultery." His disciples said to him, "If such is the case of a man with his wife, it is better not to marry." But he said to them, "Not everyone can accept this teaching, but only those to whom it is given. For there are eunuchs who have been so from birth, and there are eunuchs who have been made eunuchs by others, and there are eunuchs who have made themselves eunuchs for the sake of the kingdom of heaven. Let anyone accept this who can."

- Whether we marry or remain single, we are called to live wholeheartedly. I pray with thanks for all the people I know who have been able to live out their desires and dreams. I pray with compassion for all who have been disappointed by the changing circumstances of their lives.

- God's desire is for man and woman to come together in body, mind, and soul. In the commitment of marriage, the two are deeply united. Jesus doesn't seem to give a last word on marriage and unfaithfulness here. He looks with compassion on our human faults and failings. His heart reaches out to all who are in any way connected with marital difficulties and breakup.

Saturday 19th August
Matthew 19:13–15

Little children were being brought to him in order that he might lay his hands on them and pray. The disciples spoke sternly to those who brought them; but Jesus said, "Let the little children come to me, and do not stop them; for it is to such as these that the kingdom of heaven belongs." And he laid his hands on them and went on his way.

- I have lost my innocence; my trust in God is shaky; I don't experience much joy in life. Help me, Lord, to become again like a trusting little child before you, for nothing is impossible for you. Amen.

- I bring before Jesus everything in my life that is growing, delicate, or even a dream for me. I allow him to bless my hopes, and I listen to him as he values my desires. I think of how I might look out more for the "children" around me.

The Twentieth Week of Ordinary Time
August 20—August 26

Something to think and pray about each day this week:

Jesus' Values

With whom does Jesus identify? The hungry, the thirsty, the stranger, the naked, the sick, the prisoner, the least of his brothers and sisters. If we love these brothers and sisters with an effective love that tries to ease their burdens, then we love Jesus. If we do not try to ease their burdens, then, Jesus says, we do not love him. This is indeed a hard saying, especially in a world such as ours in which we are so aware of the sufferings of so many millions of the brothers and sisters of Jesus because of the mass media. If at the end we come to such a hard saying, perhaps we may wish that we had never asked to know the values of Jesus because the task seems so impossible. We may all feel that we will be put with the goats. How can we respond? First, we need to realize that we are asking to know the values of Jesus to love him more and follow him more closely. We cannot change our hearts by our own willpower. If Jesus reveals to us what he values, then he will also give us the desire to want to share his values, the desire to be given a heart like his. We are asking for a gift, in other words.

—William A. Barry, SJ, *Seek My Face*

The Presence of God

To be present is to arrive as one is and open up to the other.
At this instant, as I arrive here, God is present waiting for me.
God always arrives before me, desiring to connect with me
even more than my most intimate friend.
I take a moment and greet my loving God.

Freedom

I am free. When I look at these words in writing, they seem to create in me a feeling of awe. Yes, a wonderful feeling of freedom. Thank you, God.

Consciousness

To be conscious about something is to be aware of it.
Dear Lord, help me to remember that you gave me life.
Thank you for the gift of life.
Teach me to slow down, to be still and enjoy the pleasures created for me.
To be aware of the beauty that surrounds me. The marvel of mountains, the calmness of lakes, the fragility of a flower petal. I need to remember that all these things come from you.

The Word

The word of God comes to us through the Scriptures. May the Holy Spirit enlighten my mind and heart to respond to the Gospel teachings. (Please turn to the Scripture on the following pages. Inspiration points are there should you need them. When you are ready, return here to continue.)

Conversation

I begin to talk to Jesus about the piece of Scripture I have just read. What part of it strikes a chord in me? Perhaps the words of a friend—or some story I have heard recently—will slowly rise to the surface in my consciousness. If so, does the story throw light on what the Scripture passage may be trying to say to me?

Conclusion

Glory be to the Father, and to the Son, and to the Holy Spirit,
As it was in the beginning, is now and ever shall be,
World without end. Amen.

Sunday 20th August
Twentieth Sunday in Ordinary Time
Matthew 15:21–28

Jesus left that place and went away to the district of Tyre and Sidon. Just then a Canaanite woman from that region came out and started shouting, "Have mercy on me, Lord, Son of David; my daughter is tormented by a demon." But he did not answer her at all. And his disciples came and urged him, saying, "Send her away, for she keeps shouting after us." He answered, I was sent only to the lost sheep of the house of Israel. But she came and knelt before him, saying, "Lord, help me." He answered, "It is not fair to take the children's food and throw it to the dogs." She said, "Yes, Lord, yet even the dogs eat the crumbs that fall from their masters' table." Then Jesus answered her, "Woman, great is your faith! Let it be done for you as you wish." And her daughter was healed instantly.

- This is an extraordinary story. While the woman stands her ground, Jesus changes his position. Perhaps he himself comes to a fuller understanding of his own mission as he watches and listens to the Canaanite woman. Is there anyone I judge too hastily?

- *He did not answer her at all.* It would have been easy for this woman to give up in bitterness. She feels trebly handicapped: a woman alone in a man's world; a Gentile and therefore unclean; and with an afflicted daughter. But in spite of Jesus' silence she trusts him, keeps at him, and bests him in debate. Lord, may I never be discouraged by your silence.

Monday 21st August
Matthew 19:16–22

Then someone came to Jesus and said, "Teacher, what good deed must I do to have eternal life?" And he said to him, "Why do you ask me about what is good? There is only one who is good. If you wish to enter into life, keep the commandments." He said to him, "Which ones?" And Jesus said, "You shall not murder; You shall not commit adultery; You shall not steal; You shall not bear false witness; Honour your father and mother; also, You shall love your neighbour as yourself." The young man said to him, "I have kept all these; what do I still lack?" Jesus said to him, "If you wish to be perfect, go, sell your possessions, and give the money to the poor, and you will have treasure in heaven; then come, follow me." When the young man heard this word, he went away grieving, for he had many possessions.

- Interestingly, the commandments Jesus recites to the rich young man do not include the first three, which all relate to our relationship with God. Instead, he lists those that address our relationships with one another. The message is clear: we do not live in isolation. Love for our neighbor is the door to eternal life. What attachments in my life are holding me back from a deeper relationship with my neighbor and with God?

- The young man was doing his best but realized that there was something missing, something holding him back. My time of prayer will sometimes bring me in touch with a message from Jesus, a word from God, that challenges and causes a certain sorrow; I may realize that God is less interested in what I do than in who I am becoming.

Tuesday 22nd August
Matthew 19:23–30

Then Jesus said to his disciples, "Truly I tell you, it will be hard for a rich person to enter the kingdom of heaven. Again I tell you, it is easier for a camel to go through the eye of a needle than for someone who is rich to enter the kingdom of God." When the disciples heard this, they were greatly astounded and said, "Then who can be saved?" But Jesus looked at them and said, "For mortals it is impossible, but for God all things are possible." Then Peter said in reply, "Look, we have left everything and followed you. What then will we have?" Jesus said to them, "Truly I tell you, at the renewal of all things, when the Son of Man is seated on the throne of his glory, you who have followed me will also sit on twelve thrones, judging the twelve tribes of Israel. And everyone who has left houses or brothers or sisters or father or mother or children or fields, for my name's sake, will receive a hundredfold, and will inherit eternal life. But many who are first will be last, and the last will be first."

- The trouble with possessions is that they can too easily possess us. Jesus calls for radical change in our lives, a change that can seem unattainable. However, he reminds us that, while something may seem impossible for mortals, for God, all things are possible.

- Do I believe that God will ask nothing of me that I am not, with his help, capable of doing?

Wednesday 23rd August
Matthew 20:1–16

Jesus said to his disciples, "For the kingdom of heaven is like a landowner who went out early in the morning to hire laborers for his vineyard. After agreeing with the laborers for the usual daily wage, he sent them into his vineyard. When he went out about nine o'clock, he saw others standing idle in the marketplace; and he said to them, 'You also go into the vineyard, and I will pay you whatever is right.' So they went. When he went out again about noon and about three o'clock, he did the same. And about five o'clock he went out and found others standing around; and he said to them, 'Why are you standing here idle all day?' They said to him, 'Because no one has hired us.' He said to them, 'You also go into the vineyard.' When evening came, the owner of the vineyard said to his manager, 'Call the laborers and give them their pay, beginning with the last and then going to the first.' When those hired about five o'clock came, each of them received the usual daily wage. Now when the first came, they thought they would receive more; but each of them also received the usual daily wage. And when they received it, they grumbled against the landowner, saying, 'These last worked only one hour, and you have made them equal to us who have borne the burden of the day and the scorching heat.' But he replied to one of them, 'Friend, I am doing you no wrong; did you not agree with me for the usual daily wage? Take what belongs to you and go; I choose to give to this last the same as I give to you. Am I not allowed to do what I choose with what belongs to me? Or are you envious because I am generous?' So the last will be first, and the first will be last."

- Envy is arguably the most poisonous of the deadly sins. Not only do the envious loathe others for what they have, but they loathe themselves for not having it. We are all coworkers in God's vineyard. We can each be confident that he will deal not only justly but generously with us. Are there times when I selfishly consider myself more deserving than others?

- Do I feel envious of some who have been given a talent that I do not have? But God tells no one any story but their own. Lord, you know best. Let me say a simple "Amen" to the way you are guiding my life.

Thursday 24th August
John 1:45–51

Philip found Nathanael and said to him, "We have found him about whom Moses in the law and also the prophets wrote, Jesus son of Joseph from Nazareth." Nathanael said to him, "Can anything good come out of Nazareth?" Philip said to him, "Come and see." When Jesus saw Nathanael coming toward him, he said of him, "Here is truly an Israelite in whom there is no deceit!" Nathanael asked him, "Where did you get to know me?" Jesus answered, "I saw you under the fig tree before Philip called you." Nathanael replied, "Rabbi, you are the Son of God! You are the King of Israel!" Jesus answered, "Do you believe because I told you that I saw you under the fig tree? You will see greater things than these." And he said to him, "Very truly, I tell you, you will see heaven opened and the angels of God ascending and descending upon the Son of Man."

- Philip does not waste time in arguing with Nathaniel. Come and see, he says. Lord, I pray that I might lead others to you by the way I live. Jesus saw in Nathaniel a quality that surprised and appealed to him. What quality in me might delight Jesus?

- Jesus sees me, too, "under the fig trees," and he recognizes what is in my heart. I relax in the knowledge that I am known and loved.

Friday 25th August
Matthew 22:34–40

When the Pharisees heard that he had silenced the Sadducees, they gathered together, and one of them, a lawyer, asked him a question to test him. "Teacher, which commandment in the law is the greatest?" He said to him, "'You shall love the Lord your God with all your heart, and with all your soul, and with all your mind.' This is the greatest and first commandment. And a second is like it: 'You shall love your neighbor as yourself.' On these two commandments hang all the law and the prophets."

- The understanding of Christian love does not solely focus on passion or affection but also on acts of mercy. I cannot choose how I feel, but I can choose how I act.

- Right here is a simple summary of the Gospel. Simple as this message seems, I know how difficult it is to live out. I ask God for the help I need to love fully and freely. Life in balance is loving God and loving others. I consider how I sometimes wobble and, in my prayer, seek again the path that Jesus puts before me.

Saturday 26th August
Matthew 23:1–12

Then Jesus said to the crowds and to his disciples, "The scribes and the Pharisees sit on Moses' seat; therefore, do whatever they teach you and follow it; but do not do as they do, for they do not practice what they teach. They tie up heavy burdens, hard to bear, and lay them on the shoulders of others; but they themselves are unwilling to lift a finger to move them. They do all their deeds to be seen by others; for they make their phylacteries broad and their fringes long. They love to have the place of honor at banquets and the best seats in the synagogues, and to be greeted with respect in the marketplaces, and to have people call them rabbi. But you are not to be called rabbi, for you have one teacher, and you are all students. And call no one your father on earth, for you have one Father—the one in heaven. Nor are you to be called instructors, for you have one instructor, the Messiah. The greatest among you will be your servant. All who exalt themselves will be humbled, and all who humble themselves will be exalted."

- Religion can be heavy going! Jesus came to lighten our religious loads and focus us on loving and serving others. We can load religious burdens and expectations on others, even in our judgments on them. I ask God to help me to resist any fundamentalist rejection of others and to help me to appreciate good wherever I find it.

- There may seem to be a contradiction between obedience and independence. I pray that I may have the humility to imitate, to receive instruction, and to follow even as I accept the dignity that God gives me by speaking in love directly to my heart.

August 27—September 2

Something to think and pray about each day this week:

Translating Purpose into Practice

Authenticity is the first test of my values and purpose. If I say I'm here on earth to repair the world or to be holy, do I really, really mean it? Do these ideas make me live and work differently, or do they ultimately hold no more significance than an empty slogan emblazoned across a glossy corporate annual report? Can I say that I'm here on earth for a reason, or am I simply drifting along, grasping after whatever suits a short-term need or a current fad? If authenticity of purpose is the first test, then putting purpose into practice is the second and equally daunting challenge. For the loftier our purpose, the more we test our imagination to find everyday ways to demonstrate that purpose in how we live. I may be inspired enough to commit to building the civilization of love, but can I live that extraordinary-sounding purpose throughout life's very ordinary routines of commuting to work, answering office e-mail, keeping a house clean, balancing a checkbook, and doing chores? Our values are the answer; they are the means by which we translate purpose into practice all day, every day.

—Chris Lowney, *Heroic Living*

The Presence of God

Be still and know that I am God. Lord, may your Spirit guide me to seek your loving presence more and more. For it is there I find rest and refreshment from this busy world.

Freedom

By God's grace I was born to live in freedom. Free to enjoy the pleasures he created for me. Dear Lord, grant that I may live as you intended, with complete confidence in your loving care.

Consciousness

In God's loving presence I unwind the past day,
starting from now and looking back, moment by moment.
I gather in all the goodness and light, in gratitude.
I attend to the shadows and what they say to me,
seeking healing, courage, forgiveness.

The Word

The word of God comes to us through the Scriptures. May the Holy Spirit enlighten my mind and heart to respond to the Gospel teachings. (Please turn to the Scripture on the following pages. Inspiration points are there should you need them. When you are ready, return here to continue.)

Conversation

Jesus, you always welcomed little children when you walked on this earth. Teach me to have a childlike trust in you. To live in the knowledge that you will never abandon me.

Conclusion

Glory be to the Father, and to the Son, and to the Holy Spirit,
As it was in the beginning, is now and ever shall be,
World without end. Amen.

Sunday 27th August
Twenty-First Sunday in Ordinary Time
Matthew 16:13–20

Now when Jesus came into the district of Caesarea Philippi, he asked his disciples, "Who do people say that the Son of Man is?" And they said, "Some say John the Baptist, but others Elijah, and still others Jeremiah or one of the prophets." He said to them, "But who do you say that I am?" Simon Peter answered, "You are the Messiah, the Son of the living God." And Jesus answered him, "Blessed are you, Simon son of Jonah! For flesh and blood has not revealed this to you, but my Father in heaven. And I tell you, you are Peter, and on this rock I will build my church, and the gates of Hades will not prevail against it. I will give you the keys of the kingdom of heaven, and whatever you bind on earth will be bound in heaven, and whatever you loose on earth will be loosed in heaven." Then he sternly ordered the disciples not to tell anyone that he was the Messiah.

- Jesus could trust Peter to be honest—he would say what was on his mind and in his heart. As Jesus asks me the same question, I answer honestly, knowing that nothing I say will alienate Jesus.

- Am I open to Jesus' question, "Who do *you* say that I am?" This text has been used so often for apologetic purposes that it is hard to recapture the drama, the uncertain silence, that must have followed Jesus' question. He wondered what they would say and wonders what I say to the same question. Lord, I linger with this question: *What are you to me?*

Monday 28th August
Matthew 23:13–22

Jesus said, "But woe to you, scribes and Pharisees, hypocrites! For you lock people out of the kingdom of heaven. For you do not go in yourselves, and when others are going in, you stop them. Woe to you, scribes and Pharisees, hypocrites! For you cross sea and land to make a single convert, and you make the new convert twice as much a child of hell as yourselves. Woe to you, blind guides, who say, 'Whoever swears by the sanctuary is bound by nothing, but whoever swears by the gold of the sanctuary is bound by the oath.' You blind fools! For which is greater, the gold or the sanctuary that has made the gold sacred? And you say,

'Whoever swears by the altar is bound by nothing, but whoever swears by the gift that is on the altar is bound by the oath.' How blind you are! For which is greater, the gift or the altar that makes the gift sacred? So whoever swears by the altar, swears by it and by everything on it; and whoever swears by the sanctuary, swears by it and by the one who dwells in it; and whoever swears by heaven, swears by the throne of God and by the one who is seated upon it."

- What a terrible thing to say! What was going on in Jesus' mind? Consider how much it must have distressed him to see the Pharisees look for attention and distract people from the God about whom they appeared to speak. Much as Jesus is loving, patient, and kind, he has an energy and desire for people to wake up! Jesus, let me hear your call to life.

- Jesus continues his sevenfold condemnation of bad leaders. He wants people to be free, whereas bad leaders have a disastrous impact on those they are meant to serve. Lord, let me use my freedom well. Do not let me dominate others in argument or actions.

Tuesday 29th August
The Passion of Saint John the Baptist
Mark 6:17–29

Herod himself had sent men who arrested John, bound him, and put him in prison on account of Herodias, his brother Philip's wife, because Herod had married her. For John had been telling Herod, "It is not lawful for you to have your brother's wife." And Herodias had a grudge against him, and wanted to kill him. But she could not, for Herod feared John, knowing that he was a righteous and holy man, and he protected him. When he heard him, he was greatly perplexed; and yet he liked to listen to him. But an opportunity came when Herod on his birthday gave a banquet for his courtiers and officers and for the leaders of Galilee. When his daughter Herodias came in and danced, she pleased Herod and his guests; and the king said to the girl, "Ask me for whatever you wish, and I will give it." And he solemnly swore to her, "Whatever you ask me, I will give you, even half of my kingdom." She went out and said to her mother, "What should I ask for?" She replied, "The head of John the baptizer." Immediately she rushed back to the king and requested, "I want you to give me at once the head of John the Baptist on a platter." The king was deeply grieved; yet out of regard for his oaths and for the guests, he did not want to refuse her. Immediately the king sent a soldier of the guard with orders to bring John's head. He went and beheaded him in the prison, brought his head on a platter, and gave it to the girl. Then the girl gave it to her mother. When his disciples heard about it, they came and took his body, and laid it in a tomb.

- John the Baptist was beheaded because he spoke truth to power. The man who prepared the way for Jesus was executed at the whim of a corrupt ruler. Those who work for justice in the world or witness to their faith today often face difficult and even life-threatening situations. I pause to remember them in prayer.

- When it came to John the Baptist, Herod was what we would call conflicted. He would not repent and follow John, yet he tried to protect him and wanted to listen to him. In the end, Herod chose against John. Wavering between opposite loyalties or principles usually comes to a bad ending. Am I wavering today?

Wednesday 30th August
Matthew 23:27–32

Jesus said, "Woe to you, scribes and Pharisees, hypocrites! For you are like whitewashed tombs, which on the outside look beautiful, but inside they are full of the bones of the dead and of all kinds of filth. So you also on the outside look righteous to others, but inside you are full of hypocrisy and lawlessness. Woe to you, scribes and Pharisees, hypocrites! For you build the tombs of the prophets and decorate the graves of the righteous, and you say, 'If we had lived in the days of our ancestors, we would not have taken part with them in shedding the blood of the prophets.' Thus you testify against yourselves that you are descendants of those who murdered the prophets. Fill up, then, the measure of your ancestors."

- Are my words and actions, like those of the Pharisees, driven by a preoccupation with truth and orthodoxy or by justice, mercy, and love? How often do I close my eyes to those in need? How can I be of service to those less fortunate than myself?

- Jesus challenges the scribes and Pharisees to look at what is going on in their inner selves, the part they hide from one another, and indeed, from themselves. Father, we, too, can live in an unrealistic way, doing our own thing and having no concern for how we treat those whose paths we cross.

Thursday 31st August
Matthew 24:42–51

Jesus said to his disciples, "Keep awake therefore, for you do not know on what day your Lord is coming. But understand this: if the owner of the house had known in what part of the night the thief was coming, he would have stayed awake and would not have let his house be broken into. Therefore you also must be ready, for the Son of Man is coming at an unexpected hour. Who then is the faithful and wise slave, whom his master has put in charge of his household, to give the other slaves their allowance of food at the proper time? Blessed is that slave whom his master will find at work when he arrives. Truly I tell you, he will put that one in charge of all his possessions. But if that wicked slave says to himself, My master is delayed and he begins to beat his fellow-slaves, and eats and drinks with drunkards, the master of that slave will come on a day when he does not expect him and at an hour that he does not know. He will cut him in pieces and put him with the hypocrites, where there will be weeping and gnashing of teeth."

- Throughout the Gospels, Jesus speaks about being awake and paying attention. Jesus' call to build a world of justice and peace cannot be delayed. The time is now. Am I so preoccupied with busyness and my own cares and concerns that I sometimes forget to watch and pray?

- The grace and presence of God can hit us at any time. A moment in the countryside, a prayer at Mass, a hug with a loved one, a support in trouble—all can be doors opening to God. Some have recalled the presence of God at a deathbed. Note the moments when the Lord came your way and left an afterglow that has lasted for years.

Friday 1st September
Matthew 25:1–13

Jesus said to his disciples, "Then the kingdom of heaven will be like this. Ten bridesmaids took their lamps and went to meet the bridegroom. Five of them were foolish, and five were wise. When the foolish took their lamps, they took no oil with them; but the wise took flasks of oil with their lamps. As the bridegroom was delayed, all of them became drowsy and slept. But at midnight there was a shout, 'Look! Here is the bridegroom! Come out to meet him.' Then all those bridesmaids got up and trimmed their lamps. The foolish said to the wise, 'Give us some of your oil, for our lamps are going out.' But the wise replied, 'No! there will not be enough for you and for us; you had better go to the dealers and buy some for yourselves.' And while they went to buy it, the bridegroom came, and those who were ready went with him into the wedding banquet; and the door was shut. Later the other bridesmaids came also, saying, 'Lord, lord, open to us.' But he replied, 'Truly I tell you, I do not know you.' Keep awake therefore, for you know neither the day nor the hour."

• As Christians we wait in readiness, we wait in hope, and we wait together. I may be alone at my computer, but I am conscious of the thousands of my sisters and brothers who are also praying at this very moment. I include them in my prayer today.

• Father, you wait patiently for us to turn to you and accept all that you are offering us through the power of your Holy Spirit. Help us to keep our lamps lit with the oil of prayer. With that light to help us, we can do good works and share your love with others.

Saturday 2nd September
Matthew 25:14–30

Jesus said to his disciples, "For it is as if a man, going on a journey, summoned his slaves and entrusted his property to them; to one he gave five talents, to another two, to another one, to each according to his ability. Then he went away. The one who had received the five talents went off at once and traded with them, and made five more talents. In the same way, the one who had the two talents made two more talents. But the one who had received the one talent went off and dug a hole in the ground and hid his master's money. After a long time the master of those slaves came and settled accounts with them. Then the one who had received the five talents came forward, bringing five more talents, saying, 'Master, you handed over to me five talents; see, I have made five more talents.' His master said to him, 'Well done, good and trustworthy slave; you have been trustworthy in a few things, I will put you in charge of many things;

enter into the joy of your master.' And the one with the two talents also came forward, saying, 'Master, you handed over to me two talents; see, I have made two more talents.' His master said to him, 'Well done, good and trustworthy slave; you have been trustworthy in a few things, I will put you in charge of many things; enter into the joy of your master.' Then the one who had received the one talent also came forward, saying, 'Master, I knew that you were a harsh man, reaping where you did not sow, and gathering where you did not scatter seed; so I was afraid, and I went and hid your talent in the ground. Here you have what is yours.' But his master replied, 'You wicked and lazy slave! You knew, did you, that I reap where I did not sow, and gather where I did not scatter? Then you ought to have invested my money with the bankers, and on my return I would have received what was my own with interest. So take the talent from him, and give it to the one with the ten talents. For to all those who have, more will be given, and they will have an abundance; but from those who have nothing, even what they have will be taken away. As for this worthless slave, throw him into the outer darkness, where there will be weeping and gnashing of teeth.'"

• The anxiety-ridden servant with his timid inactivity suffers the paralysis of a closed mind. The consequence? An atrophied disciple! Discipleship requires courage and risk-taking. Lord, let me discover my unique talents and use them in wholehearted activity and worthwhile deeds of love.

• Help me, God, to appreciate how I make a difference in the world. Refine me so that who I am may give glory to you. The servants did not judge one another's results, nor did they look to the markets. Each stood honestly before the master, as I do now.

The Twenty-Second Week of Ordinary Time
September 3—September 9

Something to think and pray about each day this week:

Disordered Affections

Sometimes we're driven by the I-want-it-so-badly virus: I so wanted to get to the top of the company, or to attract that attractive person, or to be rich, or to be recognized as important, or to have the best house, or to have a more exciting life. In fact, we sometimes delude ourselves into thinking that the object of our affection (the job, the car, the partner, the house) must be right for us precisely because we want it so badly. Sometimes our desires are in fact good indicators of where we need to go or what course we need to take. But sometimes just the opposite is true. What I want so badly may scratch an ego itch but do nothing to further my purpose in life; it might even lead me astray of my purpose. Greed, pride, or a host of other debilitating drives can take a powerful hold on us and are all the more pernicious because we're not fully aware of how deeply they may have affected our thinking. That's what Ignatius meant by an attachment to disordered affections that can undermine our judgment.

—Chris Lowney, *Heroic Leadership*

The Presence of God

I pause for a moment and think of the love and the grace that God showers on me: I am created in the image and likeness of God; I am God's dwelling place.

Freedom

Lord, you created me to live in freedom. May your Holy Spirit guide me to follow you freely. Instill in my heart a desire to know and love you more each day.

Consciousness

How am I really feeling? Lighthearted? Heavyhearted? I may be very much at peace, happy to be here.

Equally, I may be frustrated, worried, or angry.

I acknowledge how I really am. It is the real me that the Lord loves.

The Word

I read the word of God slowly, a few times over, and I listen to what God is saying to me. (Please turn to the Scripture on the following pages. Inspiration points are there should you need them. When you are ready, return here to continue.)

Conversation

I know with certainty there were times when you carried me, Lord. When it was through your strength I got through the dark times in my life.

Conclusion

I thank God for these moments we have spent together and for any insights I have been given concerning the text.

Sunday 3rd September
Twenty-Second Sunday in Ordinary Time
Matthew 16:21–27

From that time on, Jesus began to show his disciples that he must go to Jerusalem and undergo great suffering at the hands of the elders and chief priests and scribes, and be killed, and on the third day be raised. And Peter took him aside and began to rebuke him, saying, "God forbid it, Lord! This must never happen to you." But he turned and said to Peter, "Get behind me, Satan! You are a stumbling block to me; for you are setting your mind not on divine things but on human things." Then Jesus told his disciples, "If any want to become my followers, let them deny themselves and take up their cross and follow me. For those who want to save their life will lose it, and those who lose their life for my sake will find it. For what will it profit them if they gain the whole world but forfeit their life? Or what will they give in return for their life? For the Son of Man is to come with his angels in the glory of his Father, and then he will repay everyone for what has been done."

- If we are to be followers of Jesus, we need to let him lead, accepting that he will not lead us away from suffering, pain, or difficulty. I pray that I may let go and grow in trust of God's love for me.

- Peter has just been congratulated as the rock on which Jesus will build his church. He is comfortable in a theology of grace and glory. But he is blind to the whole reality. Lord, help me receive the whole story from you, today and every day.

Monday 4th September
Luke 4:16–30

When he came to Nazareth, where he had been brought up, he went to the synagogue on the sabbath day, as was his custom. He stood up to read, and the scroll of the prophet Isaiah was given to him. He unrolled the scroll and found the place where it was written:

"The Spirit of the Lord is upon me,
because he has anointed me
to bring good news to the poor.
He has sent me to proclaim release to the captives

and recovery of sight to the blind,
to let the oppressed go free,
to proclaim the year of the Lord's favor."

And he rolled up the scroll, gave it back to the attendant, and sat down. The eyes of all in the synagogue were fixed on him. Then he began to say to them, "Today this Scripture has been fulfilled in your hearing." All spoke well of him and were amazed at the gracious words that came from his mouth. They said, "Is not this Joseph's son?" He said to them, "Doubtless you will quote to me this proverb, 'Doctor, cure yourself!' And you will say, 'Do here also in your home town the things that we have heard you did at Capernaum.'" And he said, "Truly I tell you, no prophet is accepted in the prophet's home town. But the truth is, there were many widows in Israel in the time of Elijah, when the heaven was shut up for three years and six months, and there was a severe famine over all the land; yet Elijah was sent to none of them except to a widow at Zarephath in Sidon. There were also many lepers in Israel in the time of the prophet Elisha, and none of them was cleansed except Naaman the Syrian." When they heard this, all in the synagogue were filled with rage. They got up, drove him out of the town, and led him to the brow of the hill on which their town was built, so that they might hurl him off the cliff. But he passed through the midst of them and went on his way.

• Familiarity with Jesus left his listeners unimpressed. The word of God made flesh was reading the word of God to them, and it fell upon deaf ears. Today, let me consciously look for the extraordinary amidst the ordinary.

• If you were asked to proclaim one piece of Scripture to your community, what would it be? As you think about your choice, notice how you choose it.

Tuesday 5th September
Luke 4:31–37

Jesus went down to Capernaum, a city in Galilee, and was teaching them on the sabbath. They were astounded at his teaching, because he spoke with authority. In the synagogue there was a man who had the spirit of an unclean demon, and he cried out with a loud voice, "Let us alone! What have you to do with us, Jesus of Nazareth? Have you come to destroy us? I know who you are, the Holy One of God." But Jesus rebuked him, saying, "Be silent, and come out of him!" When the demon had thrown him down before them, he came out of him without having done him any harm. They were all amazed and kept saying to one another, "What kind of utterance is this? For with authority and power he commands the unclean spirits, and out they come!" And a report about him began to reach every place in the region.

- Lord, the people were astounded at hearing you. Let me, too, be amazed by your words, especially when you reveal the goodness of your Father towards me. Jolt me from my dullness. Let me experience your disturbing freshness, your vision of how we should live.

- Can I bring the evil that I confront in my life—and in our world—before Jesus? How do I feel when I consider these things? Confidence in God? Doubt and fear? Perhaps I should talk this over with him.

Wednesday 6th September
Luke 4:38–44

After leaving the synagogue he entered Simon's house. Now Simon's mother-in-law was suffering from a high fever, and they asked him about her. Then he stood over her and rebuked the fever, and it left her. Immediately she got up and began to serve them. As the sun was setting, all those who had any who were sick with various kinds of diseases brought them to him; and he laid his hands on each of them and cured them. Demons also came out of many, shouting, "You are the Son of God!" But he rebuked them and would not allow them to speak, because they knew that he was the Messiah. At daybreak he departed and went into a deserted place. And the crowds were looking for him; and when they reached him, they wanted to prevent him from leaving them. But he said to them, "I must proclaim the good news of the kingdom of God to the other cities also; for I was sent for this purpose." So he continued proclaiming the message in the synagogues of Judea.

- It may seem surprising that Jesus turned away the crowds who went looking for him. His point of view was different from what might be expected. He spoke from the still point of his life, from his core relationship with his Father. I need my moments of stillness and reflection to anchor myself and rediscover my true identity and direction.

- Jesus' ministry of healing and liberation continues. In response to the intercession of others, Peter's mother-in-law is healed of her fever. Lord, today I bring to you the many people who are sick in mind, body, or spirit. Lay your healing hands upon them and renew their spirits.

Thursday 7th September
Luke 5:1–11

Once while Jesus was standing beside the lake of Gennesaret, and the crowd was pressing in on him to hear the word of God, he saw two boats there at the shore of the lake; the fishermen had gone out of them and were washing their nets. He got into one of the boats, the one belonging to Simon, and asked him to put out a little way from the shore. Then he sat down and taught the crowds from the boat. When he had finished speaking, he said to Simon, "Put out into the deep water and let down your nets for a catch." Simon answered, "Master, we have worked all night long but have caught nothing. Yet if you say so, I will let down the nets." When they had done this, they caught so many fish that their nets were beginning to break. So they signalled to their partners in the other boat to come and help them. And they came and filled both boats, so that they began to sink. But when Simon Peter saw it, he fell down at Jesus' knees, saying, "Go away from me, Lord, for I am a sinful man!" For he and all who were with him were amazed at the catch of fish that they had taken; and so also were James and John, sons of Zebedee, who were partners with Simon. Then Jesus said to Simon, "Do not be afraid; from now on you will be catching people." When they had brought their boats to shore, they left everything and followed him.

- This miracle reveals the power and generosity of God. Jesus knew what would please Simon, who would never forget this catch of fish! God's grace comes to us tailor-made to fit our situation. Can I recall a moment when my efforts to do good were rewarded beyond my dreams? Did I recognize then that God was busily at work through me?

- Peter invited Jesus into one of his most precious and important possessions—his boat. This was the means of his livelihood and gave him status among the others. Peter also allowed Jesus to tell him where to fish, handing over control of this boat and his own life to Jesus. In prayer we invite Jesus into the most personal and important places of our lives.

Friday 8th September
The Nativity of the Blessed Virgin Mary
Matthew 1:18–23

Now the birth of Jesus the Messiah took place in this way. When his mother Mary had been engaged to Joseph, but before they lived together, she was found to be with child from the Holy Spirit. Her husband Joseph, being a righteous man and unwilling to expose her to public disgrace, planned to dismiss her quietly. But just when he had resolved to do this, an angel of the Lord appeared to him in a dream and said, "Joseph, son of David, do not be afraid to take Mary as your wife, for the child conceived in her is from the Holy Spirit. She will bear a son, and you are to name him Jesus, for he will save his people from their sins." All this took place to fulfill what had been spoken by the Lord through the prophet: "Look, the virgin shall conceive and bear a son, and they shall name him Emmanuel," which means, "God is with us."

- Joseph occupies a central place in this Gospel. He decides to be kind toward Mary and divorce her in secret. A dream upturns his original decision. God intervenes, and more is asked of Joseph. He is called to revisit and revise his original intentions. Lord, I thank you for Joseph's generous, courageous risk-taking. May I respond as he did, when you invite me to risk.

- There is a model in Joseph's story for making decisions and dealing with doubts. Pray about it, carry it as a question, pester God about it. This is the story of Joseph's utterly unique vocation, as foster father of the Son of God.

Saturday 9th September
Luke 6:1–5

One sabbath while Jesus was going through the grain fields, his disciples plucked some heads of grain, rubbed them in their hands, and ate them. But some of the Pharisees said, "Why are you doing what is not lawful on the sabbath?" Jesus answered, "Have you not read what David did when he and his companions were hungry? He entered the house of God and took and ate the bread of the Presence, which it is not lawful for any but the priests to eat, and gave some to his companions?" Then he said to them, "The Son of Man is lord of the sabbath."

- Every time is a good time to do good, and laws are good only when they are in the service of love. God's central concern is the well-being and happiness of humankind. Let these be my central concern likewise. Pope Francis urges us not to be afraid of making mistakes in our efforts to do good.

- Jesus hears what distracts me and also what calls me to truth. The accusing party is not always others or authority; sometimes we don't allow ourselves to get away with anything but spend time chiding, scolding, and not letting go. I ask Jesus' help to be able to listen to what is really important.

September 10—September 16

Something to think and pray about each day this week:

A Place of Grace

In the latter years of her life, in the backyard of her home in northern Florida, my grandmother had a porch swing. She liked to sit and swing and hum old church hymns such as "Rock of Ages, Cleft for Me." I can still see her there, wearing a white scarf over her head, a concession to chemotherapy's unrelenting march. When as a young adult I visited her, she would always ask me to sit with her on the swing for a spell. She would pat my leg and call me "darlin'." As long as my grandmother lived—and in spite of her pain—there was always a place for me on the swing. If I were asked to explain grace, I would paint the picture of my grandmother's swing. There, I never had to deliberate or explain or worry, regardless of the weight I carried. The porch swing—my grandmother's presence—bestowed grace without conditions.

—Terry Hershey, *Sanctuary: Creating a Space for Grace in Your Life*

The Presence of God

Jesus, help me to be fully alive to your Holy Presence. Enfold me in your love. Let my heart become one with yours.

Freedom

I will ask God's help,
to be free from my own preoccupations,
to be open to God in this time of prayer,
to come to know, love, and serve God more.

Consciousness

I ask how I am within myself today? Am I particularly tired, stressed, or off form? If any of these characteristics apply, can I try to let go of the concerns that disturb me?

The Word

God speaks to each of us individually. I listen attentively to hear what God is saying to me. Read the text a few times, then listen. (Please turn to the Scripture on the following pages. Inspiration points are there should you need them. When you are ready, return here to continue.)

Conversation

Sometimes I wonder what I might say if I were to meet you in person, Lord.
I think I might say, Thank you, Lord, for always being there for me.

Conclusion

Glory be to the Father, and to the Son, and to the Holy Spirit,
As it was in the beginning, is now and ever shall be,
World without end. Amen.

Sunday 10th September
Twenty-Third Sunday in Ordinary Time
Matthew 18:15–20

Jesus said to his disciples, "If another member of the church sins against you, go and point out the fault when the two of you are alone. If the member listens to you, you have regained that one. But if you are not listened to, take one or two others along with you, so that every word may be confirmed by the evidence of two or three witnesses. If the member refuses to listen to them, tell it to the church; and if the offender refuses to listen even to the church, let such a one be to you as a Gentile and a tax collector. Truly I tell you, whatever you bind on earth will be bound in heaven, and whatever you loose on earth will be loosed in heaven. Again, truly I tell you, if two of you agree on earth about anything you ask, it will be done for you by my Father in heaven. For where two or three are gathered in my name, I am there among them."

- Jesus is Emmanuel, God with us. He is with us in our church community. His message is one of reconciliation, not retribution. We are asked to regain our brother or sister. Regaining is more than stopping someone's offensive behavior; it is converting that person—bringing about a true change in attitude.

- Jesus promises his continuing presence. Even as I pray alone, I am united with others who pray at this time, with all of those who read this Gospel today. I grow in awareness that Jesus wants to be present to me, is present to me, loves me, and calls me to life.

Monday 11th September
Luke 6:6–11

On another sabbath Jesus entered the synagogue and taught, and there was a man there whose right hand was withered. The scribes and the Pharisees watched him to see whether he would cure on the sabbath, so that they might find an accusation against him. Even though he knew what they were thinking, he said to the man who had the withered hand, "Come and stand here." He got up and stood there. Then Jesus said to them, "I ask you, is it lawful to do good or to do harm on the sabbath, to save life or to destroy it?" After looking around at all of them, he said to him, "Stretch out your hand." He did so, and his hand was restored.

But they were filled with fury and discussed with one another what they might do to Jesus.

- The Pharisees are filled with fury because with Jesus the rule of love is taking over from the rule of law, and so their control of people is being challenged. I ask the Lord that love may win out in the choices that I make.

- Lord, our church suffers today from those who use their position and power to dominate others. Reveal to me the ways you call me to stretch out my hand to empower those around me.

Tuesday 12th September
Luke 6:12–19

Now during those days Jesus went out to the mountain to pray; and he spent the night in prayer to God. And when day came, he called his disciples and chose twelve of them, whom he also named apostles: Simon, whom he named Peter, and his brother Andrew, and James, and John, and Philip, and Bartholomew, and Matthew, and Thomas, and James son of Alphaeus, and Simon, who was called the Zealot, and Judas son of James, and Judas Iscariot, who became a traitor. He came down with them and stood on a level place, with a great crowd of his disciples and a great multitude of people from all Judea, Jerusalem, and the coast of Tyre and Sidon. They had come to hear him and to be healed of their diseases; and those who were troubled with unclean spirits were cured. And all in the crowd were trying to touch him, for power came out from him and healed all of them.

- Consider what was in Jesus' heart: the hope, trust, and love that he had for his disciples as he chose them to be close to him. Allow Jesus to look on you with the same hope, trust, and love. Hear yourself called; ask for grace to be able to respond fully from your heart.

- Luke's Gospel highlights the centrality of prayer in the life and mission of Jesus. His decisions and choices emerge from lengthy periods of communion with the one he calls "Abba." Lord, I come to you in this time of prayer. Let me hear again your call to me. Let me sense your power at work in and through me.

Wednesday 13th September
Luke 6:20–26

Jesus looked up at his disciples and said: "Blessed are you who are poor, for yours is the kingdom of God. Blessed are you who are hungry now, for you will be filled. Blessed are you who weep now, for you will laugh. Blessed are you when people hate you, and when they exclude you, revile you, and defame you on account of the Son of Man. Rejoice on that day and leap for joy, for surely your reward is great in heaven; for that is what their ancestors did to the prophets. But woe to you who are rich, for you have received your consolation. Woe to you who are full now, for you will be hungry. Woe to you who are laughing now, for you will mourn and weep. Woe to you when all speak well of you, for that is what their ancestors did to the false prophets."

- The kingdom of God is mysterious because it is God's project working out silently in human history. But from this text we know some of those who will be in it. The poor and the hungry will be there. So will those who weep and also the dominated, the persecuted, the outcasts of the earth. What an extraordinary group!

- Those who are at the bottom of the human pyramid will be rejoicing and leaping for joy at God's goodness to them. When my heart is breaking because of the misery of so many today, I must not think that God has forgotten them. Instead I thank God that for them the best is yet to come, and I ask to be included among them, at least as someone who cares about them.

Thursday 14th September
John 3:13–17

No one has ascended into heaven except the one who descended from heaven, the Son of Man. And just as Moses lifted up the serpent in the wilderness, so must the Son of Man be lifted up, that whoever believes in him may have eternal life. For God so loved the world that he gave his only Son, so that everyone who believes in him may not perish but may have eternal life. Indeed, God did not send the Son into the world to condemn the world, but in order that the world might be saved through him.

- In his final "Yes" of abandonment to the Father, Christ breathed out his spirit on us, enabling us to be his witnesses and to love the teeming world as he does. Each person I see is a brother or sister for whom Christ died.

- In John's Gospel the cross reveals the vast breadth and width of God's love. It reverses all human values. Once a symbol of shame, it becomes the symbol of glory. The love revealed is not exclusive, for just a few. Rather, it is a redemptive love that embraces the whole world. As I gaze on the cross, may I be lifted up into all that is true, good, and beautiful.

Friday 15th September
John 19:25–27

Meanwhile, standing near the cross of Jesus were his mother, and his mother's sister, Mary the wife of Clopas, and Mary Magdalene. When Jesus saw his mother and the disciple whom he loved standing beside her, he said to his mother, "Woman, here is your son." Then he said to the disciple, "Here is your mother." And from that hour the disciple took her into his own home.

- Even at the moment of his death, Jesus' heart is open to those who suffer. He recognizes the grieving of Mary and John and asks them to make space in their lives for one another. Jesus asked Mary and John to make room in their lives for new relationships of care; could it be that I sometimes receive the same invitation?

- William Butler Yeats's poem helps me plumb the depths of Mary's thoughts on Calvary: What is this flesh I purchased with my pains, / This fallen star my milk sustains, / This love that makes my heart's blood stop / Or strikes a sudden chill into my bones / And makes my hair stand up?

Saturday 16th September
Luke 6:43–49

Jesus said to his disciples, "No good tree bears bad fruit, nor again does a bad tree bear good fruit; for each tree is known by its own fruit. Figs are not gathered from thorns, nor are grapes picked from a bramble bush. The good person out of the good treasure of the heart produces good, and the evil person out of evil treasure produces evil; for it is out of the abundance of the heart that the mouth speaks. Why do you call me Lord,

Lord, and do not do what I tell you? I will show you what someone is like who comes to me, hears my words, and acts on them. That one is like a man building a house, who dug deeply and laid the foundation on rock; when a flood arose, the river burst against that house but could not shake it, because it had been well built. But the one who hears and does not act is like a man who built a house on the ground without a foundation. When the river burst against it, immediately it fell, and great was the ruin of that house."

- What is "the good treasure" in my heart? Have I any treasure there at all? I ask the Holy Spirit to help me search within and understand what my good treasure is.

- For Jesus' audience, fig trees symbolized fertility, peace, and prosperity. Grapes symbolized joy. Brambles and thorns served only as firewood. Fruit, like character, takes time to ripen and mature. Jesus connects soundness of heart with good fruit. Lord, help me mature and bear good fruit.

The Twenty-Fourth Week of Ordinary Time
September 17—September 23

Something to think and pray about each day this week:

What God Really Wants

St. Ignatius recognized that God's will is not a precise blueprint, but neither is it a vague "whatever you want" blank check. God has a "plan" in the sense that he has an idea of the kind of person you can be and an idea of the life that would bring you the most joy. The broad outlines of God's idea are the same for everyone—to love and serve God and neighbor. But the particulars are unique to each of us. Finding God's will means discovering God's unique love for us, his desire to help us grow into our most authentic selves, and the way we can best serve him and his people. That's why we get rid of disordered affections. It's like a cook peeling an artichoke to get to the heart, or a sculptor chipping away at marble to find the beautiful form inside. Beneath the love of money, possessions, honor, and pride, we will find what we *really* want. And here is Ignatius's great insight. When we find what we really want, we find what God wants, too. It's a pretty remarkable idea, so I'll say it again: *when we discover what we really want, we discover what God wants, too.*

—Jim Manney, *God Finds Us*

The Presence of God

"I stand at the door and knock," says the Lord. What a wonderful privilege that the Lord of all creation desires to come to me. I welcome his presence.

Freedom

Saint Ignatius thought that a thick and shapeless tree trunk would never believe that it could become a statue, admired as a miracle of sculpture, and would never submit itself to the chisel of the sculptor,
who sees by her genius what she can make of it.
I ask for the grace to let myself be shaped by my loving Creator.

Consciousness

Knowing that God loves me unconditionally, I can afford to be honest about how I am. What are my fears and desires? What do I expect from God? What am I willing to give to God—from my emotions and talents, thoughts and energy? And how do I feel now? I share my feelings openly with the Lord.

The Word

I take my time to read the word of God, slowly, a few times, allowing myself to dwell on anything that strikes me. (Please turn to the Scripture on the following pages. Inspiration points are there should you need them. When you are ready, return here to continue.)

Conversation

Do I notice myself reacting as I pray with the word of God? Do I feel challenged, comforted, angry? Imagining Jesus sitting or standing by me, I speak out my feelings, as one trusted friend to another.

Conclusion

I thank God for these moments we have spent together and for any insights I have been given concerning the text.

Sunday 17th September
Twenty-Fourth Sunday in Ordinary Time
Matthew 18:21–35

Then Peter came and said to him, "Lord, if another member of the church sins against me, how often should I forgive? As many as seven times?" Jesus said to him, "Not seven times, but, I tell you, seventy-seven times. For this reason the kingdom of heaven may be compared to a king who wished to settle accounts with his slaves. When he began the reckoning, one who owed him ten thousand talents was brought to him; and, as he could not pay, his lord ordered him to be sold, together with his wife and children and all his possessions, and payment to be made. So the slave fell on his knees before him, saying, 'Have patience with me, and I will pay you everything.' And out of pity for him, the lord of that slave released him and forgave him the debt. But that same slave, as he went out, came upon one of his fellow slaves who owed him a hundred denarii; and seizing him by the throat, he said, 'Pay what you owe.' Then his fellow slave fell down and pleaded with him, 'Have patience with me, and I will pay you.' But he refused; then he went and threw him into prison until he should pay the debt. When his fellow slaves saw what had happened, they were greatly distressed, and they went and reported to their lord all that had taken place. Then his lord summoned him and said to him, 'You wicked slave! I forgave you all that debt because you pleaded with me. Should you not have had mercy on your fellow slave, as I had mercy on you?' And in anger his lord handed him over to be tortured until he should pay his entire debt. So my heavenly Father will also do to every one of you, if you do not forgive your brother or sister from your heart."

- When he speaks about the kingdom of God, Jesus invites us to use our imagination. I use my imagination and allow myself to be drawn into this story; I think of how I am forgiven and consider how well I offer that forgiveness to others.

- The king in the story wanted first only to settle accounts with his debtors. He did not set out to let the debt go. Compassion took over later, and he cancelled the debt. He would never think of it again. The Lord is like that with us: totally forgiving and not remembering our sins. Help me, Lord, to forget my sins as you have, so that I can be free to love and forgive others.

Monday 18th September
Luke 7:1–10

After Jesus had finished all his sayings in the hearing of the people, he entered Capernaum. A centurion there had a slave whom he valued highly, and who was ill and close to death. When he heard about Jesus, he sent some Jewish elders to him, asking him to come and heal his slave. And Jesus went with them, but when he was not far from the house, the centurion sent friends to say to him, "Lord, do not trouble yourself, for I am not worthy to have you come under my roof; therefore I did not presume to come to you. But only speak the word, and let my servant be healed." When Jesus heard this he was amazed at him, and turning to the crowd that followed him, he said, "I tell you, not even in Israel have I found such faith." When those who had been sent returned to the house, they found the slave in good health.

- Is it not disconcerting to see this outsider so much in tune with Christ and so concerned for his servant? And is Jesus hinting to me that I need only to ask him and he will help me?

- Though we see only through a glass darkly, we know that Jesus is somehow attentive to each one of God's scattered children. Worldly status means nothing to him. In the story, I can be the dying servant who desperately needs help. Or I can be the centurion who intercedes for someone else. Whatever way I pray this scene, let its surprising outcome not be lost on me.

Tuesday 19th September
Luke 7:11–17

Soon afterwards Jesus went to a town called Nain, and his disciples and a large crowd went with him. As he approached the gate of the town, a man who had died was being carried out. He was his mother's only son, and she was a widow; and with her was a large crowd from the town. When the Lord saw her, he had compassion for her and said to her, "Do not weep." Then he came forward and touched the bier, and the bearers stood still. And he said, "Young man, I say to you, rise!" The dead man sat up and began to speak, and Jesus gave him to his mother. Fear seized all of them; and they glorified God, saying, "A great prophet has risen among us!" and "God has looked favorably on his people!" This word about him spread throughout Judea and all the surrounding country.

- Do I walk with them in their distress? Would people feel I have a compassionate heart? Lord, allow me to be the gospel of compassion in my own time and place.

- Jesus looked at the widow with compassion—just as he looks at me now. I allow time to acknowledge who or what I mourn, to let Jesus behold me, and to receive his blessing of hope.

Wednesday 20th September
Luke 7:31–35

Jesus said, "To what then will I compare the people of this generation, and what are they like? They are like children sitting in the marketplace and calling to one another, 'We played the flute for you, and you did not dance; we wailed, and you did not weep.' For John the Baptist has come eating no bread and drinking no wine, and you say, 'He has a demon;' the Son of Man has come eating and drinking, and you say, 'Look, a glutton and a drunkard, a friend of tax collectors and sinners!' Nevertheless, wisdom is vindicated by all her children."

- Children can complain and change their minds quickly, but Jesus points out how adults can be hardheaded and impossible to please. Am I fickle, difficult to please, shifting in my beliefs and attitudes? I pray today for stability, grounded in gratitude and a teachable spirit.

- Lord, I, too, can be contrary of heart, blind and deaf to your truth. I go through periods of negativity and complaint, when nothing seems to please me. Come to me in my poverty of spirit. Reveal love's wisdom to me and let me be counted among your children.

Thursday 21st September
Matthew 9:9–13

As Jesus was walking along, he saw a man called Matthew sitting at the tax booth; and he said to him, "Follow me." And he got up and followed him. And as he sat at dinner in the house, many tax collectors and sinners came and were sitting with him and his disciples. When the Pharisees saw this, they said to his disciples, "Why does your teacher eat with tax collectors and sinners?" But when he heard this, he said, "Those who are well have no need of a physician, but those who are sick. Go and learn what this means, 'I desire mercy, not sacrifice.' For I have come to call not the righteous but sinners."

- Tax collectors were despised in Jesus' time much as drug dealers or ruthless landlords are today. With this in mind, let yourself be amazed at what happens here. Watch Jesus coming along with his ragged band of disciples. Jesus stops before the tax booth, and Matthew braces himself for trouble. Jesus catches Matthew's eye; his glance is respectful; perhaps he shows a welcoming smile. Then he says: 'Follow me!'

- Jesus was walking along, Matthew was at his place of work: a normal, everyday setting for God's grace to find an opening. Sitting at your computer is another such setting. Many tax collectors and sinners came to sit and eat with Jesus. It is characteristic of holy people that others feel easy in their company. Jesus accepted people as they were, where they were. Am I as easy and accepting?

Friday 22nd September
Luke 8:1–3

Soon afterwards Jesus went on through cities and villages, proclaiming and bringing the good news of the kingdom of God. The twelve were with him, as well as some women who had been cured of evil spirits and infirmities: Mary, called Magdalene, from whom seven demons had gone out, and Joanna, the wife of Herod's steward Chuza, and Susanna, and many others, who provided for them out of their resources.

- Saint Luke always speaks favorably of women and highlights their positive response to Jesus. He is the only Gospel writer who gives us this detail of the women who traveled with Jesus. The scene gives an image of the infant church. It is on the move and is made up of ordinary women and men who are centered on Jesus.

- How fragile a start for the church! In these times I may experience the church as fragile and ill-equipped for its great task of spreading the good news. I pray that God may bless my efforts to bring good news to those I meet.

Saturday 23rd September
Luke 8:4–15

When a great crowd gathered and people from town after town came to him, he said in a parable: "A sower went out to sow his seed; and as he sowed, some fell on the path and was trampled on, and the birds of the air ate it up. Some fell on the rock; and as it grew up, it withered for lack of moisture. Some fell among thorns, and the thorns grew with it and choked it. Some fell into good soil, and when it grew, it produced a hundredfold." As he said this, he called out, "Let anyone with ears to hear listen!" Then his disciples asked him what this parable meant. He said, "To you it has been given to know the secrets of the kingdom of God; but to others I speak in parables, so that 'looking they may not perceive, and listening they may not understand.' Now the parable is this: The seed is the word of God. The ones on the path are those who have heard; then the devil comes and takes away the word from their hearts, so that they may not believe and be saved. The ones on the rock are those who, when they hear the word, receive it with joy. But these have no root; they believe only for a while and in a time of testing fall away. As for what fell among the thorns, these are the ones who hear; but as they go on their way, they are choked by the cares and riches and pleasures of life, and their fruit does not mature. But as for that in the good soil, these are the ones who, when they hear the word, hold it fast in an honest and good heart, and bear fruit with patient endurance."

- The sower is energetic; he has work to do. He is lavish, noncalculating, generous, extravagant, even—it seems—wasteful. He does not worry that some seed will be lost. We can imagine that he is happy as he goes along. This is what God is like!

- God sows seed in my heart every day and does not get annoyed if I ignore the word today; he will go out and sow more words tomorrow. God never stops giving and does not count the cost. Joy and gratitude well up in me for this, and I thank God for such goodness to me.

The Twenty-Fifth Week of Ordinary Time
September 24—September 30

Something to think and pray about each day this week:

One Makes a Difference

This whole universe, with its trillions of galaxies, began as a tiny speck of concentrated energy, smaller than a grain of salt. When you were first conceived, you were just a single cell, a mere pinpoint of life, barely visible to the naked eye but packed full of the potential for everything you would ever become—every action, choice, and relationship. You are just a drop in the ocean, but without you the ocean will not become the ocean. You are just a grain of sand, but you are a grain of sand that tips the scales. You are just a drop of dew that soaks into the earth and is gone by noon, but that drop of dew brings life to the seed that grows in the earth. You are only one, but the Power of One is greater than you dare to dream. One is not Nothing. One makes a difference. Your choices can tip the scales of humanity a little bit more toward goodness and truth, if that is your desire.

—Margaret Silf, *Simple Faith*

The Presence of God
To be present is to arrive as one is and open up to the other.
At this instant, as I arrive here, God is present waiting for me.
God always arrives before me, desiring to connect with me
even more than my most intimate friend.
I take a moment and greet my loving God.

Freedom
I am free. When I look at these words in writing, they seem to create in me a feeling of awe. Yes, a wonderful feeling of freedom. Thank you, God.

Consciousness
To be conscious about something is to be aware of it.
Dear Lord, help me to remember that you gave me life.
Thank you for the gift of life.
Teach me to slow down, to be still and enjoy the pleasures created for me.
To be aware of the beauty that surrounds me. The marvel of mountains, the calmness of lakes, the fragility of a flower petal. I need to remember that all these things come from you.

The Word
The word of God comes to us through the Scriptures. May the Holy Spirit enlighten my mind and heart to respond to the Gospel teachings. (Please turn to the Scripture on the following pages. Inspiration points are there should you need them. When you are ready, return here to continue.)

Conversation
I begin to talk to Jesus about the piece of Scripture I have just read. What part of it strikes a chord in me? Perhaps the words of a friend—or some story I have heard recently—will slowly rise to the surface in my consciousness. If so, does the story throw light on what the Scripture passage may be trying to say to me?

Conclusion
Glory be to the Father, and to the Son, and to the Holy Spirit,
As it was in the beginning, is now and ever shall be,
World without end. Amen.

Sunday 24th September
Twenty-Fifth Sunday in Ordinary Time
Matthew 20:1–16a

Jesus said to his disciples, "For the kingdom of heaven is like a landowner who went out early in the morning to hire laborers for his vineyard. After agreeing with the laborers for the usual daily wage, he sent them into his vineyard. When he went out about nine o'clock, he saw others standing idle in the marketplace; and he said to them, 'You also go into the vineyard, and I will pay you whatever is right.' So they went. When he went out again about noon and about three o'clock, he did the same. And about five o'clock he went out and found others standing around; and he said to them, 'Why are you standing here idle all day?' They said to him, 'Because no one has hired us.' He said to them, 'You also go into the vineyard.' When evening came, the owner of the vineyard said to his manager, 'Call the laborers and give them their pay, beginning with the last and then going to the first.' When those hired about five o'clock came, each of them received the usual daily wage. Now when the first came, they thought they would receive more; but each of them also received the usual daily wage. And when they received it, they grumbled against the landowner, saying, 'These last worked only one hour, and you have made them equal to us who have borne the burden of the day and the scorching heat.' But he replied to one of them, 'Friend, I am doing you no wrong; did you not agree with me for the usual daily wage? Take what belongs to you and go; I choose to give to this last the same as I give to you. Am I not allowed to do what I choose with what belongs to me? Or are you envious because I am generous?' So the last will be first, and the first will be last."

- This story will irritate us if we cannot glimpse something of God's generosity and overflowing compassion. Here I am, Lord. You see how little I deserve, but you want to hold nothing back, if only I open my hands to receive.

- The human mind suspects injustice, while the heart of God sees only an opportunity to be generous. Help me, Lord, to let go of my presumptions so that I may see as you do and act freely from a full heart.

Monday 25th September
Luke 8:16–18

Jesus said to his disciples, "No one after lighting a lamp hides it under a jar, or puts it under a bed, but puts it on a lampstand, so that those who enter may see the light. For nothing is hidden that will not be disclosed, nor is anything secret that will not become known and come to light. Then pay attention to how you listen; for to those who have, more will be given; and from those who do not have, even what they seem to have will be taken away."

• Lord, to be a Christian today is challenging. In times of struggle I am tempted to hide my light, to remain anonymous, to be silent. Lord, when the wick of my lamp flickers and fades, strengthen its beam and let me be again a light bearer, a beacon of hope to those I daily encounter.

• This is demanding, Lord. I am not comfortable shining before others as an example of Christian living. But I am not much use to you if I hide my allegiance. Saint Francis of Assisi would tell his friars to walk through the town and preach the Gospel, sometimes by talking, more often by the example of their lives.

Tuesday 26th September
Luke 8:19–21

Then Jesus' mother and his brothers came to him, but they could not reach him because of the crowd. And he was told, "Your mother and your brothers are standing outside, wanting to see you." But he said to them, "My mother and my brothers are those who hear the word of God and do it."

• The primary word told us by Jesus is that the love of his Father for us is infinite; we are to trust this word and live by it. As Pope Francis says, "When everything is said and done, we are infinitely loved." When we know how well we are loved, and how well our neighbors are loved, we are transformed and the whole world becomes a more familial place.

• There is your family, Lord Jesus: Mary, and the others of the household—perhaps Joseph was already dead. Now you widen it. We become your family not by birth, nor by being female, nor by rituals, but by hearing and acting on God's word. You welcome me into the same intimate relationship with you as Mary your mother.

Wednesday 27th September
Luke 9:1–6

Then Jesus called the twelve together and gave them power and authority over all demons and to cure diseases, and he sent them out to proclaim the kingdom of God and to heal. He said to them, "Take nothing for your journey, no staff, nor bag, nor bread, nor money—not even an extra tunic. Whatever house you enter, stay there, and leave from there. Wherever they do not welcome you, as you are leaving that town shake the dust off your feet as a testimony against them." They departed and went through the villages, bringing the good news and curing diseases everywhere.

- Jesus suggests that we live in a simple way and not be encumbered by niggling concerns. It will be difficult for us to bring good news if we are concerned with our own details. We will be able to travel more lightly if we can make what matters to Jesus matter to us.

- The disciples of Jesus are to move on if they are not welcomed. Hostility can cling like dust to the feet and hinder further growth. It is the same with our personal life. Prayer invites us to let go of hostility, antipathy, and hurt, both from us to another and from another to ourselves.

Thursday 28th September
Luke 9:7–9

Now Herod the ruler heard about all that had taken place, and he was perplexed, because it was said by some that John had been raised from the dead, by some that Elijah had appeared, and by others that one of the ancient prophets had arisen. Herod said, "John I beheaded; but who is this about whom I hear such things?" And he tried to see him.

- Herod has beheaded John the Baptist; but now Jesus is on the scene and is making headlines. Herod is perplexed and anxious. He tries to see Jesus, but more from fear and bad conscience than from genuine desire. A true disciple has a faith-filled desire to know Jesus and to grow in an ever-deepening relationship with him.

- Lord, faith is a prerequisite for sight. Only by truly accepting you and embracing your way can I hope to see you. Strengthen my faith, Lord.

Friday 29th September
John 1:47–51

When Jesus saw Nathanael coming toward him, he said of him, "Here is truly an Israelite in whom there is no deceit!" Nathanael asked him, "Where did you come to know me?" Jesus answered, "I saw you under the fig tree before Philip called you." Nathanael replied, "Rabbi, you are the Son of God! You are the King of Israel!" Jesus answered, "Do you believe because I told you that I saw you under the fig tree? You will see greater things than these." And he said to him, "Very truly, I tell you, you will see heaven opened and the angels of God ascending and descending upon the Son of Man."

- Jesus, you reward Nathanael by hinting at a new level of disclosure and intimacy between yourself and him. Please be patient with me and grant that I may "see you more clearly, love you more dearly, and follow you more nearly," as the old prayer has it.

- Jesus witnessed some aspect of Nathanael that seemed to surprise him; there are hidden and secret aspects of my life, too, that are known and valued by God. Jesus lifts Nathanael's eyes from the everyday and prompts him to think of heaven; I might consider my hoped-for destination and see how my daily concerns are enlightened and brought into another perspective.

Saturday 30th September
Luke 9:43b–45

And all were astounded at the greatness of God. While everyone was amazed at all that he was doing, Jesus said to his disciples, "Let these words sink into your ears: The Son of Man is going to be betrayed into human hands." But they did not understand this saying; its meaning was concealed from them, so that they could not perceive it. And they were afraid to ask him about this saying.

- The disciples need some inspiration points here! They cannot take in the fact that Jesus will be betrayed. Why would anyone betray him when he is doing so much good and is at the height of his powers and so popular? But when I feel myself betrayed, then I am glad that his life took this form. I am strengthened by the fact that the Son of God knows the anguish from personal experience and that he has grappled with it and brought great good out of it by his love.

- Jesus says, "My grace is enough for you." Bad news may come from the doctor. We may fail in something important. We may be betrayed by friends. Yet he has gone before us and shows us the way to endure. Into your hands, O Lord, I commend my good fortune and my misfortunes.

The Twenty-Sixth Week of Ordinary Time
October 1—October 7

Something to think and pray about each day this week:

The Cost of Love Often Seems Too High

If life's purpose lies in getting what we want, as our culture insists, then freedom becomes a very big deal. Freedom, we think, is what allows us to exercise our "inalienable right" to the pursuit of happiness. With this view of freedom, it's easy to feel threatened by constraint. Our instinct is to resist it with all our might, for it impedes our ability to live the life we think we want. Yet to maximize this kind of freedom requires that we minimize or even eliminate serious relationships. For the more we rely on others or others rely on us, the less free we are to go wherever we wish to go, pursue whatever we wish to pursue, and do whatever we wish to do. Love constrains us. And in a society devoted to personal self-fulfillment, the cost of love often seems too high. Surprisingly, freedom is a very big deal in the Gospels, too. However, here it means something quite different. . . . When Jesus says that "the truth will make you free" (John 8:36), he does not mean free to pursue personal happiness. When St. Paul says that it is "for freedom Christ has set us free" (Galatians 5:1), he does not mean we now have permission to satisfy our every impulse and whim. Quite the contrary. In the Bible, the "free" person is the one no longer plagued by the burdensome quest for money, pleasure, possessions, social status, and political power—the very things that our culture says will satisfy our deepest wants and make us happy.

—Paula Huston, *A Season of Mystery*

The Presence of God

Be still and know that I am God. Lord, may your Spirit guide me to seek your loving presence more and more. For it is there I find rest and refreshment from this busy world.

Freedom

By God's grace I was born to live in freedom. Free to enjoy the pleasures he created for me. Dear Lord, grant that I may live as you intended, with complete confidence in your loving care.

Consciousness

In God's loving presence I unwind the past day,
starting from now and looking back, moment by moment.
I gather in all the goodness and light, in gratitude.
I attend to the shadows and what they say to me,
seeking healing, courage, forgiveness.

The Word

The word of God comes to us through the Scriptures. May the Holy Spirit enlighten my mind and heart to respond to the Gospel teachings. (Please turn to the Scripture on the following pages. Inspiration points are there should you need them. When you are ready, return here to continue.)

Conversation

Jesus, you always welcomed little children when you walked on this earth. Teach me to have a childlike trust in you. To live in the knowledge that you will never abandon me.

Conclusion

Glory be to the Father, and to the Son, and to the Holy Spirit,
As it was in the beginning, is now and ever shall be,
World without end. Amen.

Sunday 1st October
Twenty-Sixth Sunday in Ordinary Time
Matthew 21:28–32

Jesus said, "What do you think? A man had two sons; he went to the first and said, 'Son, go and work in the vineyard today.' He answered, 'I will not'; but later he changed his mind and went. The father went to the second and said the same; and he answered, 'I go, sir'; but he did not go. Which of the two did the will of his father?" They said, "The first." Jesus said to them, "Truly I tell you, the tax collectors and the prostitutes are going into the kingdom of God ahead of you. For John came to you in the way of righteousness and you did not believe him, but the tax collectors and the prostitutes believed him; and even after you saw it, you did not change your minds and believe him."

• Jesus says to me, "What do you think?" Do I take time out to think about where I stand in relation to God? Do I give my soul an opportunity to catch up? I ask the Lord to help me give time to thinking about the things that really matter.

• Jesus speaks this parable to me. I avoid applying it to others right now and simply accept Jesus' warmth as he sees how I have served. I listen for his invitation as he shows me where I hold back.

Monday 2nd October
Matthew 18:1–5, 10

At that time the disciples came to Jesus and asked, "Who is the greatest in the kingdom of heaven?" He called a child, whom he put among them, and said, "Truly I tell you, unless you change and become like children, you will never enter the kingdom of heaven. Whoever becomes humble like this child is the greatest in the kingdom of heaven. Whoever welcomes one such child in my name welcomes me. . . . Take care that you do not despise one of these little ones; for, I tell you, in heaven their angels continually see the face of my Father in heaven."

• Jesus cares for us individually through our guardian angel. Do I believe that I am personally cared for by God? To believe this is a great gift of faith. We are asked to trust God like little children, whose nature is to trust.

- Anything weak, small, or voiceless is likely to be overlooked in this world. I ask the Holy Spirit to shed light on my life so that I might see as Jesus sees, recognizing the small voices, the tender shoots, and the fragile beginnings where God is already at work in me.

Tuesday 3rd October
Luke 9:51–56

When the days drew near for Jesus to be taken up, he set his face to go to Jerusalem. And he sent messengers ahead of him. On their way they entered a village of the Samaritans to make ready for him; but they did not receive him, because his face was set toward Jerusalem. When his disciples James and John saw it, they said, "Lord, do you want us to command fire to come down from heaven and consume them?" But he turned and rebuked them. Then they went on to another village.

- Jesus, you will not be distracted by any setbacks. Ignite in me the flame of your steadfast Spirit so that I may follow you to the end.
- Lord, when I am rejected, I can be consumed with feelings of anger or revenge. Do not let me give in to these feelings. Instead let me turn away and move on as you do.

Wednesday 4th October
Luke 9:57–62

As they were going along the road, someone said to him, "I will follow you wherever you go." And Jesus said to him, "Foxes have holes, and birds of the air have nests; but the Son of Man has nowhere to lay his head." To another he said, "Follow me." But he said, "Lord, first let me go and bury my father." But Jesus said to him, "Let the dead bury their own dead; but as for you, go and proclaim the kingdom of God." Another said, "I will follow you, Lord; but let me first say farewell to those at my home." Jesus said to him, "No one who puts a hand to the plow and looks back is fit for the kingdom of God."

- Jesus, deepen my understanding of what it means to make a permanent commitment to you. Lead my enthusiasm to new places of determination, new understandings, new orientations so that I may abide in you as I look forward to eternal life.

- A disciple can learn to love God unconditionally only when she or he has first experienced that kind of love from God. Do I find myself hesitating or holding back in my following? How does this sit with the guarantee of God's unconditional love for me?

Thursday 5th October
Luke 10:1–12

The Lord appointed seventy others and sent them on ahead of him in pairs to every town and place where he himself intended to go. He said to them, "The harvest is plentiful, but the labourers are few; therefore ask the Lord of the harvest to send out laborers into his harvest. Go on your way. See, I am sending you out like lambs into the midst of wolves. Carry no purse, no bag, no sandals; and greet no one on the road. Whatever house you enter, first say, 'Peace to this house!' And if anyone is there who shares in peace, your peace will rest on that person; but if not, it will return to you. Remain in the same house, eating and drinking whatever they provide, for the laborer deserves to be paid. Do not move about from house to house. Whenever you enter a town and its people welcome you, eat what is set before you; cure the sick who are there, and say to them, 'The kingdom of God has come near to you.' But whenever you enter a town and they do not welcome you, go out into its streets and say, 'Even the dust of your town that clings to our feet, we wipe off in protest against you. Yet know this: the kingdom of God has come near.' I tell you, on that day it will be more tolerable for Sodom than for that town."

- To spread God's kingdom, Jesus chooses to depend on the various gifts of his chosen ones. He sends us out just as we are. We carry little except our limited strengths and our frailties. The gift of peace that we can bring, to those who accept us, is more precious than any casual roadside conversation. Lord, give me this peace, this tranquility of spirit.

- How do I feel when my goodwill is rejected? I can ask the Lord to strengthen me in my resolve to be a peace bearer and for the grace to be able to "fight nice" when I meet opposition.

Friday 6th October
Luke 10:13–16

Jesus said, "Woe to you, Chorazin! Woe to you, Bethsaida! For if the deeds of power done in you had been done in Tyre and Sidon, they would have repented long ago, sitting in sackcloth and ashes. But at the judgment it will be more tolerable for Tyre and Sidon than for you. And you, Capernaum, will you be exalted to heaven? No, you will be brought down to Hades. Whoever listens to you listens to me, and whoever rejects you rejects me, and whoever rejects me rejects the one who sent me."

- There is a strong sense of a living tradition here: "Whoever listens to you listens to me." Do I believe that the church today, no matter how imperfectly, continues the mission and ministry of Christ Jesus as he received it from his heavenly Father? This can demand great faith.

- Jesus berates the people for not recognizing him and listening to him. They have rejected him and his message. In many ways Jesus still speaks to us in ordinary loves, challenges, and events. Prayer creates within us a discerning heart so that we can hear the call of the Lord and sense the love of God in many different ways.

Saturday 7th October
Luke 10:17–24

The seventy returned with joy, saying, "Lord, in your name even the demons submit to us!" He said to them, "I watched Satan fall from heaven like a flash of lightning. See, I have given you authority to tread on snakes and scorpions, and over all the power of the enemy; and nothing will hurt you. Nevertheless, do not rejoice at this, that the spirits submit to you, but rejoice that your names are written in heaven." At that same hour Jesus rejoiced in the Holy Spirit and said, "I thank you, Father, Lord of heaven and earth, because you have hidden these things from the wise and the intelligent and have revealed them to infants; yes, Father, for such was your gracious will. All things have been handed over to me by my Father; and no one knows who the Son is except the Father, or who the Father is except the Son and anyone to whom the Son chooses to reveal him." Then turning to the disciples, Jesus said to them privately, "Blessed are the eyes that see what you see! For I tell you that many prophets and kings desired to see what you see, but did not see it, and to hear what you hear, but did not hear it."

- God values us simply because of who we are. Inner contentment, which comes from knowing and loving God, makes us indeed blessed. As I talk to the Lord I can ask for a growth in friendship with him.

- Sometimes people like to know that their names are on a park or church bench, or on the wall where they worked; they know then they might be remembered. Our names are carved on the hand of God and are written in heaven. What better place than heaven for our names to be written. We know then that we are expected!

The Twenty-Seventh Week of Ordinary Time
October 8—October 14

Something to think and pray about each day this week:

Thin Places

There are "thin places" that occur in my life that are unique, special places that I do not get to visit very often, but when I do the felt presence of God is almost overwhelming. Many of mine are places in nature, such as the beach, my grandparents' farm, and being in the North Georgia Mountains, and they invite me to understand the vastness and creative power of our creator. As I stand and soak in the beauty of nature these places offer, I also find that I understand that my mere presence in life is but one piece of God's magnificent, ongoing creative work. As the question of "thin places" remained on my heart, I found myself pondering it often during my Examen. Over time, I began to realize that there are some very basic rhythms and routines of my life that allowed me to readily and easily find God: snuggling my daughter, Abby, while sipping my morning coffee; sitting down to lunch with my kids after preschool to hear about their day; reading to my kids and our night time ritual of prayer; and savoring the few quieter moments with my hubby after the last door of my kids' room was closed. I was surprised to find that the rhythms of my life are spotted with moments that easily allow me to find God. Without realizing it, these moments are checkpoints to see how the ones I love are doing and even more importantly "still points" that allow me to savor the gifts in my life and to deepen my awareness of God in all things.

—Becky Eldredge on *dotMagis*, the blog of IgnatianSpirituality.com

The Presence of God

I pause for a moment and think of the love and the grace that God showers on me: I am created in the image and likeness of God; I am God's dwelling place.

Freedom

Lord, you created me to live in freedom. May your Holy Spirit guide me to follow you freely. Instill in my heart a desire to know and love you more each day.

Consciousness

How am I really feeling? Lighthearted? Heavyhearted? I may be very much at peace, happy to be here.
Equally, I may be frustrated, worried, or angry.
I acknowledge how I really am. It is the real me that the Lord loves.

The Word

I read the word of God slowly, a few times over, and I listen to what God is saying to me. (Please turn to the Scripture on the following pages. Inspiration points are there should you need them. When you are ready, return here to continue.)

Conversation

I know with certainty there were times when you carried me, Lord. When it was through your strength I got through the dark times in my life.

Conclusion

I thank God for these moments we have spent together and for any insights I have been given concerning the text.

Sunday 8th October
Twenty-Seventh Sunday in Ordinary Time
Matthew 21:33–43

Jesus said to them, "Listen to another parable. There was a landowner who planted a vineyard, put a fence around it, dug a wine press in it, and built a watchtower. Then he leased it to tenants and went to another country. When the harvest time had come, he sent his slaves to the tenants to collect his produce. But the tenants seized his slaves and beat one, killed another, and stoned another. Again he sent other slaves, more than the first; and they treated them in the same way. Finally he sent his son to them, saying, 'They will respect my son.' But when the tenants saw the son, they said to themselves, 'This is the heir; come, let us kill him and get his inheritance.' So they seized him, threw him out of the vineyard, and killed him. Now when the owner of the vineyard comes, what will he do to those tenants?" They said to him, "He will put those wretches to a miserable death, and lease the vineyard to other tenants who will give him the produce at the harvest time." Jesus said to them, "Have you never read in the Scriptures: 'The stone that the builders rejected has become the cornerstone; this was the Lord's doing, and it is amazing in our eyes'? Therefore I tell you, the kingdom of God will be taken away from you and given to a people that produces the fruits of the kingdom."

- Jesus reminds us that the kingdom does not belong to us—it is a gift of God. I consider what it is that I think I own and consider how it is that all good comes from God's hands. So I give thanks.

- Lord, what fruits of the kingdom will you bring out of my life? Help me cultivate faith and pay attention to your gifts to me.

Monday 9th October
Luke 10:25–37

Just then a lawyer stood up to test Jesus. "Teacher," he said, "what must I do to inherit eternal life?" He said to him, "What is written in the law? What do you read there?" He answered, "You shall love the Lord your God with all your heart, and with all your soul, and with all your strength, and with all your mind; and your neighbor as yourself." And he said to him, "You have given the right answer; do this, and you will live." But wanting to justify himself, he asked Jesus, "And who is my neighbor?"

Jesus replied, "A man was going down from Jerusalem to Jericho, and fell into the hands of robbers, who stripped him, beat him, and went away, leaving him half dead. Now by chance a priest was going down that road; and when he saw him, he passed by on the other side. So likewise a Levite, when he came to the place and saw him, passed by on the other side. But a Samaritan while traveling came near him; and when he saw him, he was moved with pity. He went to him and bandaged his wounds, having poured oil and wine on them. Then he put him on his own animal, brought him to an inn, and took care of him. The next day he took out two denarii, gave them to the innkeeper, and said, 'Take care of him; and when I come back, I will repay you whatever more you spend.' Which of these three, do you think, was a neighbor to the man who fell into the hands of the robbers?" He said, "The one who showed him mercy." Jesus said to him, "Go and do likewise."

• When Jesus is asked the question, "Who is my neighbor?" he does not answer with a definition but by telling a story. This beautiful passage from the Gospel shows how the answer must come from the heart, not the head. In my prayer I can ask the Lord to help me, through my heart, to realize where today's path goes.

• Let this story hit you anew. Ask, *What makes me go to the other side? What makes me avoid some types of people in need?* I pray that I may identify any blocks in myself that cause me to ignore or belittle others' needs.

Tuesday 10th October
Luke 10:38–42

Now as they went on their way, Jesus entered a certain village, where a woman named Martha welcomed him into her home. She had a sister named Mary, who sat at the Lord's feet and listened to what he was saying. But Martha was distracted by her many tasks; so she came to him and asked, "Lord, do you not care that my sister has left me to do all the work by myself? Tell her then to help me." But the Lord answered her, "Martha, Martha, you are worried and distracted by many things; there is need of only one thing. Mary has chosen the better part, which will not be taken away from her."

- Here am I, sitting at Jesus' feet, ready to receive his word into my heart. I bring to the center of my attention not what Jesus asks me to do but who Jesus asks me to become: a loving heart, formed in God's image.

- Once again, Jesus acts contrary to acceptable Jewish practice. He is alone, perhaps, in the home of two women who are not his relatives. Furthermore, he is teaching them! Lord, if we do not meet, I shall never come to know you. But knowing you is what life is about.

Wednesday 11th October
Luke 11:1–4

Jesus was praying in a certain place, and after he had finished, one of his disciples said to him, "Lord, teach us to pray, as John taught his disciples." He said to them, "When you pray, say: Father, hallowed be your name. Your kingdom come. Give us each day our daily bread. And forgive us our sins, for we ourselves forgive everyone indebted to us. And do not bring us to the time of trial."

- When the incarnate Son of God, the one closest to the Father, is asked to put into words the elements of true prayer, he responds with what we now call the Lord's Prayer or the Our Father. Identify one phrase of this prayer and meditate on it today.

- It is difficult to forgive even small hurts. What about the hurts of injustice, abuse, neglect? Jesus encourages us to think of these in prayer. One step toward forgiveness is to pray for someone—even when we can't talk to that person or think kindly of him or her.

Thursday 12th October
Luke 11:5–13

And he said to them, "Suppose one of you has a friend, and you go to him at midnight and say to him, 'Friend, lend me three loaves of bread; for a friend of mine has arrived, and I have nothing to set before him.' And he answers from within, 'Do not bother me; the door has already been locked, and my children are with me in bed; I cannot get up and give you anything.' I tell you, even though he will not get up and give him anything because he is his friend, at least because of his persistence he will get up and give him whatever he needs. So I say to you, Ask, and it will be given to you; search, and you will find; knock, and the door will be opened for you. For everyone who asks receives, and everyone who searches finds, and for everyone who knocks, the door will be opened. Is there anyone among you who, if your child asks for a fish, will give a snake instead of a fish? Or if the child asks for an egg, will give a scorpion? If you then, who are evil, know how to give good gifts to your children, how much more will the heavenly Father give the Holy Spirit to those who ask him!"

- Jesus wants me to persevere in my requests and says that he will give me what I need but not always what I want. I ask Jesus to guide me in knowing the difference.

- We may have been praying for ourselves or others for many years, and now we're tired of asking. Prayer is always heard by God but not always answered as we might wish. God, what do I receive from you when I pray and pray? Your presence? Understanding? Compassion?

Friday 13th October
Luke 11:15–26

Some of them said, "He casts out demons by Beelzebul, the ruler of the demons." Others, to test him, kept demanding from him a sign from heaven. But he knew what they were thinking and said to them, "Every kingdom divided against itself becomes a desert, and house falls on house. If Satan also is divided against himself, how will his kingdom stand?—for you say that I cast out the demons by Beelzebul. Now if I cast out the demons by Beelzebul, by whom do your exorcists cast them out? Therefore they will be your judges. But if it is by the finger of God that I cast out the demons, then the kingdom of God has come to you. When a strong man, fully armed, guards his castle, his property is safe. But when one stronger than he attacks him and overpowers him, he takes away his armor in which he trusted and divides his plunder. Whoever is not with me is against me, and whoever does not gather with me scatters. When the unclean spirit has gone out of a person, it wanders through waterless regions looking for a resting place, but not finding any, it says, 'I will return to my house from which I came.' When it comes, it finds it swept and put in order. Then it goes and brings seven other spirits more evil than itself, and they enter and live there; and the last state of that person is worse than the first."

- Jesus reminds us that when we have received help under his guidance, we should be careful to stay in his company lest we are tempted to revert to our old ways. I can speak to the Lord and ask him to help me remain open to goodness.

- What are my demons? Can I name even one of them? Whatever makes me unfree can be called a demon. Demons possess us, whereas angels liberate us for love and service. When I feel driven to work too hard or to spend too much money on myself, I am in danger of being possessed by either urge. Lord, liberate me, please!

Saturday 14th October
Luke 11:27–28

While Jesus was saying this, a woman in the crowd raised her voice and said to him, "Blessed is the womb that bore you and the breasts that nursed you!" But he said, "Blessed rather are those who hear the word of God and obey it!"

- There is an echo here of Mary's Magnificat: *Henceforth all generations shall call me blessed.* Luke points to Mary as the one who pondered God's words, kept them in her heart, and reflected on them when she went down to Nazareth. To receive the word of God is a greater gift than to receive the body of Jesus in the womb. Jesus, help me welcome your word today.

- Mary is richly blessed by giving birth to Jesus but, even more, by hearing his word and receiving it as the years go by. Can I enter prayer today with the attitude of listening and pondering what God says to me?

The Twenty-Eighth Week of Ordinary Time
October 15—October 21

Something to think and pray about each day this week:

Silence as Sacred Space

I was hesitant at first, but it made sense that if God worked through all things, God certainly worked through my imagination. It was then that I realized the true beauty of silent prayer. Every week I was given a set of Bible verses to contemplate. More than that, I was asked to imagine myself within the Bible stories. It was there that I "met" God for the first time. He revealed himself to me in a number of creative ways that made me seek God more, ways that fueled my desire to know God more deeply. Ironically, my silent prayer was incredibly loud, interactive, and engaging. It was also emotional and intimate. The silence allowed God to speak to my heart in mysterious ways. I interacted with God in ways that I never thought possible. We shared intimate moments and furthered our relationship. In my Scripture contemplations, Jesus treated me as one of his disciples and entrusted me with tasks to further his mission. He trusted me. He embraced me. He stuck up for me. He loved me. The silence was a sacred space for me to be with Jesus.

—Jurell Sison on *dotMagis*, the blog of IgnatianSpirituality.com

The Presence of God

Jesus, help me to be fully alive to your Holy Presence. Enfold me in your love. Let my heart become one with yours.

Freedom

I will ask God's help,
to be free from my own preoccupations,
to be open to God in this time of prayer,
to come to know, love, and serve God more.

Consciousness

I ask how I am within myself today? Am I particularly tired, stressed, or off form? If any of these characteristics apply, can I try to let go of the concerns that disturb me?

The Word

God speaks to each of us individually. I listen attentively to hear what God is saying to me. Read the text a few times, then listen. (Please turn to the Scripture on the following pages. Inspiration points are there should you need them. When you are ready, return here to continue.)

Conversation

Sometimes I wonder what I might say if I were to meet you in person, Lord.
I think I might say, Thank you, Lord, for always being there for me.

Conclusion

Glory be to the Father, and to the Son, and to the Holy Spirit,
As it was in the beginning, is now and ever shall be,
World without end. Amen.

Sunday 15th October
Twenty-Eighth Sunday in Ordinary Time
Matthew 22:1–14

Once more Jesus spoke to them in parables, saying: "The kingdom of heaven may be compared to a king who gave a wedding banquet for his son. He sent his slaves to call those who had been invited to the wedding banquet, but they would not come. Again he sent other slaves, saying, 'Tell those who have been invited: Look, I have prepared my dinner, my oxen and my fat calves have been slaughtered, and everything is ready; come to the wedding banquet.' But they made light of it and went away, one to his farm, another to his business, while the rest seized his slaves, maltreated them, and killed them. The king was enraged. He sent his troops, destroyed those murderers, and burned their city. Then he said to his slaves, 'The wedding is ready, but those invited were not worthy. Go therefore into the main streets, and invite everyone you find to the wedding banquet.' Those slaves went out into the streets and gathered all whom they found, both good and bad; so the wedding hall was filled with guests. But when the king came in to see the guests, he noticed a man there who was not wearing a wedding robe, and he said to him, 'Friend, how did you get in here without a wedding robe?' And he was speechless. Then the king said to the attendants, 'Bind him hand and foot, and throw him into the outer darkness, where there will be weeping and gnashing of teeth. For many are called, but few are chosen.'"

- O Lord, how we need your constant invitation to come to you and learn from you. Rid us of our garments of selfishness, our judgmental attitudes, our stubborn hearts, and clothe us instead with your garments of salvation.

- As generous and open-ended as God's invitation is, it is not to be exploited or taken for granted. For my part, I ask God to help me respond as best I can, to prepare my heart to receive God's gifts.

Monday 16th October
Luke 11:29–32

When the crowds were increasing, Jesus began to say, "This generation is an evil generation; it asks for a sign, but no sign will be given to it except the sign of Jonah. For just as Jonah became a sign to the people of

Nineveh, so the Son of Man will be to this generation. The queen of the South will rise at the judgment with the people of this generation and condemn them, because she came from the ends of the earth to listen to the wisdom of Solomon, and see, something greater than Solomon is here! The people of Nineveh will rise up at the judgment with this generation and condemn it, because they repented at the proclamation of Jonah, and see, something greater than Jonah is here!"

- People are coming to Jesus looking for signs. He compares himself to Solomon and Jonah, who were signs from God in their lifetimes. He, however, speaks with greater authority than these. What signs in your life are leading you to Jesus? Who are your advisors and whose voice do you listen to when you think about the deep meaning of your life?

- Jesus tells it as it is. When "the crowds were increasing," he challenged them to ask themselves why they were coming to see and listen to him. Why do I come to prayer each day? Something greater is here.

Tuesday 17th October
Luke 11:37–41

While Jesus was speaking, a Pharisee invited him to dine with him; so he went in and took his place at the table. The Pharisee was amazed to see that he did not first wash before dinner. Then the Lord said to him, "Now you Pharisees clean the outside of the cup and of the dish, but inside you are full of greed and wickedness. You fools! Did not the one who made the outside make the inside also? So give for alms those things that are within; and see, everything will be clean for you."

- It can be too easy to conform to others' expectations. We miss out by not developing our own inner life. I ask Jesus for the gift of inner freedom from which good judgment comes.

- Jesus tells us that holiness lies in wholeness and integrity; we are invited to be of one piece, without deep contradictions. I bring my life before God fully and openly, asking that any divisions in me be healed—that I be made whole.

Wednesday 18th October
Luke 10:1–9

After this the Lord appointed seventy others and sent them on ahead of him in pairs to every town and place where he himself intended to go. He said to them, "The harvest is plentiful, but the laborers are few; therefore ask the Lord of the harvest to send out laborers into his harvest. Go on your way. See, I am sending you out like lambs into the midst of wolves. Carry no purse, no bag, no sandals; and greet no one on the road. Whatever house you enter, first say, 'Peace to this house!' And if anyone is there who shares in peace, your peace will rest on that person; but if not, it will return to you. Remain in the same house, eating and drinking whatever they provide, for the laborer deserves to be paid. Do not move about from house to house. Whenever you enter a town and its people welcome you, eat what is set before you; cure the sick who are there, and say to them, 'The kingdom of God has come near to you.'"

- Jesus appoints each of his followers to go out to heal and to preach the kingdom of God. He needs help and doesn't wait for us to sort out issues of personal frailty. He has selected us, and he says to us, "Go!" People will be surprised, and we will experience a variety of receptions as we try to share Jesus' love and values. Lord, help me be willing to go—now.

- The Lord sends me out as his ambassador! When people see me coming, do they think of me as bringing good news? "The kingdom of God" means that God's ways of relating to people are to prevail. I ask that all my interactions with others be life-giving and liberating rather than unhelpful.

Thursday 19th October
Luke 11:47–54

Jesus said: "Woe to you! For you build the tombs of the prophets whom your ancestors killed. So you are witnesses and approve of the deeds of your ancestors; for they killed them, and you build their tombs. Therefore also the Wisdom of God said, 'I will send them prophets and apostles, some of whom they will kill and persecute,' so that this generation may be charged with the blood of all the prophets shed since the foundation of the world, from the blood of Abel to the blood of Zechariah, who perished between the altar and the sanctuary. Yes, I tell you, it will be charged against this generation. Woe to you lawyers! For you have taken away the key of knowledge; you did not enter yourselves, and you hindered those who were entering." When he went outside, the scribes and the Pharisees began to be very hostile toward him and to cross-examine him about many things, lying in wait for him, to catch him in something he might say.

- Many prophets before Jesus suffered death for telling the truth; this would be Jesus' fate as well. It is a great freedom to be open to the truth and not embedded in our prejudices. I ask the Lord for the kind of security in my relationship with him that enables me to be more open-minded.

- The lawyers who confront Jesus use the law as a weapon to attack others and to save themselves. This prevents others from entering the kingdom of God. Am I trapped by laws of my own making?

Friday 20th October
Luke 12:1–7

Meanwhile, when the crowd gathered by the thousands, so that they trampled on one another, Jesus began to speak first to his disciples, "Beware of the yeast of the Pharisees, that is, their hypocrisy. Nothing is covered up that will not be uncovered, and nothing secret that will not become known. Therefore whatever you have said in the dark will be heard in the light, and what you have whispered behind closed doors will be proclaimed from the housetops. I tell you, my friends, do not fear those who kill the body, and after that can do nothing more. But I will warn you whom to fear: fear him who, after he has killed, has authority to cast into hell. Yes, I tell you, fear him! Are not five sparrows sold for two pennies? Yet not one of them is forgotten in God's sight. But even the hairs of your head are all counted. Do not be afraid; you are of more value than many sparrows."

- We appreciate meeting an authentic person. Before God, all pretense is eventually uncovered because God misses nothing. Our relationship with God supports us in our search for authenticity.

- God has an eye for the details, for the monsters as well as the molecules. We mortals are born and die by the millions, many of us disregarded or forgotten. Yet the Lord cherishes each of us personally. Without that faith I would despair. So I come back to this truth: in God's eyes each of us is precious.

Saturday 21st October
Luke 12:8–12

Jesus said to the disciples, "And I tell you, everyone who acknowledges me before others, the Son of Man also will acknowledge before the angels of God; but whoever denies me before others will be denied before the angels of God. And everyone who speaks a word against the Son of Man will be forgiven; but whoever blasphemes against the Holy Spirit will not be forgiven. When they bring you before the synagogues, the rulers, and the authorities, do not worry about how you are to defend yourselves or what you are to say; for the Holy Spirit will teach you at that very hour what you ought to say."

- Not only does Jesus promise his constant presence in the lives of his faithful ones, but he also promises the help and inspiration of the Holy Spirit, especially in times of need. How do I feel when I consider that I may always call upon the help of the Holy Spirit?

- Jesus speaks to his disciples in anticipation of conflict and persecution ahead. When I read his words, is my response one of being encouraged and challenged, or am I frightened and unnerved? Why do I react in this way? What words of comfort are here for me?

The Twenty-Ninth Week of Ordinary Time
October 22—October 28

Something to think and pray about each day this week:

God's Presence

Prayer is a matter of relationship. Intimacy is the basic issue, not answers to problems or resolutions "to be better." Many of life's problems and challenges have no answers; we can only live with and through them. Problems and challenges, however, can be faced and lived through with more peace and resilience if people know that they are not alone. A man's wife will not return from the dead, but the pain is more bearable when he has poured out his sorrow, his anger, and his despair to God and has experienced God's intimate presence.

—William A. Barry, SJ, *Letting God Come Close*

The Presence of God

"I stand at the door and knock," says the Lord. What a wonderful privilege that the Lord of all creation desires to come to me. I welcome his presence.

Freedom

Saint Ignatius thought that a thick and shapeless tree trunk would never believe that it could become a statue, admired as a miracle of sculpture, and would never submit itself to the chisel of the sculptor,
who sees by her genius what she can make of it.
I ask for the grace to let myself be shaped by my loving Creator.

Consciousness

Knowing that God loves me unconditionally, I can afford to be honest about how I am. What are my fears and desires? What do I expect from God? What am I willing to give to God—from my emotions and talents, thoughts and energy? And how do I feel now? I share my feelings openly with the Lord.

The Word

I take my time to read the word of God, slowly, a few times, allowing myself to dwell on anything that strikes me. (Please turn to the Scripture on the following pages. Inspiration points are there should you need them. When you are ready, return here to continue.)

Conversation

Do I notice myself reacting as I pray with the word of God? Do I feel challenged, comforted, angry? Imagining Jesus sitting or standing by me, I speak out my feelings, as one trusted friend to another.

Conclusion

I thank God for these moments we have spent together and for any insights I have been given concerning the text.

Sunday 22nd October
Twenty-Ninth Sunday in Ordinary Time
Matthew 22:15–21

Then the Pharisees went and plotted to entrap Jesus in what he said. So they sent their disciples to him, along with the Herodians, saying, "Teacher, we know that you are sincere, and teach the way of God in accordance with truth, and show deference to no one; for you do not regard people with partiality. Tell us, then, what you think. Is it lawful to pay taxes to the emperor, or not?" But Jesus, aware of their malice, said, "Why are you putting me to the test, you hypocrites? Show me the coin used for the tax." And they brought him a denarius. Then he said to them, "Whose head is this, and whose title?" They answered, "The emperor's." Then he said to them, "Give therefore to the emperor the things that are the emperor's, and to God the things that are God's."

- To be a good citizen and to serve God are not in contradiction, since God works through all human systems and institutions to build the final community of love. God needs me to help build good relationships wherever I find myself.

- Some people have tried to use this reply of Jesus to justify revolution against an oppressive regime, others to bolster their conservatism. Lord, you hungered for justice, but you sought change by peaceful means. Help me do the same.

Monday 23rd October
Luke 12:13–21

Someone in the crowd said to Jesus, "Teacher, tell my brother to divide the family inheritance with me." But he said to him, "Friend, who set me to be a judge or arbitrator over you?" And he said to them, "Take care! Be on your guard against all kinds of greed; for one's life does not consist in the abundance of possessions." Then he told them a parable: "The land of a rich man produced abundantly. And he thought to himself, 'What should I do, for I have no place to store my crops?' Then he said, 'I will do this: I will pull down my barns and build larger ones, and there I will store all my grain and my goods. And I will say to my soul, Soul, you have ample goods laid up for many years; relax, eat, drink, be merry.' But God said to him, 'You fool! This very night your life is being demanded of you. And the things you have prepared, whose will they be?' So it is with those who store up treasures for themselves but are not rich toward God."

- What are we, in fact, living for? The demands of our way of life can make it difficult to put first things first. It is only in our relationship to Jesus that we can discover who we truly are, as Jesus sees us.

- In this parable, Jesus attacks greed and egotism. This rich man is living for this world and this life only, thinking only of himself, with no awareness of others' needs. All the rich man's ambitious planning is in vain because that same night he is to die. Who will inherit his substantial fortune, since he cannot take it with him, though he has lived as if he could? I ask Jesus to show me the real values and riches in my own life.

Tuesday 24th October
Luke 12:35–38

Jesus said to his disciples, "Be dressed for action and have your lamps lit; be like those who are waiting for their master to return from the wedding banquet, so that they may open the door for him as soon as he comes and knocks. Blessed are those slaves whom the master finds alert when he comes; truly I tell you, he will fasten his belt and have them sit down to eat, and he will come and serve them. If he comes during the middle of the night, or near dawn, and finds them so, blessed are those slaves."

- It's a great gift to be alert to the fact that we have come from God and we are going back to God. This helps put our whole life into a proper perspective. Closeness to Jesus is what keeps this awareness alive.

- Are these words only about the end time, or is Jesus knocking at my door on a daily basis? Am I being challenged to recognize him in the guise of a stranger, a person who is ill or who needs an encouraging word or a gentle touch? Do I treasure these opportunities as an encounter with Christ? Lord, make me vigilant so that I may recognize your face in my encounters today.

Wednesday 25th October

Luke 12:39–48

Jesus said to his disciples, "But know this: if the owner of the house had known at what hour the thief was coming, he would not have let his house be broken into. You also must be ready, for the Son of Man is coming at an unexpected hour." Peter said, "Lord, are you telling this parable for us or for everyone?" And the Lord said, "Who then is the faithful and prudent manager whom his master will put in charge of his slaves, to give them their allowance of food at the proper time? Blessed is that slave whom his master will find at work when he arrives. Truly I tell you, he will put that one in charge of all his possessions. But if that slave says to himself, 'My master is delayed in coming,' and if he begins to beat the other slaves, men and women, and to eat and drink and get drunk, the master of that slave will come on a day when he does not expect him and at an hour that he does not know, and will cut him in pieces, and put him with the unfaithful. That slave who knew what his master wanted, but did not prepare himself or do what was wanted, will receive a severe beating. But one who did not know and did what deserved a beating will receive a light beating. From everyone to whom much has been given, much will be required; and from one to whom much has been entrusted, even more will be demanded."

- Today's Gospel reading continues the message of being awake, alert, and ready. Each day is a microcosm of life, and we are called to live it as fully and as meaningfully as possible. "The glory of God is the human person fully alive!" So says Saint Irenaeus.

- Prayer times are our moments of being ready: in common worship, personal prayer time, and casual moments. The Lord can touch our lives at any time with a mood of peace, a challenge, or a word of Scripture. Prayer is God's gift to us and God's work within us.

Thursday 26th October

Luke 12:49–53

Jesus said to the crowds, "I came to bring fire to the earth, and how I wish it were already kindled! I have a baptism with which to be baptized, and what stress I am under until it is completed! Do you think that I have come to bring peace to the earth? No, I tell you, but rather division!

From now on five in one household will be divided, three against two and two against three; they will be divided: father against son and son against father, mother against daughter and daughter against mother, mother-in-law against her daughter-in-law and daughter-in-law against mother-in-law."

- Jesus uses the image of fire to speak of this great desire in his heart to save us. Not everyone would receive his message, and hence it would bring division in many relationships. How important to me is the good news that Jesus has brought? It helps me realize how much I must mean to him when I consider what it cost him.

- Lord, you disturb me, shake me out of complacency, and make my heart burn within me. Your message is not just about being nice. It means being angry at times, confronting injustice, making a stand.

Friday 27th October
Luke 12:54–59

Jesus also said to the crowds, "When you see a cloud rising in the west, you immediately say, 'It is going to rain'; and so it happens. And when you see the south wind blowing, you say, 'There will be scorching heat'; and it happens. You hypocrites! You know how to interpret the appearance of earth and sky, but why do you not know how to interpret the present time? And why do you not judge for yourselves what is right? Thus, when you go with your accuser before a magistrate, on the way make an effort to settle the case, or you may be dragged before the judge, and the judge hand you over to the officer, and the officer throw you in prison. I tell you, you will never get out until you have paid the very last penny."

- Weather forecasting has improved immensely. However, one's life is not so easy to predict. The ability to be honest with myself and to be in touch with the movements in my heart and mind provide a wonderful and solid foundation for interior growth. In my prayer I ask the Lord for the gift of sensitivity.

- Jesus clearly feels that many of his listeners are too complacent about the call to conversion and that they need to be shaken up. In what way am I complacent? How is God calling me to live a new and better life, and what are my resistances? Can I allow Jesus to challenge my resistance?

Saturday 28th October
Luke 6:12–16

Now during those days Jesus went out to the mountain to pray; and he spent the night in prayer to God. And when day came, he called his disciples and chose twelve of them, whom he also named apostles: Simon, whom he named Peter, and his brother Andrew, and James, and John, and Philip, and Bartholomew, and Matthew, and Thomas, and James son of Alphaeus, and Simon, who was called the Zealot, and Judas son of James, and Judas Iscariot, who became a traitor.

- It seems that Jesus and his Father spent the whole night in conversation about the choosing of the twelve apostles. Can I imagine how the conversation went? Do I ever consult God about the decisions I have to make, especially those that would have a long-term effect?

- Whenever I see the names of the disciples listed, I dare to include mine among them as I acknowledge that Jesus calls me to be a disciple too. I am not being presumptuous or vain but ask again for the humility I need to be his follower. I thank God for people upon whom I have relied and from whom I have received blessings; their discipleship has built me up in faith, and I pray that I may do likewise for others.

The Thirtieth Week of Ordinary Time
October 29—November 4

Something to think and pray about each day this week:

Loved Sinners

We have not always made choices that lead us to praise, honor, and serve God. We have not always acted as if we believe that we are loved. We have not always treated everything in our lives as a gift. We come to the humbling awareness that we are sinners, that we have often been ungrateful and unfaithful. We have failed to respond to God's offer of love by failing to love God and love our neighbor. Sin is the failure to bother to love. Sin is not simply the things we do but also the things we fail to do. St. Ignatius traces all this to a lack of gratitude—failure to recognize everything as a gift to be cherished, fostered, and shared. For Ignatius, ingratitude is the greatest sin and the root of all sin. It is, in the end, the failure to love as God has loved us. This realization leads us to sorrow. Ignatius invites us to pray for sorrow and shame, for a deep interior knowledge of our sinfulness, of the disorder in our lives, and of our ingratitude and lack of response to God's offer of life. This sorrow leads us to contrition and repentance—a turning toward God, whom we have offended. We realize that we have distanced ourselves from the one we most desire. We are sinners, but we are forgiven. The two are connected. Only when we claim our sinfulness and stand in sorrow before God can we truly experience God's mercy. We are loved sinners. God loves us even when we are sinners. Only when we know the depth of our sin do we know the depth of God's mercy. We are not as good as we thought, but we are much more loved than we ever imagined.

—Gerald M. Fagin, SJ, *Discovering Your Dream*

The Presence of God
To be present is to arrive as one is and open up to the other.
At this instant, as I arrive here, God is present waiting for me.
God always arrives before me, desiring to connect with me
even more than my most intimate friend.
I take a moment and greet my loving God.

Freedom
I am free. When I look at these words in writing, they seem to create in me a feeling of awe. Yes, a wonderful feeling of freedom. Thank you, God.

Consciousness
To be conscious about something is to be aware of it.
Dear Lord, help me to remember that you gave me life.
Thank you for the gift of life.
Teach me to slow down, to be still and enjoy the pleasures created for me. To be aware of the beauty that surrounds me. The marvel of mountains, the calmness of lakes, the fragility of a flower petal. I need to remember that all these things come from you.

The Word
The word of God comes to us through the Scriptures. May the Holy Spirit enlighten my mind and heart to respond to the Gospel teachings. (Please turn to the Scripture on the following pages. Inspiration points are there should you need them. When you are ready, return here to continue.)

Conversation
I begin to talk to Jesus about the piece of Scripture I have just read. What part of it strikes a chord in me? Perhaps the words of a friend—or some story I have heard recently—will slowly rise to the surface in my consciousness. If so, does the story throw light on what the Scripture passage may be trying to say to me?

Conclusion
Glory be to the Father, and to the Son, and to the Holy Spirit,
As it was in the beginning, is now and ever shall be,
World without end. Amen.

Sunday 29th October
Thirtieth Sunday in Ordinary Time
Matthew 22:34–40

When the Pharisees heard that Jesus had silenced the Sadducees, they gathered together, and one of them, a lawyer, asked him a question to test him. "Teacher, which commandment in the law is the greatest?" He said to him, "'You shall love the Lord your God with all your heart, and with all your soul, and with all your mind.' This is the greatest and first commandment. And a second is like it: 'You shall love your neighbor as yourself.' On these two commandments hang all the law and the prophets."

- Isn't it possible for my heart, soul, and mind to want different things sometimes? Jesus calls me to integrity and to wholeness. As I am drawn into relationship with him, I come to love what he loves, to desire what he desires, and to think as he thinks.

- I can do nothing to make God love me more. God's love shines on me as the sun shines on Earth. Real prayer includes resting gratefully in that love. I have a treasure in my heart, which is the limitless love of God for me. But I must share it with my neighbor. I ask to be a true escort of God's love to others.

Monday 30th October
Luke 13:10–17

Now Jesus was teaching in one of the synagogues on the sabbath. And just then there appeared a woman with a spirit that had crippled her for eighteen years. She was bent over and was quite unable to stand up straight. When Jesus saw her, he called her over and said, "Woman, you are set free from your ailment." When he laid his hands on her, immediately she stood up straight and began praising God. But the leader of the synagogue, indignant because Jesus had cured on the sabbath, kept saying to the crowd, "There are six days on which work ought to be done; come on those days and be cured, and not on the sabbath day." But the Lord answered him and said, "You hypocrites! Does not each of you on the sabbath untie his ox or his donkey from the manger, and lead it away to give it water? And ought not this woman, a daughter of Abraham whom Satan bound for eighteen long years, be set free from this bondage on the sabbath day?"

When he said this, all his opponents were put to shame; and the entire crowd was rejoicing at all the wonderful things that he was doing.

- This woman was crippled and bent over, a condition that robbed her of dignity and her rightful place in the community: She was unable to stand up straight and face the world. Once again, Jesus' intervention made all the difference. Immediately the woman stood up straight and began a whole new way of being and living. I acknowledge my need for healing and place myself before God today.

- As a person of faith, this woman praises God, who has given her freedom. The synagogue leader is saying, in a way, that the Sabbath is not an appropriate time for God to manifest his compassion and mercy. Jesus claims that God's actions cannot be restricted by humans. God's mercy and healing know no limits of time or place, if we but turn to God in a spirit of trust.

Tuesday 31st October
Luke 13:18–21

Jesus said, "What is the kingdom of God like? And to what should I compare it? It is like a mustard seed that someone took and sowed in the garden; it grew and became a tree, and the birds of the air made nests in its branches." And again he said, "To what should I compare the kingdom of God? It is like yeast that a woman took and mixed in with three measures of flour until all of it was leavened."

- The secret of the kingdom of God is to allow Jesus to grow in us. As we do so, we come to love him and depend on him as our traveling companion. Like the birds making their nests in the branches of the trees, we, too, nestle in the heart of Jesus and find nourishment in his care.

- Our attention is naturally drawn to what is biggest and best; it is easy to overlook things that are small, frail, and humble. Perhaps I can think of prayers I have said, of hopes I once had, and recognize how those seeds have grown. I may be able to trace the "yeast" of a vision, a desire, a dream, and see how it has inspired me and others.

Wednesday 1st November
All Saints
Matthew 5:1–12a

When Jesus saw the crowds, he went up the mountain; and after he sat down, his disciples came to him. Then he began to speak, and taught them, saying:

"Blessed are the poor in spirit, for theirs is the kingdom of heaven.

Blessed are those who mourn, for they will be comforted.

Blessed are the meek, for they will inherit the earth.

Blessed are those who hunger and thirst for righteousness, for they will be filled.

Blessed are the merciful, for they will receive mercy.

Blessed are the pure in heart, for they will see God.

Blessed are the peacemakers, for they will be called children of God.

Blessed are those who are persecuted for righteousness' sake, for theirs is the kingdom of heaven.

Blessed are you when people revile you and persecute you and utter all kinds of evil against you falsely on my account. Rejoice and be glad, for your reward is great in heaven, for in the same way they persecuted the prophets who were before you."

• Note that the word Beatitudes means blessings. These are not commandments to be obeyed but blessings to be sought. Is there any one in particular you would like to have? Pray for it today.

• Four times we are told that those who appear to be the most unfortunate in this world are actually the ones who are blessed by God. God will right the wrongs they suffer and bring them justice. This turns all worldly values upside down. Have I yet experienced the upturning of my worldly values?

Thursday 2nd November
The Commemoration of All the Faithful Departed (All Souls' Day)
John 6:35–40

Jesus said to them, "I am the bread of life. Whoever comes to me will never be hungry, and whoever believes in me will never be thirsty. But I said to you that you have seen me and yet do not believe. Everything that the Father gives me will come to me, and anyone who comes to me I will never drive away; for I have come down from heaven, not to do my own will, but the will of him who sent me. And this is the will of him who sent me, that I should lose nothing of all that he has given me, but raise it up on the last day. This is indeed the will of my Father, that all who see the Son and believe in him may have eternal life; and I will raise them up on the last day."

• For Christians the dead are not gone from our lives forever; they continue to exist and to be part of our community. The Gospel can underpin our prayer. It offers us Christ's assurance that he will raise us all on the last day because that is the will of his Father.

• The whole life of Jesus is a response to the magnetic attraction of the Father's will. Remaining completely faithful to the Father is what nourishes and sustains him. When we pray, we seek to find and do the Father's will ourselves, not to bring God around to doing ours. Jesus has come to draw each one of us to the Father. Everything he says and does is for this purpose.

Friday 3rd November
Luke 14:1–6

On one occasion when Jesus was going to the house of a leader of the Pharisees to eat a meal on the sabbath, they were watching him closely. Just then, in front of him, there was a man who had dropsy. And Jesus asked the lawyers and Pharisees, "Is it lawful to cure people on the sabbath, or not?" But they were silent. So Jesus took him and healed him, and sent him away. Then he said to them, "If one of you has a child or an ox that has fallen into a well, will you not immediately pull it out on a sabbath day?" And they could not reply to this.

• Can I visualize the setting where Jesus meets the man suffering from dropsy and cures him with a hostile audience of lawyers and Pharisees looking on? What feelings and motivations are going on in the various characters? Why do the Pharisees react as they do? What does the man with dropsy make of it? As an onlooker, what do I make of it?

• "If one of you has a child or an ox that has fallen into a well, will you not immediately pull it out on a sabbath day?" Maybe prayer can be a time to bring people in our mind and heart to God and see them with the compassionate eye of Jesus.

Saturday 4th November
Luke 14:1, 7–11

On one occasion when Jesus was going to the house of a leader of the Pharisees to eat a meal on the sabbath, they were watching him closely. . . . When he noticed how the guests chose the places of honor, he told them a parable. "When you are invited by someone to a wedding banquet, do not sit down at the place of honor, in case someone more distinguished than you has been invited by your host; and the host who invited both of you may come and say to you, 'Give this person your place,' and then in disgrace you would start to take the lowest place. But when you are invited, go and sit down at the lowest place, so that when your host comes, he may say to you, 'Friend, move up higher'; then you will be honored in the presence of all who sit at the table with you. For all who exalt themselves will be humbled, and those who humble themselves will be exalted."

- When Jesus recommends genuine humility—and his parable is not about banquet etiquette!—what is he calling me to? What is so great about this humility? Jesus picks out that uneasy moment when I walk to the table and wonder is there a place for me. Do I remember either the elation of being considered more special than I thought I was or the deflation of being thought more ordinary than seemed right to me?

- Lord, if I am happy in my own skin, I'll be good company for whoever is beside me. I do not ask to make an entrance like a celebrity, nor do I want to be overlooked completely. Give me contentment and an eye for the needs of whoever sits by me.

The Thirty-First Week of Ordinary Time
November 5—November 11

Something to think and pray about each day this week:

Our Life with the Saints

God's invitation to live out our unique vocations is part of what makes the world so rich. "How gloriously different are the saints," wrote C. S. Lewis. Problems arise when we begin to believe that we have to be someone *else* to be holy. We try to use someone else's map to heaven when God has already planted in our soul all the directions we need. In that way, we ignore our own call to sanctity. When admirers used to visit Calcutta to see Mother Teresa, she would tell many of them, "Find your own Calcutta." This is not to say that we aren't called to emulate the saints or, more to the point, Jesus. Reading the Gospels and the lives of the saints are fine ways of discovering new paths to holiness. That is part of the discovery process Merton speaks of. After all, it was in reading about Merton's journey that I discovered something of what my own journey must be. Through reading, conversation, and prayer, I grow gradually into the person I am meant to be. My life with the saints helps me see more clearly and embrace more eagerly whatever God has in store for me. In order to continue on our journey to sanctity, we have to hold lightly others' interpretation of holiness. Not only that, once we set aside the notion that we're supposed to be someone else, we must begin the long process of discovering who we really are and what we are meant to do.

—James Martin, SJ, *My Life with the Saints*

The Presence of God

Be still and know that I am God. Lord, may your Spirit guide me to seek your loving presence more and more. For it is there I find rest and refreshment from this busy world.

Freedom

By God's grace I was born to live in freedom. Free to enjoy the pleasures he created for me. Dear Lord, grant that I may live as you intended, with complete confidence in your loving care.

Consciousness

In God's loving presence I unwind the past day,
starting from now and looking back, moment by moment.
I gather in all the goodness and light, in gratitude.
I attend to the shadows and what they say to me,
seeking healing, courage, forgiveness.

The Word

The word of God comes to us through the Scriptures. May the Holy Spirit enlighten my mind and heart to respond to the Gospel teachings. (Please turn to the Scripture on the following pages. Inspiration points are there should you need them. When you are ready, return here to continue.)

Conversation

Jesus, you always welcomed little children when you walked on this earth. Teach me to have a childlike trust in you. To live in the knowledge that you will never abandon me.

Conclusion

Glory be to the Father, and to the Son, and to the Holy Spirit,
As it was in the beginning, is now and ever shall be,
World without end. Amen.

Sunday 5th November
Thirty-First Sunday in Ordinary Time
Matthew 23:1–12

Then Jesus said to the crowds and to his disciples, "The scribes and the Pharisees sit on Moses' seat; therefore, do whatever they teach you and follow it; but do not do as they do, for they do not practice what they teach. They tie up heavy burdens, hard to bear, and lay them on the shoulders of others; but they themselves are unwilling to lift a finger to move them. They do all their deeds to be seen by others; for they make their phylacteries broad and their fringes long. They love to have the place of honor at banquets and the best seats in the synagogues, and to be greeted with respect in the marketplaces, and to have people call them rabbi. But you are not to be called rabbi, for you have one teacher, and you are all students. And call no one your father on earth, for you have one Father—the one in heaven. Nor are you to be called instructors, for you have one instructor, the Messiah. The greatest among you will be your servant. All who exalt themselves will be humbled, and all who humble themselves will be exalted."

- Passages such as this one in Saint Matthew have led to anti-Jewish sentiments, hatred, and persecution. But Jesus' criticisms are valid for religious leaders anywhere who lose sight of the ideal of service to their people. I pray for our leaders, that they may never be distracted by human honor or forget whom it is they serve.

- Jesus, you gave the religious leaders of your day a hard time. But how do you find me? Do I play games to make people think that I am important? How much do I value my public image? Do I misuse my authority? Help me instead to be a humble servant to the needy, just like you.

Monday 6th November
Luke 14:12–14

Jesus said also to the one who had invited him, "When you give a luncheon or a dinner, do not invite your friends or your brothers or your relatives or rich neighbors, in case they may invite you in return, and you would be repaid. But when you give a banquet, invite the poor, the crippled, the lame, and the blind. And you will be blessed, because they cannot repay you, for you will be repaid at the resurrection of the righteous."

- Jesus, how often my giving is corrupted by self-interest and the hope of favors in return. You gave to me without hope of return. I can do you no favors, but you taught me that love means giving without expectations, that there is more happiness in giving than in receiving.

- In prayer we offer to God what we do for God, knowing that this is reward enough. Although he promises reward, Jesus wants us to do good simply because it is good. Giving without hope of reward means letting go of even my rational satisfaction.

Tuesday 7th November
Luke 14:15–24

One of the dinner guests, on hearing this, said to Jesus, "Blessed is anyone who will eat bread in the kingdom of God!" Then Jesus said to him, "Someone gave a great dinner and invited many. At the time for the dinner he sent his slave to say to those who had been invited, 'Come; for everything is ready now.' But they all alike began to make excuses. The first said to him, 'I have bought a piece of land, and I must go out and see it; please accept my apologies.' Another said, 'I have bought five yoke of oxen, and I am going to try them out; please accept my apologies.' Another said, 'I have just been married, and therefore I cannot come.' So the slave returned and reported this to his master. Then the owner of the house became angry and said to his slave, 'Go out at once into the streets and lanes of the town and bring in the poor, the crippled, the blind, and the lame.' And the slave said, 'Sir, what you ordered has been done, and there is still room.' Then the master said to the slave, 'Go out into the roads and lanes, and compel people to come in, so that my house may be filled. For I tell you, none of those who were invited will taste my dinner.'"

- Jesus' invitation to the banquet is for now. The time and place we meet Jesus and the mystery of God is now. Only the present is alive; the past is gone and the future yet to come. Prayer of any sort is entering into the "now" of God.

- It is easy to become familiar with comforts, to lose the savor of good things. I pray that I might have the generosity of the host who threw the banquet open. I think of how I embody the welcome and freedom that offer the goodness of God to all. Like the people invited to feast, I often resist God's invitation. I take time now just to be present with God, who loves my company.

Wednesday 8th November
Luke 14:25–33

Now large crowds were traveling with Jesus; and he turned and said to them, "Whoever comes to me and does not hate father and mother, wife and children, brothers and sisters, yes, and even life itself, cannot be my disciple. Whoever does not carry the cross and follow me cannot be my disciple. For which of you, intending to build a tower, does not first sit down and estimate the cost, to see whether he has enough to complete it? Otherwise, when he has laid a foundation and is not able to finish, all who see it will begin to ridicule him, saying, 'This fellow began to build and was not able to finish.' Or what king, going out to wage war against another king, will not sit down first and consider whether he is able with ten thousand to oppose the one who comes against him with twenty thousand? If he cannot, then, while the other is still far away, he sends a delegation and asks for the terms of peace. So therefore, none of you can become my disciple if you do not give up all your possessions."

- For most of us, the cross is not inflicted from outside but is part of our makeup: the body's and mind's infirmities, the addictions, temptations, and recurrent desires that rob us of freedom. Carrying my cross means learning to accept these troubles and deal with them.

- Before all else, our minds and hearts belong to the Lord. We must do all in our power to seek him first, and all else will fall into place. Teach us to follow you faithfully, O Lord. Prepare our way and help us put our feet on the path that leads to freedom.

Thursday 9th November
John 2:13–22

The Passover of the Jews was near, and Jesus went up to Jerusalem. In the temple he found people selling cattle, sheep, and doves, and the money changers seated at their tables. Making a whip of cords, he drove all of them out of the temple, both the sheep and the cattle. He also poured out the coins of the money changers and overturned their tables. He told those who were selling the doves, "Take these things out of here! Stop making my Father's house a marketplace!" His disciples remembered that it was written, "Zeal for your house will consume me." The Jews then said to him, "What sign can you show us for doing this?" Jesus answered them, "Destroy this temple, and in three days I will raise it up." The Jews then said, "This temple has been under construction for forty-six years, and will you raise it up in three days?" But he was speaking of the temple of his body. After he was raised from the dead, his disciples remembered that he had said this; and they believed the Scripture and the word that Jesus had spoken.

• Commerce was necessary to sustain the worship of God in his temple. Animals had to be sold for sacrifice, Roman money changed into Jewish money to pay the temple tax. But where should this commerce take place? Not within the temple precinct! Does Jesus express his anger appropriately? What might desecrate our places of worship today?

• Jesus, you got really angry in the temple! Are there things about me that make you angry? My heart is your temple; do I clutter it up so much that there is little space for you? When I see things going on that are wrong, do I do anything about them?

Friday 10th November
Luke 16:1–8

Then Jesus said to the disciples, "There was a rich man who had a manager, and charges were brought to him that this man was squandering his property. So he summoned him and said to him, 'What is this that I hear about you? Give me an accounting of your management, because you cannot be my manager any longer.' Then the manager said to himself, 'What will I do, now that my master is taking the position away from me? I am not strong enough to dig, and I am ashamed to beg. I have decided what to do so that, when I am dismissed as manager, people may welcome me into their homes.' So, summoning his master's debtors one by one, he asked the first, 'How much do you owe my master?' He answered, 'A hundred jugs of olive oil.' He said to him, 'Take your bill, sit down quickly, and make it fifty.' Then he asked another, 'And how much do you owe?' He replied, 'A hundred containers of wheat.' He said to him, 'Take your bill and make it eighty.' And his master commended the dishonest manager because he had acted shrewdly; for the children of this age are more shrewd in dealing with their own generation than are the children of light."

- Lord, you are telling me to use wisely whatever wealth I have. God gave us temporal things to use. My wealth consists not in what I keep but in what I give away. You will judge me by how I use the things of which I am only a steward.

- The manager made preparations for himself in the way that seemed best to him, even dealing dishonestly, possibly to get on the better side of his employer's debtors. Jesus finds value in this man's shrewdness. Lord, do I make an effort to handle what happens to me? Do I prepare myself for what is next? In what way might I be shrewd or wise?

Saturday 11th November
Luke 16:9–15

Jesus said to his disciples, "And I tell you, make friends for yourselves by means of dishonest wealth so that when it is gone, they may welcome you into the eternal homes. Whoever is faithful in a very little is faithful also in much; and whoever is dishonest in a very little is dishonest also in much. If then you have not been faithful with the dishonest wealth, who will entrust to you the true riches? And if you have not been faithful with what belongs to another, who will give you what is your own? No slave can serve two masters; for a slave will either hate the one and love the other, or be devoted to the one and despise the other. You cannot serve God and wealth." The Pharisees, who were lovers of money, heard all this, and they ridiculed him. So he said to them, "You are those who justify yourselves in the sight of others; but God knows your hearts; for what is prized by human beings is an abomination in the sight of God."

- Wealth can be understood literally, but it can also be given a metaphorical meaning. It can stand for anything that distracts us from the service of God, anything that may have become a substitute for God, anything that seduces us like a false and deceitful lover.

- Rather than read the word of Scripture as you might read a newspaper, you might allow the Gospel words to "read" you. Jesus' words are like the words of a friend or a loved one. I take time now to be in the presence of God who loves me, laying aside other distractions or bringing them before God.

The Thirty-Second Week of Ordinary Time
November 12—November 18

Something to think and pray about each day this week:

Like Home, Only Better
My son is very worried heaven will be like church, which, like most four-year-old boys, he finds insufferable. I think a lot of us fear heaven will be boring. We don't want to spend eternity floating around on a cloud. We want trees and beaches and grass and sky and dogs and horses. We want to work and play and love. We want bodies and we want to use them. God knows our longing for Eden, and he wants to give it back to us. He will remake the earth without the sea—that ancient metaphor for chaos, death. So I tell my son, as I tell myself, it will be just like home, only better.

—Jessica Mesman Griffith, *2016: A Book of Grace-Filled Days*

The Presence of God
I pause for a moment and think of the love and the grace that God showers on me: I am created in the image and likeness of God; I am God's dwelling place.

Freedom
Lord, you created me to live in freedom. May your Holy Spirit guide me to follow you freely. Instill in my heart a desire to know and love you more each day.

Consciousness
How am I really feeling? Lighthearted? Heavyhearted? I may be very much at peace, happy to be here.
Equally, I may be frustrated, worried, or angry.
I acknowledge how I really am. It is the real me that the Lord loves.

The Word
I read the word of God slowly, a few times over, and I listen to what God is saying to me. (Please turn to the Scripture on the following pages. Inspiration points are there should you need them. When you are ready, return here to continue.)

Conversation
I know with certainty there were times when you carried me, Lord. When it was through your strength I got through the dark times in my life.

Conclusion
I thank God for these moments we have spent together and for any insights I have been given concerning the text.

Sunday 12th November
Thirty-Second Sunday in Ordinary Time
Matthew 25:1–13

Jesus said to his disciples, "Then the kingdom of heaven will be like this. Ten bridesmaids took their lamps and went to meet the bridegroom. Five of them were foolish, and five were wise. When the foolish took their lamps, they took no oil with them; but the wise took flasks of oil with their lamps. As the bridegroom was delayed, all of them became drowsy and slept. But at midnight there was a shout, 'Look! Here is the bridegroom! Come out to meet him.' Then all those bridesmaids got up and trimmed their lamps. The foolish said to the wise, 'Give us some of your oil, for our lamps are going out.' But the wise replied, 'No! there will not be enough for you and for us; you had better go to the dealers and buy some for yourselves.' And while they went to buy it, the bridegroom came, and those who were ready went with him into the wedding banquet; and the door was shut. Later the other bridesmaids came also, saying, 'Lord, lord, open to us.' But he replied, 'Truly I tell you, I do not know you.' Keep awake therefore, for you know neither the day nor the hour."

• Does Jesus have trouble waking me up when he arrives? I ask for the grace to be alert and responsive to the constant coming of God into my life. We are the light of the world, Jesus says. As I move among people today, I imagine that light radiates from me toward them, and from them to me. Does this change the atmosphere in which I live?

• I pray for all who have given up hope, for those for whom the waiting seemed too much to ask. Jesus suggests that there is a proper time to prepare. I look to the "oil and lamps" of my life and ask God to replenish and restock my reserves.

Monday 13th November
Luke 17:1–6

Jesus said to his disciples, "Occasions for stumbling are bound to come, but woe to anyone by whom they come! It would be better for you if a millstone were hung around your neck and you were thrown into the sea than for you to cause one of these little ones to stumble. Be on your guard! If another disciple sins, you must rebuke the offender, and if there is repentance, you must forgive. And if the same person sins against you seven times a day, and turns back to you seven times and says, 'I repent' you must forgive." The apostles said to the Lord, "Increase our faith!" The Lord replied, "If you had faith the size of a mustard seed, you could say to this mulberry tree, 'Be uprooted and planted in the sea' and it would obey you."

- The image of the millstone around the neck sends shivers down the spine. I pray for the little ones who have been made to stumble in our present-day church. Occasions for stumbling are bound to come. Jesus picked himself up three times and continued on the Way of the Cross. Can I come to terms with my own stumbling ways?

- Jesus, we are so quick to "name and blame," so quick to judge, so prone to hold on to grudges that we have against another person, even though this may have happened so long ago. Teach us how to forgive, Father, as you have forgiven us.

Tuesday 14th November
Luke 17:7–10

Jesus said to his disciples, "Who among you would say to your slave who has just come in from plowing or tending sheep in the field, 'Come here at once and take your place at the table'? Would you not rather say to him, 'Prepare supper for me, put on your apron and serve me while I eat and drink; later you may eat and drink'? Do you thank the slave for doing what was commanded? So you also, when you have done all that you were ordered to do, say, 'We are worthless slaves; we have done only what we ought to have done!'"

- Slavery was an accepted part of most ancient cultures, and Jesus' listeners would easily understand the point he is making here. In the modern world we see it as unjust. So, to apply this model, as Jesus does, to the relationship between God and ourselves is likely to make us uneasy. But can we at least accept that our obedience to God is required by the very nature of who God is? That it is not something to boast about or seek a reward for? Especially since our obedience is that of a son or daughter to a loving Father?

- Dear Lord, you didn't spend your time boasting about all you did and all you suffered. You were like a slave, serving us all, washing our feet, dying for us. Make me a bit more like you in your humility and self-forgetfulness.

Wednesday 15th November
Luke 17:11–19

On the way to Jerusalem Jesus was going through the region between Samaria and Galilee. As he entered a village, ten lepers approached him. Keeping their distance, they called out, saying, "Jesus, Master, have mercy on us!" When he saw them, he said to them, "Go and show yourselves to the priests." And as they went, they were made clean. Then one of them, when he saw that he was healed, turned back, praising God with a loud voice. He prostrated himself at Jesus' feet and thanked him. And he was a Samaritan. Then Jesus asked, "Were not ten made clean? But the other nine, where are they? Was none of them found to return and give praise to God except this foreigner?" Then he said to him, "Get up and go on your way; your faith has made you well."

- The lepers are regarded as unclean and forced to live outside of towns and villages. Even when approaching Jesus, they keep at a distance. Curing a leper restores that person to his or her community. How do poverty, depression, and other kinds of illness rob people of community today?

- I have done it myself, Lord. I go looking for something, advertising my need, seeking sympathy. And when somebody helps me, part of me is muttering, *He was only doing his job, or what you'd expect of a neighbor.* I take kindness for granted and do not bother to say thank you.

Thursday 16th November
Luke 17:20–25

Once Jesus was asked by the Pharisees when the kingdom of God was coming, and he answered, "The kingdom of God is not coming with things that can be observed; nor will they say, 'Look, here it is!' or 'There it is!' For, in fact, the kingdom of God is among you." Then he said to the disciples, "The days are coming when you will long to see one of the days of the Son of Man, and you will not see it. They will say to you, 'Look there!' or 'Look here!' Do not go, do not set off in pursuit. For as the lightning flashes and lights up the sky from one side to the other, so will the Son of Man be in his day. But first he must endure much suffering and be rejected by this generation."

- Jesus encourages his disciples not to get worked up, or even overly curious, about the end times and the (second) coming of the Son of Man but to concentrate on the here and now and ponder Jesus' own teaching: that the Son of Man must first endure much suffering and be rejected by this generation. This they will soon see acted out in Jerusalem.

- The kingdom of God means the presence, love, and goodness of God. How have I experienced God in my life today? Am I allowing God to take me over more and more? It is thus that the kingdom of God comes to flower in my heart.

Friday 17th November
Luke 17:26–37

Jesus said to his disciples, "Just as it was in the days of Noah, so too it will be in the days of the Son of Man. They were eating and drinking, and marrying and being given in marriage, until the day Noah entered the ark, and the flood came and destroyed all of them. Likewise, just as it was in the days of Lot: they were eating and drinking, buying and selling, planting and building, but on the day that Lot left Sodom, it rained fire and sulphur from heaven and destroyed all of them—it will be like that on the day that the Son of Man is revealed. On that day, anyone on the housetop who has belongings in the house must not come down to take them away; and likewise anyone in the field must not turn back. Remember Lot's wife. Those who try to make their life secure will lose it, but those who lose their life will keep it. I tell you, on that night there will be two in one bed; one will be taken and the other left. There will be two women grinding meal together; one will be taken and the other left." Then they asked him, "Where, Lord?" He said to them, "Where the corpse is, there the vultures will gather."

- Jesus wants his listeners to notice how life was going on normally, people engaging in their everyday activities, when the disaster struck. No warning, no premonition, no time to plan an escape! So, too, the Son of Man will come suddenly and unexpectedly. The only way to be prepared is to live a good life, one based on love. Then the coming of the Son of Man will not be a disaster but our final liberation.

- Everything in this life is passing; we are on a pilgrimage back to our heavenly home and so we are not to be tied to anything or anyone to the detriment of forgetting who we are and where we are bound. Lord of heaven and earth, just as you led the Israelites out of Egypt, lead us, too, as we seek to do your will to "love you more dearly and follow you more nearly" all the days of our life.

Saturday 18th November

Luke 18:1–8

Then Jesus told them a parable about their need to pray always and not to lose heart. He said, "In a certain city there was a judge who neither feared God nor had respect for people. In that city there was a widow who kept coming to him and saying, 'Grant me justice against my opponent.' For a while he refused; but later he said to himself, 'Though I have no fear of God and no respect for anyone, yet because this widow keeps bothering me, I will grant her justice, so that she may not wear me out by continually coming.'" And the Lord said, "Listen to what the unjust judge says. And will not God grant justice to his chosen ones who cry to him day and night? Will he delay long in helping them? I tell you, he will quickly grant justice to them. And yet, when the Son of Man comes, will he find faith on earth?"

- Our persistence in prayer does not change God's mind. Instead it prepares our own hearts by strengthening our desire for God! Jesus wishes us to pray always and not lose heart. Help me to be constant, Lord. Renew my failing confidence when your answer is "Wait. . . . wait . . . wait a little longer."

- Saint Luke shows that Jesus prayed consistently during his public life and his passion. I am Jesus' disciple, and he needs me to be a person of prayer also. Jesus, when you search my heart, do you find any faith inside it? Stretch my small heart so that I may take the risk of entrusting myself more to you.

The Thirty-Third Week of Ordinary Time
November 19—November 25

Something to think and pray about each day this week:

The Power of Gratitude

Gratitude is quite possibly the greatest weapon God gives us against despair. When we take the time to be grateful, it diverts our gaze toward the light rather than the darkness. This theme of gratitude in the bleakest moments is all over the Bible. As they began their ministry, the apostles were persecuted, flogged, and threatened. Their response to this, though, was to rejoice that they were considered worthy to suffer dishonor for the sake of God. They saw the light in the midst of darkness, and it gave them what they needed to keep on with their ministry. In the Gospel of Luke, Jesus is described as "anxious" to eat the Passover meal with the apostles, and he gives thanks during that meal. He knew it was his last, he knew one of his apostles would betray him, and yet he found a little bit of light in that dark day. St. Ignatius clearly recognized the power of gratitude. He suggested gratitude as a central part of the Examen, ensuring that retreatants, the Jesuits, and all whom they guide and teach come into the practice of seeing the good that God grants them each day of their lives. It's perfect training for those periods of desolation—a light toward consolation.

—Cara Callbeck on *dotMagis*, the blog of IgnatianSpirituality.com

The Presence of God
Jesus, help me to be fully alive to your Holy Presence. Enfold me in your love. Let my heart become one with yours.

Freedom
I will ask God's help,
to be free from my own preoccupations,
to be open to God in this time of prayer,
to come to know, love, and serve God more.

Consciousness
I ask how I am within myself today? Am I particularly tired, stressed, or off form? If any of these characteristics apply, can I try to let go of the concerns that disturb me?

The Word
God speaks to each of us individually. I listen attentively to hear what God is saying to me. Read the text a few times, then listen. (Please turn to the Scripture on the following pages. Inspiration points are there should you need them. When you are ready, return here to continue.)

Conversation
Sometimes I wonder what I might say if I were to meet you in person, Lord.
I think I might say, Thank you, Lord, for always being there for me.

Conclusion
Glory be to the Father, and to the Son, and to the Holy Spirit,
As it was in the beginning, is now and ever shall be,
World without end. Amen.

Sunday 19th November
Thirty-Third Sunday in Ordinary Time
Matthew 25:14–30

Jesus said to his disciples, "For it is as if a man, going on a journey, summoned his slaves and entrusted his property to them; to one he gave five talents, to another two, to another one, to each according to his ability. Then he went away. The one who had received the five talents went off at once and traded with them, and made five more talents. In the same way, the one who had the two talents made two more talents. But the one who had received the one talent went off and dug a hole in the ground and hid his master's money. After a long time the master of those slaves came and settled accounts with them. Then the one who had received the five talents came forward, bringing five more talents, saying, 'Master, you handed over to me five talents; see, I have made five more talents.' His master said to him, 'Well done, good and trustworthy slave; you have been trustworthy in a few things, I will put you in charge of many things; enter into the joy of your master.'" And the one with the two talents also came forward, saying, 'Master, you handed over to me two talents; see, I have made two more talents.' His master said to him, 'Well done, good and trustworthy slave; you have been trustworthy in a few things, I will put you in charge of many things; enter into the joy of your master.' Then the one who had received the one talent also came forward, saying, 'Master, I knew that you were a harsh man, reaping where you did not sow, and gathering where you did not scatter seed; so I was afraid, and I went and hid your talent in the ground. Here you have what is yours.' But his master replied, 'You wicked and lazy slave! You knew, did you, that I reap where I did not sow, and gather where I did not scatter? Then you ought to have invested my money with the bankers, and on my return I would have received what was my own with interest. So take the talent from him, and give it to the one with the ten talents. For to all those who have, more will be given, and they will have an abundance; but from those who have nothing, even what they have will be taken away. As for this worthless slave, throw him into the outer darkness, where there will be weeping and gnashing of teeth.'"

- What can I take from your story, Lord? The talents with which I grew up are different from other people's: more than some, fewer than others'. Am I to take risks with them? Try out different paths, with the danger of failing?

- If we have a readiness humbly to receive God's grace, then God can bless us. People who prefer to rely on themselves will ultimately find themselves with very little. When we know that what we have is not ours, we allow God to give us more; if we get where we are purely by our own efforts, we do not get very far at all.

Monday 20th November
Luke 18:35–43

As Jesus approached Jericho, a blind man was sitting by the roadside begging. When he heard a crowd going by, he asked what was happening. They told him, "Jesus of Nazareth is passing by." Then he shouted, "Jesus, Son of David, have mercy on me!" Those who were in front sternly ordered him to be quiet; but he shouted even more loudly, "Son of David, have mercy on me!" Jesus stood still and ordered the man to be brought to him; and when he came near, he asked him, "What do you want me to do for you?" He said, "Lord, let me see again." Jesus said to him, "Receive your sight; your faith has saved you." Immediately he regained his sight and followed him, glorifying God; and all the people, when they saw it, praised God.

- I imagine myself as the blind beggar sitting helpless by the side of the road. All I can do is shout loudly when I learn that Jesus is passing. Even when Jesus asks me to come forward, others have to lead me. How do I feel as I hear Jesus' respectful and sensitive question: What do you want me to do for you?

- The poor can be a nuisance because they disturb our comfortable lives. I talk with Jesus about my attitude toward the needy. I see that Jesus reverses human values and puts this blind beggar first. I ask for grace to do the same.

Tuesday 21st November
The Presentation of the Blessed Virgin Mary
Luke 19:1–10

Jesus entered Jericho and was passing through it. A man was there named Zacchaeus; he was a chief tax collector and was rich. He was trying to see who Jesus was, but on account of the crowd he could not, because he was short in stature. So he ran ahead and climbed a sycamore tree to see him, because he was going to pass that way. When Jesus came to the place, he looked up and said to him, "Zacchaeus, hurry and come down; for I must stay at your house today." So he hurried down and was happy to welcome him. All who saw it began to grumble and said, "He has gone to be the guest of one who is a sinner." Zacchaeus stood there and said to the Lord, "Look, half of my possessions, Lord, I will give to the poor; and if I have defrauded anyone of anything, I will pay back four times as much." Then Jesus said to him, "Today salvation has come to this house, because he too is a son of Abraham. For the Son of Man came to seek out and to save the lost."

• Where do I fall short so that I cannot see Jesus? What particular tree can I climb to see him more clearly? The practice of prayer is like a tree; it gives me a daily glimpse of the Lord as he passes. How do I feel when Jesus invites himself to my kitchen? How does the conversation go?

• Zacchaeus used his imagination to see above the heads of those who came between him and Jesus. Do I allow anyone to prevent my seeing Jesus? Jesus saw what was holding Zacchaeus back from living fully and freely. I ask Jesus to speak to me about my life, to help and to heal me.

Wednesday 22nd November
Luke 19:11–28

Jesus went on to tell a parable, because he was near Jerusalem, and because they supposed that the kingdom of God was to appear immediately. So he said, "A nobleman went to a distant country to get royal power for himself and then return. He summoned ten of his slaves, and gave them ten pounds, and said to them, 'Do business with these until I come back.' But the citizens of his country hated him and sent a delegation after him, saying, 'We do not want this man to rule over us.' When he returned, having received royal power, he ordered these slaves, to whom he had given the money, to be summoned so that he might find out what they had gained by trading. The first came forward and said, 'Lord, your pound has made ten more pounds.' He said to him, 'Well done, good slave! Because you have been trustworthy in a very small thing, take charge of ten cities.' Then the second came, saying, 'Lord, your pound has made five pounds.' He said to him, 'And you, rule over five cities.' Then the other came, saying, 'Lord, here is your pound. I wrapped it up in a piece of cloth, for I was afraid of you, because you are a harsh man; you take what you did not deposit, and reap what you did not sow.' He said to him, 'I will judge you by your own words, you wicked slave! You knew, did you, that I was a harsh man, taking what I did not deposit and reaping what I did not sow? Why then did you not put my money into the bank? Then when I returned, I could have collected it with interest.' He said to the bystanders, 'Take the pound from him and give it to the one who has ten pounds.' (And they said to him, 'Lord, he has ten pounds!') 'I tell you, to all those who have, more will be given; but from those who have nothing, even what they have will be taken away. But as for these enemies of mine who did not want me to be king over them—bring them here and slaughter them in my presence.'" After he had said this, he went on ahead, going up to Jerusalem.

- Some aspects of this parable jar us: the ruthless nobleman with slaves, the king who would slaughter reluctant subjects. But the central theme remains: God bids us use what we are given, the individual talents that mark us. He wants us to make a difference, not relax into a comfort zone.

- There is a sense of departure in this story of Jesus. Soon he will go away; in fact, he tells the story when he is near Jerusalem, where he will be soon killed. The nobleman gives what he has to the servants; it's as if his work is to be done now by others. The same is true for Jesus and ourselves now; we are the ones entrusted with the mission and the life of Jesus for today.

Thursday 23rd November
Luke 19:41–44

As Jesus came near and saw the city, he wept over it, saying, "If you, even you, had only recognized on this day the things that make for peace! But now they are hidden from your eyes. Indeed, the days will come upon you, when your enemies will set up ramparts around you and surround you, and hem you in on every side. They will crush you to the ground, you and your children within you, and they will not leave within you one stone upon another; because you did not recognize the time of your visitation from God."

- Jesus weeps over Jerusalem as a mother weeps over her child. Jesus, who was there to help you carry your burdens? Who was there in moments of sadness or loneliness? Yet you are so near to us, just waiting for us to call on you to comfort us in the darkest moments of our lives. Thank you for your great love for us.

- I know what it is like when friends can't see what is good for them. As I listen to Jesus yearning for Jerusalem, I allow his gaze to fall lovingly on me. What does he long for me to wake up to?

Friday 24th November
Luke 19:45–48

Then Jesus entered the temple and began to drive out those who were selling things there; and he said, "It is written, 'My house shall be a house of prayer'; but you have made it a den of robbers.'" Every day he was teaching in the temple. The chief priests, the scribes, and the leaders of the people kept looking for a way to kill him; but they did not find anything they could do, for all the people were spellbound by what they heard.

- My poor heart is a "house of prayer." God is active there, transforming me, even though I notice the changes only later. In praying with Scripture, am I ever spellbound by what I read?

- In listening to Jesus, the minds of the people are opening as the minds of the officials are closing. I think of my habitual reactions and ask Jesus to shape them. Jesus calls me to the clarity with which he saw the world.

Saturday 25th November
Luke 20:27–40

Some Sadducees, those who say there is no resurrection, came to him and asked him a question, "Teacher, Moses wrote for us that if a man's brother dies, leaving a wife but no children, the man shall marry the widow and raise up children for his brother. Now there were seven brothers; the first married, and died childless; then the second and the third married her, and so in the same way all seven died childless. Finally the woman also died. In the resurrection, therefore, whose wife will the woman be? For the seven had married her." Jesus said to them, "Those who belong to this age marry and are given in marriage; but those who are considered worthy of a place in that age and in the resurrection from the dead neither marry nor are given in marriage. Indeed they cannot die anymore, because they are like angels and are children of God, being children of the resurrection. And the fact that the dead are raised Moses himself showed, in the story about the bush, where he speaks of the Lord as the God of Abraham, the God of Isaac, and the God of Jacob. Now he is God not of the dead, but of the living; for to him all of them are alive." Then some of the scribes answered, "Teacher, you have spoken well." For they no longer dared to ask him another question.

- The Sadducees scorned the idea of rising from the dead. Jesus lifts them from the tangles in which their theology has trapped them. "He is God not of the dead but of the living, for to him all are alive." We are part of that cosmos that transcends space and time and embraces not merely Abraham, Isaac, and Jacob but my parents and all my ancestors to the beginning of creation. In the resurrection we will share the eternal *Now* of God.

- I watch as Jesus tries to raise the minds of his questioners to a higher level. I ask him to share his vision, so that I may see something of the wonderful plans God has for us all.

The Thirty-Fourth and Last Week of Ordinary Time
November 26—December 2

Something to think and pray about each day this week:

Forced Gratitude?

Gratitude, of course, cannot be forced. "You should be grateful," we growl at our kids, as they limply move the food around on their plates. "Do you know how many children in the world go to bed hungry? They would be overjoyed to have a dinner like that." Somehow this doesn't make the braised eggplant any more appetizing, at least to the children who sit around my dinner table. We know that gratitude can't be forced, of course, but we still find ourselves trying to coerce our kids to be more grateful. And we do the same to ourselves, too. We're aware that we have so much to be grateful for: my children's lives, a ready supply of food and water, cozy and secure homes. We enjoy these "basics"—and countless luxuries besides—while so many people in the world struggle just to survive the day. We secretly chide ourselves: *I should be more grateful.* But try as we may, we're just not feeling it. We wonder if there's something wrong with us. Is my heart hardened somehow? Is it really not such a great gift to have these needs met? Will I ever feel content and satisfied?

—Jennifer Grant, *Wholehearted Living*

The Presence of God

"I stand at the door and knock," says the Lord. What a wonderful privilege that the Lord of all creation desires to come to me. I welcome his presence.

Freedom

Saint Ignatius thought that a thick and shapeless tree trunk would never believe that it could become a statue, admired as a miracle of sculpture, and would never submit itself to the chisel of the sculptor,
who sees by her genius what she can make of it.
I ask for the grace to let myself be shaped by my loving Creator.

Consciousness

Knowing that God loves me unconditionally, I can afford to be honest about how I am. What are my fears and desires? What do I expect from God? What am I willing to give to God—from my emotions and talents, thoughts and energy? And how do I feel now? I share my feelings openly with the Lord.

The Word

I take my time to read the word of God, slowly, a few times, allowing myself to dwell on anything that strikes me. (Please turn to the Scripture on the following pages. Inspiration points are there should you need them. When you are ready, return here to continue.)

Conversation

Do I notice myself reacting as I pray with the word of God? Do I feel challenged, comforted, angry? Imagining Jesus sitting or standing by me, I speak out my feelings, as one trusted friend to another.

Conclusion

I thank God for these moments we have spent together and for any insights I have been given concerning the text.

Sunday 26th November
Our Lord Jesus Christ, King of the Universe
Matthew 25:31–46

Jesus said to his disciples, "When the Son of Man comes in his glory, and all the angels with him, then he will sit on the throne of his glory. All the nations will be gathered before him, and he will separate people one from another as a shepherd separates the sheep from the goats, and he will put the sheep at his right hand and the goats at the left. Then the king will say to those at his right hand, 'Come, you that are blessed by my Father, inherit the kingdom prepared for you from the foundation of the world; for I was hungry and you gave me food, I was thirsty and you gave me something to drink, I was a stranger and you welcomed me, I was naked and you gave me clothing, I was sick and you took care of me, I was in prison and you visited me.' Then the righteous will answer him, 'Lord, when was it that we saw you hungry and gave you food, or thirsty and gave you something to drink? And when was it that we saw you a stranger and welcomed you, or naked and gave you clothing? And when was it that we saw you sick or in prison and visited you?' And the king will answer them, 'Truly I tell you, just as you did it to one of the least of these who are members of my family, you did it to me.' Then he will say to those at his left hand, 'You that are accursed, depart from me into the eternal fire prepared for the devil and his angels; for I was hungry and you gave me no food, I was thirsty and you gave me nothing to drink, I was a stranger and you did not welcome me, naked and you did not give me clothing, sick and in prison and you did not visit me.' Then they also will answer, 'Lord, when was it that we saw you hungry or thirsty or a stranger or naked or sick or in prison, and did not take care of you?' Then he will answer them, 'Truly I tell you, just as you did not do it to one of the least of these, you did not do it to me.' And these will go away into eternal punishment, but the righteous into eternal life."

- This message is simple, Lord. You will judge me on my love of and service to others. You are there in the poor, the sick, the prisoners, the strangers. May I recognize your face.

- Saint Matthew's hearers struggled with what would happen to non-Jews, because they themselves were the Chosen People. Jesus says that with his coming into the world, everyone is a "chosen" person.

Everyone is to be treated with limitless respect. Jesus is already present, but in disguise, in every person. What do I see when I see the needy? Do I focus on the hidden glory of others? How would I fare if human history were to be terminated today?

Monday 27th November
Luke 21:1–4

Jesus looked up and saw rich people putting their gifts into the treasury; he also saw a poor widow put in two small copper coins. He said, "Truly I tell you, this poor widow has put in more than all of them; for all of them have contributed out of their abundance, but she out of her poverty has put in all she had to live on."

- Jesus points out that the poor widow gives more than anyone else because she gives her last penny. She has left herself nothing to live on. Jesus allows us to draw our own conclusions and discover what meaning the event has for us. What are my conclusions? Can I share them with him in prayer?

- I ask for God's help to see the best in the small and impoverished everyday gestures that I might notice. I bring these moments before God for blessing. Talk of recession makes us cautious. Generosity can be a sign of the goodness of God. In a time of constraint, it may be all the more necessary.

Tuesday 28th November
Luke 21:5–11

When some were speaking about the temple, how it was adorned with beautiful stones and gifts dedicated to God, Jesus said, "As for these things that you see, the days will come when not one stone will be left upon another; all will be thrown down." They asked him, "Teacher, when will this be, and what will be the sign that this is about to take place?" And he said, "Beware that you are not led astray; for many will come in my name and say, 'I am he!' and, 'The time is near!' Do not go after them. When you hear of wars and insurrections, do not be terrified; for these things must take place first, but the end will not follow immediately." Then he said to them, "Nation will rise against nation, and kingdom against kingdom; there will be great earthquakes, and in various places famines and plagues; and there will be dreadful portents and great signs from heaven."

- Given the significance of the temple for Jewish religion and culture, Jesus' words could be seen as symbolizing the end of their messianic hopes. Nothing could ever be the same again. Did I have to deal with painful endings during the past few years? Deaths of loved ones, failed relationships, illness, job loss? Where was God for me during these crises? Did any of these endings bring me freedom or open up new opportunities?

- The reading from today warns about the end times. But I am not to be terrified, because God's providence will see me through whatever evils may beset our world. I pray: "Jesus, you care about the whole world. Even though the human story seems to be full of disasters, you are laboring so that it may end in triumph. Give me courage and energy to play my little part, so that at the end I may rejoice with you."

Wednesday 29th November
Luke 21:12–19

Jesus said to his disciples, "But before all this occurs, they will arrest you and persecute you; they will hand you over to synagogues and prisons, and you will be brought before kings and governors because of my name. This will give you an opportunity to testify. So make up your minds not to prepare your defense in advance; for I will give you words and a wisdom that none of your opponents will be able to withstand or contradict. You will be betrayed even by parents and brothers, by relatives and friends; and they will put some of you to death. You will be hated by all because of my name. But not a hair of your head will perish. By your endurance you will gain your souls."

- Sporadic persecution of Christians had already begun when Luke was writing his Gospel. Similar persecution is also happening in many parts of the world today. Are those of us living in more tolerant countries sensitive to the sufferings of our fellow Christians who find themselves hated by all because of Jesus' name? Are we in effective solidarity with them? Do we pray for them? Engage in advocacy on their behalf?

- Jesus does not promise that life will be easy for his disciples. What he does promise is that he will give us words and wisdom to hold fast to the good news. This good news includes the promise of our resurrection.

Thursday 30th November
Matthew 4:18–22

As Jesus walked by the Sea of Galilee, he saw two brothers, Simon, who is called Peter, and Andrew his brother, casting a net into the sea—for they were fishermen. And he said to them, "Follow me, and I will make you fish for people." Immediately they left their nets and followed him. As he went from there, he saw two other brothers, James son of Zebedee and his brother John, in the boat with their father Zebedee, mending their nets, and he called them. Immediately they left the boat and their father, and followed him.

- This scene offers us a picture of how Jesus calls each of us. Note that the initiative is entirely his. Jesus wants you and me to follow him, not just as companions but as sharers in his mission. Christian spirituality is not simply about "Jesus and me" but about "Jesus, me, and those to whom he sends me." Each of us is a fisher: a witness, a prophet, an evangelizer, a healer, a communicator of the good news.

- What was it like for Andrew to hear his call? A mix of emotions? Delighted in being singled out (we all want to be wanted!) but maybe a bit hesitant about leaving behind his means of livelihood? What is the cost of discipleship for me?

Friday 1st December
Luke 21:29–33

Then Jesus told them a parable: "Look at the fig tree and all the trees; as soon as they sprout leaves you can see for yourselves and know that summer is already near. So also, when you see these things taking place, you know that the kingdom of God is near. Truly I tell you, this generation will not pass away until all things have taken place. Heaven and earth will pass away, but my words will not pass away."

- Through Gospel contemplation we allow ourselves to absorb the attitudes and values of Jesus. These then become the criteria by which we evaluate a situation. In a way we are looking for signs. These will not be cosmic disturbances in the heavens but inner movements of spiritual consolation or desolation. As the liturgical year ends, is there anything in my life that I need to discern? If so, I pray that I may recognize the signs and interpret them correctly.

- How do I respond to the new developments in our world, particularly the frightening ones? What does Jesus' affirmation of the nearness of the kingdom of God say to these concerns?

Saturday 2nd December
Luke 21:34–36

Jesus said to the disciples, "Be on guard so that your hearts are not weighed down with dissipation and drunkenness and the worries of this life, and that day does not catch you unexpectedly, like a trap. For it will come upon all who live on the face of the whole earth. Be alert at all times, praying that you may have the strength to escape all these things that will take place, and to stand before the Son of Man."

- Do I ever suspect that I am not in touch with my deepest self? That I tend to drift rather than live reflectively? Prayer invites us to journey inward to the still point of the soul. Do I always accept this invitation, or does fear hold me back? Or lack of faith?

- It is surprising how much of Jesus' advice about preparing for the Second Coming is also relevant to our day-to-day living. For example: Be on guard so that your hearts are not weighed down with dissipation and drunkenness and the worries of this life. Is anything weighing me down right now? It may be something sinful or it may not. Do I want to be free of this burden? Might Jesus be able and willing to help me?

Continue the Conversation

If you enjoyed this book, then connect with Loyola Press to continue the conversation, engage with other readers, and find out about new and upcoming books from your favorite spiritual writers.

Visit us at **LoyolaPress.com** to create an account and register for our newsletters.

Or scan the code on the left with your smartphone.

Connect with us through:

Facebook
facebook.com
/loyolapress

Twitter
twitter.com
/loyolapress

YouTube
youtube.com
/loyolapress